GRAMMAR AND VOCABULARY

'This flexible, choose-your-own-way course catches the reader's attention from the first page and paves a lively way for independent learning. Students should enjoy the experience.'
Angela Downing, Universidad Complutense de Madrid, Spain.

'This book is an excellently clear introduction to the core concepts in grammar and vocabulary. I would happily use this book with students beginning their study of lexis and grammar.'
Susan Hunston, University of Birmingham, UK

Routledge English Language Introductions cover core areas of language study and are one-stop resources for students.

Assuming no prior knowledge, books in the series offer an accessible overview of the subject, with activities, study questions, sample analyses, commentaries and key readings – all in the same volume. The innovative and flexible 'two-dimensional' structure is built around four sections – introduction, development, exploration and extension – which offer self-contained stages for study. Each topic can also be read across these sections, enabling the reader to build gradually on the knowledge gained.

Grammar and Vocabulary: A resource book for students

❏ is a comprehensive introduction to the study of the grammar and vocabulary of contemporary English
❏ covers the core areas of grammar and vocabulary: words and sentences, word classes, word structure, slots and fillers, sentence patterns, clause and phrase, grammar rules, and vocabularies
❏ draws on a range of real texts from newspaper articles, adverts, poems and websites
❏ provides classic readings by the key names in the discipline, from Halliday to Quirk and from Ayto to Trudgill.

This is an accessible and user-friendly textbook for all students of English language and linguistics.

The accompanying website providing weblinks and extra resources for lecturers, teachers and students, can be found at:
http://www.routledge.com/textbooks/grammar

Howard Jackson is Professor of English Language and Linguistics and Director of Academic Affairs in the Faculty of Computing, Information and English at the University of Central England. His publications include *Grammar and Meaning* (1990) and *Words, Meaning and Vocabulary* and *Investigating English Language* (co-authored with Peter Stockwell) (2000).

Series Editor: Peter Stockwell
Series Consultant: Ronald Carter

ROUTLEDGE ENGLISH LANGUAGE INTRODUCTIONS

SERIES EDITOR: PETER STOCKWELL

Peter Stockwell is Senior Lecturer in the School of English Studies at the University of Nottingham, UK, where his interests include sociolinguistics, stylistics and cognitive poetics. His recent publications include Cognitive Poetics: An Introduction (Routledge, 2002), The Poetics of Science Fiction, Investigating English Language (with Howard Jackson), and Contextualized Stylistics (edited with Tony Bex and Michael Burke).

SERIES CONSULTANT: RONALD CARTER

Ronald Carter is Professor of Modern English Language in the School of English Studies at the University of Nottingham, UK. He is the co-series editor of the forthcoming *Routledge Applied Linguistics* series, series editor of *Interface*, and was co-founder of the Routledge *Intertext* series.

OTHER TITLES IN THE SERIES:

Sociolinguistics
Peter Stockwell

Pragmatics and Discourse
Joan Cutting

FORTHCOMING:

World Englishes
Jennifer Jenkins

Phonetics and Phonology
Beverley Collins & Inger Mees

Psycholinguistics
John Field

Child Language
Jean Stilwell Peccei

Stylistics
Paul Simpson

GRAMMAR AND VOCABULARY

A resource book for students

A

B

C

D

HOWARD JACKSON

London and New York

First published 2002 by Routledge
11 New Fetter Lane, London EC4P 4EE

Simultaneously published in the USA and Canada
by Routledge
29 West 35th Street, New York, NY 10001

Routledge is an imprint of the Taylor & Francis Group

© 2002 Howard Jackson

Typeset in 10/12.5pt Minion by Graphicraft Limited, Hong Kong
Printed and bound in Great Britain by TJ International, Padstow, Cornwall

British Library Cataloguing in Publication Data
A catalogue record for this book is available from the British Library

Library of Congress Cataloging in Publication Data
A catalog record for this book has been requested

ISBN 0-415-23170-1 (hbk)
ISBN 0-415-23171-X (pbk)

FOR LYDIA

HOW TO USE THIS BOOK

The Routledge English Language Introductions are 'flexi-texts' that you can use to suit your own style of study. The books are divided into four sections:

A Introduction – sets out the key concepts for the area of study. The units of this section take you step-by-step through the foundational terms and ideas, carefully providing you with an initial toolkit for your own study. By the end of the section, you will have a good overview of the whole field.

B Development – adds to your knowledge and builds on the key ideas already introduced. Units in this section might also draw together several areas of interest. By the end of this section, you will already have a good and fairly detailed grasp of the field, and will be ready to undertake your own exploration and thinking.

C Exploration – provides examples of language data and guides you through your own investigation of the field. The units in this section will be more open-ended and exploratory, and you will be encouraged to try out your ideas and think for yourself, using your newly acquired knowledge.

D Extension – offers you the chance to compare your expertise with key readings in the area. These are taken from the work of important writers, and are provided with guidance and questions for your further thought.

You can read this book like a traditional textbook, 'vertically' straight through from beginning to end. This will take you comprehensively through the broad field of study. However, the Routledge English Language Introductions have been carefully designed so that you can read them in another dimension, 'horizontally' across the numbered units. For example, Units A1, A2, A3 and so on correspond with Units B1, B2, B3, and with Units C1, C2, C3 and D1, D2, D3, and so on. Reading A5, B5, C5, D5 will take you rapidly from the key concepts of a specific area, to a level of expertise in that precise area, all with a very close focus. You can match your way of reading with the best way that you work.

The glossary/index at the end, together with the suggestions for Further Reading, will help to keep you orientated. Each textbook has a supporting website with extra commentary, suggestions, additional material and support for teachers and students.

GRAMMAR AND VOCABULARY

The aim of this book in the series is to open up to you the fascinating study of the grammar and vocabulary of the English language, and to encourage you to analyse the language that you hear and read in your daily life. My hope is that you will become enthused by the study of language and will want to continue to explore more. This book is simply an introduction.

Each unit in the book is composed of a limited amount of exposition, and a number of 'activities' ✪. The activities are nearly always followed by a 'commentary', which either provides answers to the questions of the activity or discusses possible solutions to problems posed in the activity. The book is designed to be interactive. You should do each activity before you read the commentary that follows it. In this way, your learning and understanding will develop more effectively.

As with any academic subject, grammar has its own terminology. Some of this will be familiar to you – terms like 'word' or 'sentence' – but it is likely that you will not all have had the same exposure to terms like 'clause' or 'Subject', not to mention 'morpheme' or 'lexeme'. Terminology is introduced in this book as it is needed. The Glossary provides an index of terms, a brief explanation, and reference to the unit or units where the term is explained in detail. In Section A: Introduction, you will find that a term introduced in one unit is used again in subsequent units, so that you become familiar with it and build up a conception of how it is used in the description of grammar. Do not be fazed by the terminology! It will soon become a familiar friend – and enable you to talk confidently about grammar and vocabulary.

Finally, let me say a word about using the units in Section D: Extension. As already mentioned, these are a set of readings from other books. They are intended to extend your understanding of the topics discussed in the related series of Sections A, B and C. Sometimes they put a different perspective on what has been considered, sometimes they fill in some of the theoretical background, sometimes they discuss a related question or issue. An introduction to the reading sets it in the context of the unit series, and after the reading some suggestions are made about how you can follow it up by further investigation. You may find that you need to read the extract more than once to grasp what the author is saying, and to make the connections with the rest of the book. You may find that you want to leave units in Section D until you have finished studying all the other units. As with the book as a whole, you should use the method and sequence of study that suits you best.

I hope you will find your study stimulating, enlightening and enjoyable.

CONTENTS

CONTENTS **CROSS-REFERENCED**

 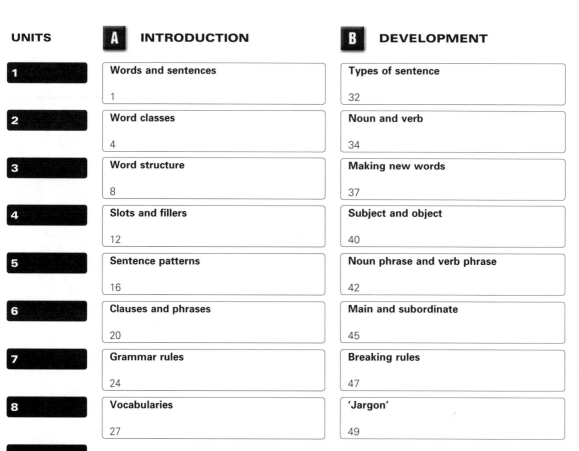

CONTENTS **CROSS-REFERENCED**

LIST OF TABLES

LIST OF FIGURES

ACKNOWLEDGEMENTS

We are grateful for the following permissions:

The *Guardian* to use the following texts (© the *Guardian*): in C2.3, 'Cyberspace is proving tricky' (26/11/00, p.26); in C3.1, 'Driving ban cut for rail "victim"' (16/12/00, p.9); in C4.1 and C4.2, Obituary of Victor Borge by Dennis Barker (27/12/00, p.17); in C4.3, 'Aircraft maker Airbus...' by Keith Harper (1/1/01, p.16); in C5.3, 'European capitals...' (4/1/01, p.17); in C8.3, 'Busting the bus jargon', from 'The Editor' (5/1/01).

'Goodbye' (in Unit C7.2) from the *Collected Poems* by John Betjeman, published by John Murray; included in the eBook by permission of Desmond Elliott, Administrator of the Estate of Sir John Betjeman.

Continuum Publishing for using part of a transcribed dialogue in Unit C7.1 from: *Spoken English – A Practical Guide* by Christine Cheepen and James Monaghan (Pinter, 1990).

The Ramblers for their advertisement entitled 'Breathing Space' in Unit C7.2.

'anyone lived in a pretty how town' (in Unit C7.2) is reprinted from *Complete Poems 1904–62*, by E. E. Cummings, edited by George J. Firmage, by permission of W. W. Norton & Company; Copyright © 1991 by the Trustees for the E. E. Cummings Trust and George James Firmage.

Dalesman Publishing Co. Ltd to reproduce the anecdote, 'At the Barber's' (in Unit C8.1) from Peter Wright's *The Lanky Twang* (Dalesman, 1972).

Professor Flor Aarts to reproduce the reading in Unit D1 from *English Syntactic Structures*.

Max Niemeyer Verlag GmbH to reproduce the reading in Unit D4 from Thomas Herbst's article, 'Designing an English valency dictionary' in *The Perfect Learner's Dictionary (?)*, edited by Thomas Herbst and Kerstin Popp (Niemeyer, 1999).

Taylor & Francis to reproduce the reading in Unit D5 from *Essentials of Grammatical Theory* by David Allerton (Routledge, 1979); and to reproduce the reading in D7, Peter Trudgill's article, 'Standard English: what it isn't', in *Standard English, The Widening Debate*, edited by Tony Bex and Richard J. Watts (Routledge, 1999); also to Professor Peter Trudgill, University of Fribourg, Switzerland, for his kind permission.

Edward Arnold (Publishers) Ltd to reproduce the reading in Unit D6 from *An Introduction to Functional Grammar* by Michael Halliday (Arnold, 1985).

Mr John Ayto for the 'Introduction' © John Ayto 1999, reprinted from *Twentieth Century Words*, by permission of Oxford University Press, in Unit D8.

Pearson Education to reproduce the reading in Unit D3 from Appendix I of *A Comprehensive Grammar of the English Language* by Randolph Quirk, Sidney Greenbaum, Geoffrey Leech and Jan Svartvik (Longman, 1985).

John Benjamins Publishing Co. to reproduce the reading in Unit D5 from *Pattern Grammar: A Corpus-Driven Approach to the Lexical Grammar of English* by Susan Hunston and Gill Francis (Benjamins, 2000).

I am also grateful to Dr Mahendra Verma, University of York, for help with Indian English in Unit C8.1.

INTRODUCTION

KEY CONCEPTS IN GRAMMAR AND VOCABULARY

WORDS AND SENTENCES

The terms 'word' and 'sentence' are, no doubt, familiar to you. You have a pretty clear idea of what a word is – a sequence of letters bounded by spaces – and of what a sentence is – a sequence of words, the first of which begins with a capital letter, and the last of which is completed by a full stop, question mark or exclamation mark. But if you look again at those definitions of 'word' and 'sentence', you will notice that they derive from your experience of written language. Think now about spoken language, which, after all, is how most of us experience language most of the time. What kind of definition might 'word' and 'sentence' have for spoken language? Let us begin with sentences.

Activity 1

How many sentences are there in the following transcription of a spoken dialogue (from Svartvik and Quirk 1980: 647)?

> when I was little we had a garden and we had in Persia and we had about sixteen cherry trees and I used to spend the whole of the cherry season up a ladder till one day M who was our very toothless gardener got a cherry and he opened it and it was a beautiful beautiful cherry and just flicked it with his finger and there was a little worm floating around inside

The features of intonation, pausing and the like have been omitted, but you can imagine how it might be spoken.

Commentary

It is very difficult to match this spoken extract with the sentences of written text. The speaker has used a very common technique of oral story telling: the use of *and* to connect actions and events in the story. If we remove most of the *and*s, as well as the repetition of *we had*, we shall have something more like the sentences of written English:

> When I was little, we had a garden in Persia. We had about sixteen cherry trees. I used to spend the whole of the cherry season up a ladder, until one day M, who was our very toothless gardener, got a cherry and opened it. It was a beautiful cherry. He just flicked it with his finger. There was a little worm floating around inside.

What this demonstrates is that sentences are not primarily about how you write them, but about the kinds of structure that they have. We can talk about 'sentences' in spoken discourse, because we recognise structures that correspond to our notions of 'sentence' from written text. For example, 'We had about sixteen cherry trees' is a structure, or pattern, that is very common: a noun or pronoun subject (*we*), followed by a verb (*had*), followed by a noun phrase object (*about sixteen cherry trees*).

A 'sentence', then, is a sequence of words in a structural pattern. The study of grammar seeks to investigate and describe the kinds of structural patterning that a language uses in order to convey meaningful messages between its speakers/hearers and writers/readers. Much of this book is devoted to studying the grammar of English. Now let us examine the term 'word'.

Activity 2

Count the number of words in the following sentence:

His father wants to hand on to him his hard-earned wealth, while his mother desires to put something more valuable into his hand.

Commentary

As you approached this activity, you probably began asking yourself, 'What is meant by a "word" in this instruction?' For example, *his* occurs four times, so is it counted as one word or four? *Hand* occurs twice, but the use is different in the two occurrences: it is used first as a 'verb', after *want to*, and then as a 'noun', after *his*. The term 'word' is not as straightforward as it first looks. To carry out the instruction in Activity 2, you need to have the term specified more precisely.

In terms of running words, or word tokens, such as might be computed by the word count of a word processor – the sequences of letters bounded by spaces – the sentence in Activity 2 has twenty-three 'words'. As we have noted, some of these word tokens have the same (spelling): *his* (4), *hand* (2) – and *to* (3). If these are counted each as one word, then the number of words, or word types, in the sentence is seventeen.

But this does not exhaust the complexity of 'words'. We have noted already that *hand* is used grammatically in two different ways, as a verb and as a noun. Similarly, *to* is used in two ways: as a marker of the 'infinitive' form of the verb, in *to hand* and *to put*; and as a 'preposition' in *to him*. You will notice that *hard-earned* counts as a single word token, even though it contains two 'words', *hard* and *earned*: they have been combined into a 'compound' word. On the other hand, *hand on* is two word tokens, even though it is a single unit as far meaning is concerned (meaning 'transmit'). Notice, too, that having selected *valuable*, the 'comparative' is formed by the addition of the word *more*; whereas, if *costly* had been selected, the comparative could have been *costlier*, which would not have increased the word token count.

How, then, do we define 'word'? We need to recognise different kinds of word:

❑ Words as units of meaning, or items of vocabulary, such as the headwords in a dictionary. The term 'lexeme' is used for words in this sense. So, *hand on, hard-earned, mother, into* are lexemes.

❏ Words as defined by spelling – the sequence of letters bounded by spaces – sometimes called 'orthographic' words. The counterpart in speech – a sequence of sounds – would be a 'phonological' word.

❏ Words as representatives of family variants, such as *costly* including *costlier* and *costliest*. We talked here of a 'lemma' and its word 'forms'. So the adjective lemma COSTLY has the forms: *costly* (base), *costlier* (comparative), *costliest* (superlative).

We note, then, that words have structure: they are made up of sounds in speech and letters in writing. But they also have structure in terms of being made up of elements such as the *-er* of *costlier* or the *-est* of *costliest*, or the combination of *hard* and *earned* in *hard-earned*. Such elements are known as 'morphemes' and are discussed further in Unit A3. Words themselves enter into the structure of sentences, as we noted earlier. The words (specifically 'lexemes') of a language constitute its vocabulary; we explore this topic further in Unit A8.

Activity 3

In our discussion of the term 'sentence', we noted that sentences are best defined in terms of structure. We identified the common structure of 'We/had/about sixteen cherry trees.' This sentence, then, has three elements of structure (which are called 'phrases'), two of which comprise a single word (*we, had*) and the third a sequence of words. Now identify the elements of structure in the following sentences:

1   The bus is coming.
2   Uncle Jim is walking down the steps.
3   I will take his bag.
4   We can put his luggage in the boot.
5   He looks very fit.

Commentary

These sentences illustrate some further common sentence structures of English. The first has two elements of structure (phrases): *the bus* and *is coming*. The second has three: *Uncle Jim, is walking* and *down the steps*. The third has three: *I, will take* and *his bag*. The fourth sentence has four phrases: *We, can put, his luggage* and *in the boot*. And the fifth has three: *He, looks* and *very fit*. You can perhaps perceive some clear patterns and regularities emerging. We explore this further in Units A4 and A5.

Activity 4

In our discussion of words, we noted that some words (lemmas) have what we called 'family variants'. Our particular example was the adjective *costly*, which has a 'comparative' (*costlier*) and a 'superlative' (*costliest*) variant. Many, especially shorter, adjectives are like *costly* in having these two variants. Similarly, many nouns (e.g. *uncle*) have a 'plural' (*uncles*) and a 'possessive' (*uncle's*) variant; and most verbs (e.g. *look*) have a 'third person singular present tense' (*looks*), a 'past tense/past participle' (*looked*) and a 'present participle' (*looking*) variant. Some verbs (e.g. *show, sing*) have different 'past tense' and 'past participle' variants (*showed, shown; sang, sung*). Now list the variants for the following lemmas:

1   *green* (adjective)
2   *fill* (verb)
3   *goat* (noun)
4   *mouse* (noun)
5   *speak* (verb)
6   *buy* (verb)

Commentary

The adjective *green* has the expected variants: *greener, greenest*. Among the verbs, *fill* has the 'regular' forms: *fills, filled, filling*; *speak*, however, has regular *speaks* and *speaking* (as do nearly all verbs), but has irregular 'past tense' (*spoke*) and 'past participle' (*spoken*); *buy*, similarly, has regular *buys* and *buying*, but irregular 'past tense/past participle' (*bought*). The noun *goat* has regular variants *goats* and *goat's*; but *mouse* has an irregular 'plural' (*mice*), but a regular 'possessive' (*mouse's*). Note that where 'plural' and 'possessive' combine, *goat* has *goats'*, while *mouse* has *mice's*. These word variants, termed 'inflections' (see Unit A3), express a number of grammatical choices that speakers/writers may make: singular or plural number, present or past tense, and so on.

WORD CLASSES

The stock of English words is immense. David Crystal (1995: 119) estimates that a conservative figure would approach one million and that, if all the terminology of science were included, it could be twice that much. Each word has a particular role that it can play in the structure of sentences. There are certain grammatical patterns, of sentence and phrase, into which a word may fit, and there may be specific other words with which it may regularly co-occur, its collocational patterning. To describe the grammatical and lexical operation of each of a million words would be a daunting task, and it would turn out that the descriptions would be identical, or very similar, for large sets of words. For this reason, grammarians have traditionally grouped words into classes. The traditional term has been 'parts of speech', but this is not a very transparent term, and linguists now prefer to talk about 'word classes'.

There is substantial, though not universal, agreement about which word classes to recognise for English. They comprise: noun, verb, adjective, adverb, pronoun, determiner, preposition, conjunction. The unfamiliar member of this list is likely to be 'determiner', which we will discuss in more detail below. A list of traditional parts of speech would have included an 'interjection' class (for items like *hey!* and *cor!*), but this is no longer thought necessary; such items would be described as phenomena of spoken discourse.

The word class with the most members is that of 'noun', followed by 'verb' and 'adjective'. The 'adverb' class is also large, but contains a number of subclasses with restricted membership. These four classes are known as the 'open' word classes, because new words in the language are added to one of these. The other classes – pronoun, determiner, preposition, conjunction – have a relatively small membership, which is rarely added to. They are, therefore, known as 'closed' classes.

In general, the members of the open (also known as 'lexical') word classes provide the main referential (lexical) meaning of a sentence, while the members of the closed (also known as 'grammatical') word classes tend to have a structuring function in sentences. This is a gross generalisation; there is more of a spectrum of function from the highly lexical of most nouns and verbs, to the highly grammatical of some determiners, but with the members of some word classes having both a lexical and a grammatical function (e.g. prepositions), but sometimes more one than the other.

The class of 'determiners' includes a restricted number of words that are used to accompany nouns in noun phrases (see Unit B5, Subunit C5.1). It includes, on the one hand, 'identifiers', such as the definite and indefinite articles (*a/an, the*), the possessive identifiers (*my, our, your, his, her, its, their*) and the demonstrative identifiers (*this/these, that/those*); and on the other, 'quantifiers', such as the numerals (*one/two/fifty, first/second/fiftieth*) and indefinite quantifiers (*some, few, several, plenty of,* etc.).

Activity 1

Remove the pronouns, determiners, prepositions and conjunctions from the following, to see how much is lost in terms of meaning. If you are not sure which word class an item belongs to, look it up in a dictionary. (The Collins dictionaries, the tenth edition of the Concise Oxford, and the New Oxford Dictionary include 'determiner' among their word class labels.)

An investigation has been launched at Blackpool Pleasure Beach after 14 people were injured in a rollercoaster accident at the resort. Two teenage boys needed surgery and have been kept in hospital after being cut free from the crushed rear carriage of The Big One ride. Twelve other people were injured and treated for whiplash after the two carriages collided on the world's tallest rollercoaster.

Commentary

If we remove all the pronouns, determiners, prepositions and conjunctions, the text will look like this:

investigation has been launched, Blackpool Pleasure beach, people were injured, rollercoaster accident, resort. teenage boys needed surgery, have been kept hospital, being cut free, crushed rear carriage, Big One ride. other people were injured, treated whiplash, carriages collided, world's tallest rollercoaster.

We should probably also omit the 'auxiliary verbs' (see Subunit C5.2, Unit B2), because they are also essentially 'grammatical' words; in which case, the text will read as follows:

investigation launched, Blackpool Pleasure beach, people injured, rollercoaster accident, resort. teenage boys needed surgery, kept hospital, cut free, crushed rear carriage, Big One ride. other people injured, treated whiplash, carriages collided, world's tallest rollercoaster.

You will notice that the words remaining are the main meaning-bearing ones, but some meaning is lost by the omission of some of the 'grammatical' words, especially the prepositions and conjunctions (*at, after, in, and, from, of, for, on*) and the numbers (*14, two, twelve*). The words that are missed least are probably the indefinite and definite articles (*a/an, the*).

Activity 2

What is a noun? How do we decide which words in English belong to the word class of 'nouns'? A traditional definition is that a noun is 'the name of a person, place or thing'. This is a 'semantic' or 'notional' definition. Try applying it to the following words, all of which we would want to assign to the noun class.

kangaroo, emptiness, tooth, baptism, hostility, pleasure, disturbance, skiing

Commentary

Notional definitions are difficult to apply, and there is room for much disagreement. Of the words in the list above, the definition applies uncontroversially to *kangaroo* and *tooth*, which can both be said to be 'things'; but it is less easy to ascertain the 'thingness' of the remainder. They are all 'abstract' nouns of various kinds: *emptiness* refers to a 'state', *baptism* to an 'action', *enmity* and *pleasure* to 'feelings', *disturbance* to a 'happening', and *skiing* to an 'activity'. Neither 'person', 'place' or 'thing' applies very readily to any of these words. We must, therefore, reject – as linguists have done – a notional definition as a reliable criterion for determining the membership of a word class.

There are, however, other, more reliable, criteria that we can use to establish word classes. Let us remain for the moment with the noun class. If you look again at the list of words in Activity 2, there are two important characteristics that can help us. First, most of the words in this list can have a 'plural' form, for when more than one is being referred to: *kangaroos, emptinesses, teeth, baptisms, hostilities, pleasures, disturbances*. It is characteristic of nouns to have a singular and a plural form, though there is a set of nouns – the 'mass' or 'uncountable' nouns – that do not, and *skiing* is one of those. Second, some of the words have (derivational) endings that are characteristic of nouns: *-ness* (forms nouns from adjectives), *-ism* (forms nouns from verbs in *-ise/-ize*), *-ity* (forms nouns from adjectives), *-ure* (forms nouns from verbs), *-ance* (forms nouns from verbs), *-ing* (forms nouns from verbs). These 'morphological' criteria can be applied more easily: if a word has a plural form, or ends in a suffix such as *-ness, -ity, -ance*, etc., then it belongs to the noun class. Unfortunately, this is not enough to establish the noun class; there are still some 'nouns' that fall outside of these criteria.

Activity 3

There is a criterion that can be applied more widely and will establish a word class with a greater degree of certainty. Identify the nouns in the following. Are there any features of their context or position that they have in common?

There was an emperor who was fond of new clothes and spent all his money on them. One day two swindlers arrived and announced that they knew how to manufacture the most beautiful cloth imaginable. The texture and pattern were uncommonly beautiful, and the clothes made from the cloth had a wonderful quality.

Commentary

The nouns are the following: *emperor, clothes, money, day, swindlers, cloth, texture, pattern, clothes, cloth, quality.* First, notice that many of these nouns are preceded by a definite or indefinite article (e.g. *an emperor, the texture*), or by an adjective (e.g. *new clothes, a wonderful quality*), or by other 'determiners' (e.g. *his money, two swindlers*). In other words, nouns are associated with particular types of other words in the structure of noun phrases (see Unit B5). Second, nouns (and their associated words) typically occur as Subject and Object in the structure of sentences, e.g. *an emperor* (Subject), *all his money* (Object), *two swindlers* (Subject), *a wonderful quality* (Object). Alternatively, they are found after prepositions, e.g. *from the cloth.*

These criteria are syntactic; they relate to the positions in the structure of phrases and sentences where members of the word class may be found. Word classes are most reliably defined by the syntactic behaviour of their members, but morphological and notional criteria can also play a part.

Activity 4

What are the notional, morphological and syntactic criteria that could be used to define the class of 'adjectives'? Here are some examples to help you.

1   The big dog jumped over the lazy fox.
2   Foxes can be very lazy, even lazier than humans.
3   This fox is the laziest that I've met, more idle than your younger brother.
4   The fox is an agricultural menace.

Commentary

First, let us establish which are the adjectives in these sentences: *big, lazy, idle, young, agricultural.* The traditional notional definition of an adjective is: 'a describing word'. This definition is vague enough to fit the vast majority of adjectives, but it is, like most notional definitions, perhaps too vague to apply with any confidence.

In terms of morphology, you will have noticed that *lazy* appears in three forms: the 'base' form *lazy*, the 'comparative' form *lazier*, and the 'superlative' form *laziest* (see further C2.2). Many adjectives have these forms, or the alternatives with *more* and *most* (e.g. *more idle* in No.3), the so-called 'gradable' adjectives; but not all adjectives do, e.g. *priceless, single* (which are 'non-gradable'). As with nouns, there are some typical 'derivational' suffixes for adjectives, e.g. the *-al* of *agricultural* (forming adjectives from nouns), *-ful* and *-less* (*hopeful, priceless*), *-ish* (*foolish*) – also from nouns – *-able/-ible* (from verbs – *readable, compressible*).

Syntactically, adjectives occur in two positions: the 'attributive' position, before nouns, e.g. *the lazy fox, an agricultural menace*; and the 'predicative' position after verbs like *be* and *seem*, e.g. *the fox seems lazy, the diamond is priceless.* With few exceptions, adjectives may occur in either position.

Activity 5

Try the same exercise with verbs: propose notional, morphological and syntactic criteria for establishing the word class of verbs. Then check your attempt with the discussion in Unit B2.

A3 WORD STRUCTURE

In Unit A1, we noted 'words' and 'sentences' as the most basic and familiar terms used for describing language. In this unit we are going to concentrate on 'words' and what they are composed of (the study of 'morphology'). In some sense, they are composed of letters in writing and of sounds in speech; but that is not the focus of our attention. Letters and sounds are in themselves without meaning, though the substitution of one letter or sound for another does make a difference of meaning (e.g. *affect/effect*, *skip/slip*). What we are concerned with are the elements of words that in themselves have a meaningful function in the grammar of the language.

First of all, let us establish the fact that words have structure. Look at the following 'family' of words:

	examine		
re-	examine		
(re-)	examin(e)	-ation	
(re-)	examin(e)	-ation	-s
(re-)	examin(e)	-ed	
(re-)	examin(e)	-ing	

All these possible words (ten in all) have a common core element – *examine* – which is called the 'root' of the word. It is itself an independent word, but composed of a single root element. Most English words have an independent (or 'free') root element, but not all (see below). The other elements in the *examine* words (e.g. *re-*, *-ation*, *-ing*) cannot operate as independent words: they are 'bound' elements. The bound elements can occur only as attachments to a root: they are 'affixes'. Those that are attached to the left of a root (e.g. *re-*), and so are bound on their right side, are called 'prefixes'. Those that are attached to the right of a root (e.g. *-ation*), and so are bound to their left, are called 'suffixes'. You will notice that a hyphen has been used to indicate on which side an affix is bound.

Activity 1

Create a family of words by adding possible affixes to the following roots. Do not make more than six words for each family.

1 appear
2 fright
3 legal
4 teach

You can check whether the words you are proposing are possible words of English by looking them up in a good dictionary.

Now let us establish that the elements of words – which are called 'morphemes' – are not arbitrary sequences of letters or sounds but have a meaning or function. Root morphemes, which function as independent words, clearly have a meaning: they are headwords in dictionaries and are defined there. The claim for the meaningfulness of morphemes rests on the argument that morphemes recur in different words with essentially the same meaning or function.

Activity 2

From the following examples, what do you think is the meaning/function of the morphemes (1) *auto-* (2) *-ify* (3) *-ish* (4) *-wise*?

1   autobiography, autochanger, autofocus, auto-suggestion
2   beautify, clarify, falsify, purify, simplify
3   babyish, dullish, greenish, largish, stiffish
4   clockwise, crabwise, slantwise, stepwise

Commentary

The prefix *auto-* is sometimes used as an abbreviation of 'automatic'. In the examples given here, its original meaning (from Greek *autos*) is more to the fore, namely 'self'. An autobiography is life (*bio*) writing (*graphy*) about oneself (*auto*). *Autochanger* and *autofocus* refer to activities that machines (gramophone, camera) do by themselves (i.e. automatically). An auto-suggestion is self-originated. You will find that the native English prefix *self-* is much more widely used in forming new words than the Greek prefix.

The suffix *-ify* is added to adjectives (*clear, false, pure, simple*) or nouns (*beauty*) to form verbs. It has a causative meaning: 'make' or 'cause to be or become'. This suffix came into English from French, and derives ultimately from the Latin word for 'make' (*facere*).

The suffix *-ish* is added to adjectives (*dull, green, large, stiff*) without changing the word class of the item they are added to, which is unusual for suffixes in English, and to nouns (*baby*), where the word class changes from noun to adjective. With adjectives such as those illustrated, it has the meaning of 'somewhat' or 'rather', whereas with nouns like *baby* the meaning is 'like' or 'characteristic of'.

The suffix *-wise* is added to nouns to form adjectives and adverbs, with the meaning 'like' or 'in the manner of': *clockwise* 'in the manner (i.e. direction) of a clock', *crabwise* 'in the manner of (i.e. walking like) a crab', *slantwise* 'in a slanting manner', *stepwise* 'as if by steps'.

For some bound morphemes (affixes) it is difficult to be very precise about a meaning, beyond describing the function that the morpheme may have in forming new words. For example, the suffix *-ness*, which is used widely for deriving nouns from adjectives (*coldness, lateness, newness, suppleness*) has, if any at all, the meaning, 'the state or quality of being . . .'. A number of prefixes (*dis-, in-, un-*) have a general 'negative' meaning when added to adjectives or nouns (*dishonest, disrepute, infertile, indecision,* *unhappy, unsafe*) and a negative or 'undo' meaning when added to verbs (*displease, disqualify, unfreeze, unravel*).

Morphemes do not always keep the same shape (pronunciation and/or spelling) in all contexts. One of the examples in Activity 2 was *clarify*, which is a combination of the morphemes CLEAR + -IFY. As an independent word, the morpheme CLEAR is spelt 'clear' and pronounced /klɪə/; in combination with the suffix -IFY, it is spelt 'clar' and pronounced /klær/. So the morpheme CLEAR has two realisations or 'allomorphs', {clear /klɪə/} and {clar /klær/}, depending on the context ({clar /klær/} before -IFY and -ITY, {clear /klɪə/} elsewhere, e.g. *clear, clearance, clearly*). Note the convention of using capital letters to indicate morphemes, and { } to encapsulate realisations (allomorphs).

Activity 3

Many morphemes, both free and bound, have more than one realisation. The PLURAL suffix on nouns and the PAST TENSE suffix on verbs are two cases in point. From the following examples, see if you can determine what the allomorphs of each of the morphemes are and what is conditioning the variation. You need to think of the pronunciation rather than the spelling.

1 PLURAL: apples, apricots, peaches
2 PAST TENSE: climbed, jumped, vaulted

Commentary

In terms of spelling, the PLURAL morpheme has two realisations: *-s* and *-es*. The PAST TENSE morpheme could also be said to have two: *-ed* and *-d* (e.g. *saved*). However, we might analyse this differently: the PAST TENSE morpheme is always realised in spelling as *-ed*, but when added to a root ending in 'e' (*save-ed*) one of the 'e' letters elides (so *saved*).

More variation occurs in the pronunciation of these morphemes. The PLURAL morpheme is realised as /z/ in *apples*, as /s/ in *apricots*, and as /ɪz/ in *peaches*. The PAST TENSE morpheme is realised as /d/ in *climbed*, as /t/ in *jumped*, and as /ɪd/ in *vaulted*. The variation is parallel and is conditioned by the final sound of the noun or verb root. Where the final sound is the same or similar to that of the suffix, /s, z/ in the case of the PLURAL, /t, d/ for the PAST TENSE, then the /ɪ/ vowel is inserted, in order to make the suffix pronounceable (*peaches* /piːtʃɪz/, *vaulted* /vɒltɪd/). Otherwise, where the final sound of the root is a voiced sound, the suffix is voiced /z, d/ (*apples* /æpəlz/, *climbed* /klaɪmd/); and where it is voiceless, the suffix is voiceless /s, t/ (*apricots* /eɪprɪkɒts/, *jumped* /dʒʌmpt/). The allomorphs of these morphemes are said to be 'phonologically conditioned'. The variation can be expressed, perhaps more accessibly, as follows:

PLURAL = {-es /ɪz/} after root-final sibilant (/s z ʃ ʒ tʃ dʒ/)
　　　　　　{-s /z/} after other root-final voiced sounds
　　　　　　{-s /s/} after other root-final voiceless consonants
PAST 　 = {-ed /ɪd/} after root-final alveolar consonants (/t d/)
TENSE 　 {-ed /d/} after other root-final voiced sounds
　　　　　　{-ed /t/} after other voiceless consonants

Activity 4

Finally in this unit, we are going to follow up on the remark made earlier that not all roots in English are free. Which element is the root in each of the following words?

1   disgruntled
2   contain
3   xenophobe
4   linguist

Commentary

You have probably struggled to find a sensible answer to the question asked, though you have the clue that it is a bound root that you are looking for; so, it will not be an independent word. In each of the words listed there are recognisable elements; but we need to remind ourselves of two principles of word structure: (1) you cannot recognise a morpheme if the remainder of the word cannot be sensibly analysed; (2) a morpheme has a constant meaning in all the words in whose structure it appears.

If you look *disgruntled* up in a dictionary, it will tell you that it is an adjective. However, like many other adjectives, it looks like the past tense or past participle of a verb, with the *-ed* suffix. The prefix *dis-*, with its 'negative' meaning, is recognisable from other words, and *grunt* could be a free root morpheme. That leaves *-le* as an element that is not accounted for. You will find *-le* listed in dictionaries as a verb-forming suffix with the meaning 'denoting repeated or continuous action, often of a trivial nature' (*Collins English Dictionary*), e.g. in *dazzle* (DAZE + -LE), *wrestle* (WREST + -LE). We can, then, account for all the elements in *disgruntled*. However, there is no verb *gruntle* in current standard English, though there may still be in some dialects, and it does have an entry in the *Oxford English Dictionary*, indicating that it did exist at some time. Similarly, the OED has an entry for the (transitive) verb *disgruntle*, defined as 'to put into sulky dissatisfaction or ill-humour'; 'to chagrin', 'disgust'. Modern dictionaries list only the adjective *disgruntled*, and sometimes the adjective *gruntled* (meaning 'satisfied', 'contented'), which is noted to be a backformation (see B3) from *disgruntled*. What do we conclude? Although we can trace the structure of *disgruntled* historically, as far as the current standard vocabulary is concerned, it cannot be analysed into morphemes, because the verb *gruntle* has been lost to the language.

Contain presents a different, though widespread, morphological problem. On the surface it appears to be composed of two morphemes: the prefix *con-*, a variant of *com-*, meaning 'with' (as in *con-demn* (i.e. 'damn'), *con-descend*, *con-figure*); and a seeming root *tain*, as in *de-tain*, *re-tain*, *sus-tain*. However, *tain* does not occur as an independent word in English; it derives from Latin *tenere* ('to hold'); and even as a bound root, *-tain*, it is perhaps doubtful whether a common meaning, either its Latin one or some other, can be detected reliably across all the words in which it occurs. It is probably best to regard words like *contain* as not amenable to valid analysis. There are many words like this, which were borrowed from Latin into English centuries ago, and which have changed their meaning in the course of time, so that the meanings of the individual parts are no longer visible to the modern speaker of English.

Xenophobe is an altogether different kind of word. It is made up of two elements, neither of which occurs as an independent word: *xeno-*, *-phobe*. Both elements occur in other words, with a constant meaning; e.g. *xeno-* in *xenogamy, xenograft, xenotransplant,* *-phobe* in *arachnophobe, claustrophobe, neophobe*. The meaning is close to the meaning of the words in Greek, from which they are borrowed into English: *xeno-* = *xenos* 'stranger', 'foreigner', *-phobe* = *phobos* 'fear', 'dread'. The two Greek roots have been combined, to form a 'neo-classical compound' (see C3.1). They are known in English as 'combining forms' and are a type of bound root.

Linguist contains the suffix *-ist*, one of the 'agentive' suffixes in English, indicating a person who 'does' or 'is competent' in something, e.g. *scient-ist, violin-ist*. A linguist is competent in *lingua*, Latin for 'tongue', 'language'. It occurs, with the same meaning, in words like *bilingual, audio-lingual, multilingual,* but not as an independent word. Consequently, we may regard *lingu(a)-* as a bound root.

Summary

In this unit, we have established that words are composed of morphemes, realised as sequences of letters/sounds ((allo)morphs) with a constant meaning/function. A word is composed of at least one root morpheme, to which may be added affixes (prefixes and suffixes). Root morphemes are normally free, affixes are always bound.

A4 SLOTS AND FILLERS

In Units A1, B1, etc., we established that sentences have structure, and that this is, in fact, their defining feature. In this unit, and in B4 and C4, we are going to look at the nature of this structure in more detail, and at its major elements.

The elements of a sentence can be viewed grammatically from two perspectives: the type or 'category' of element that they are, and the 'function' that they perform in the structure of the sentence. The functions constitute the 'slots', and the categories are the 'fillers'. This view of the grammatical structure of sentences derives from Tagmemic Linguistics (e.g. Pike and Pike 1977). It analyses a sentence into identifiable elements, each with their specific function in the structure.

Let us begin with a simple sentence (composed of one clause) with a commonly occurring pattern:

Anglers catch fish.

Each word in this sentence represents an element, or fills a slot. *Anglers* represents the element that 'does something'; *catch* represents the 'action' that the actor performs; and *fish* represents the victim of the action. Each element consists of a single word, but they could each be expanded, while retaining the same basic structure of the sentence:

All the intrepid anglers | have caught | many excellent fish.
All the intrepid anglers from the club | have been catching | many excellent fish of a good size.

Activity 1

Now you divide the following sentences into their elements. All the sentences have the same three-part structure as 'Anglers catch fish.'

1   Jack Sprat ate no fat.
2   He pulled out a plum.
3   The old man wouldn't say his prayers.
4   A naughty boy drowned the poor pussy cat.
5   Simple Simon tasted the pieman's wares.
6   The cat chased the mice that lived in the barn.

Commentary

Following the pattern, each sentence has a doer: *Jack Sprat, He, The old man, A naughty boy, Simple Simon, The cat*; an action: *ate, pulled out, wouldn't say, drowned, tasted, chased*; and a victim: *no fat, a plum, his prayers, the poor pussy cat, the pieman's wares, the mice that lived in the barn*. You will notice that the order of the elements is the same in each case: Subject-Verb-Object, to use the technical grammatical (slot) terms.

Subject-Verb-Object is the usual order of elements in English sentences, at least in those of the most common 'declarative' type (see Unit B1), used typically for making statements (see Subunit C1.1). The order defines the slots, e.g. the Subject is the element that precedes the Verb. So 'The boy hit the girl' is a different sentence from 'The girl hit the boy.' English does not mark its nouns for Subject and Object, as does Latin for example, only its pronouns. Compare:

He hit her.
She hit him.

'Him she hit' (Object-Subject-Verb) is thus unambiguous, whereas 'The boy the girl hit' is not, because *him* is the Object form (of *he*), and *she* is the Subject form, while it is only the positions of *the boy* and *the girl* that indicate their function: Subject before the Verb, and Object following.

Activity 2

Examine the sentences at A and B below. They all have three elements, but the third element in the B sentences is different from that in the A sentences. Can you detect what the difference is?

A   The minister answered the difficult questions.
    Students must register their choice of modules.
    Michael drives fast cars.
B   The minister is an honest politician.
    Students should be hard-working.
    Michael seems a competent driver.

Commentary

The A sentences have the same structure as those we have been considering so far in this unit (Subject-Verb-Object). In the B sentences, the first element (Subject) is not the doer of an action, and the third element is not the victim. The Verb elements (*is, should be, seems*) do not represent 'actions', but rather 'states'; and the third element is descriptive of the first (Subject) element. This element is termed a

'Complement', rather than an 'Object'; it reflects back on – and complements – the Subject. For further discussion of the differences between Objects and Complements, see Subunit C4.1.

Activity 3

Now examine the sentences at C below. The third element is again different from that in either the A or B sentences above. How does it differ?

C   The minister jumped onto the podium.
    Students should assemble in the hall.
    Michael is driving to Budapest.

Commentary

The third element in each of these sentences (*onto the podium, in the hall, to Budapest*) represents a 'place'. The Verb element (*jumped, should assemble, is driving*) represents an 'action', but one involving 'movement', and the third element is the destination or place of the action. This type of element is termed an 'Adverbial'.

Adverbial elements are not exclusively concerned with place (where?) or destination (where to?). They represent all kinds of circumstantial information, including 'time' (when?), 'manner' (how?), 'reason' (why?):

The minister resigned *at 3.00 pm.*
Students should work *very diligently.*
Michael withdrew *because his engine blew up.*

The differences between Objects and Adverbials are discussed further in Subunit C4.2.

Summary

We have identified five types of slot that occur in the structure of English sentences: Subject, Verb, Object, Complement, Adverbial. The most usual kind of sentence will contain at least a Subject slot and a Verb slot. Many will also contain an Object or Complement (sometimes both), and/or one or more Adverbials. We have noted that the Subject usually precedes the Verb, while Object and Complement follow. Adverbials are more flexible in their position of occurrence, but commonly occur either as the last or first elements of sentences. The range of sentence patterns found in English is discussed in Unit A5.

While Subject and Verb are common to nearly all sentence structures, the possible occurrence of Object and Complement slots, and to a lesser extent Adverbial slots, depends on the main verb word selected for the Verb slot. For example, the verb *smile* may occur simply in a Subject-Verb structure: 'Lucy smiled.' Alternatively, the sentence may additionally contain an Adverbial slot: 'Lucy smiled contentedly', 'Lucy smiled at the bus driver.' The verb *become*, however, routinely requires a Complement slot, in addition to a Subject and Verb: 'The lawyer became angry', 'Rachel became a missionary.' And the verb *throw* usually requires an Object and an Adverbial (of place/direction): 'They threw the package into the river.' The general meaning of the verb word thus has an influence on the stucture of the sentence; this insight derives from an approach to linguistic description called 'Valency Grammar' (e.g. Allerton 1982), ultimately from the work of the French linguist, Lucien Tesnière (1953).

Activity 4
Which slots, in addition to Subject and Verb, do the following verbs typically require in the sentences in which they occur?

1 *catch*   2 *fall*   3 *seem*
4 *shine*   5 *drive*

Commentary

1   *catch* in its most usual meaning ('take into the hands and hold') requires an Object (the thing caught): 'Lucy caught the ball', 'The police caught the thief.'
2   *fall* does not require any further slot apart from the Subject ('The leaves are falling'), but it is frequently followed by an Adverbial (of place/direction), e.g. 'The child fell into the pond.' When there is no Adverbial, 'to the ground' is often implied, as in the case of 'The leaves are falling.'
3   *seem* normally requires a Complement slot: 'You seem tired', 'The weather seems rather changeable.'
4   *shine*, in one of its meanings, has no slot additional to the Subject ('The sun is shining', 'His boots were shining'); but *shine* can also be used in the sense of 'make something shine', in which case an Object slot also occurs ('He was shining his boots'). Note the relationship between 'His boots were shining' and 'He was shining his boots'; there are a number of verbs in English which can be used similarly, e.g. *break, open.*
5   *drive*, in its most obvious sense, is illustrated by our earlier example, 'Michael drives fast cars', with an Object slot; but consider also the following examples:
    a   Michael drove to Budapest (Adverbial of place/direction).
    b   Michael drove the Ferrari to Budapest (Object + Adverbial).
    c   The Ferrari drives well (Adverbial of manner).
    d   Michael drives me mad (Object + Complement).

In the case of d), of course, the meaning of *drive* is no longer literal; this is a metaphorical extension of the meaning. Notice, too, in this example that the Complement reflects back on the Object.

Fillers
We have identified five types of slot in the sentence structures of English, some of which may occur more than once (though not Subject, Verb, or Complement). The question now is: what categories of element may occur in each of these slots? We will answer this question in general terms, leaving the more detailed explanation to other units.

From the examples discussed in this unit, it is clear that a slot may be filled by a single word: the Verb slot by a verb word, Subject and Object slots by a noun or pronoun (*he, her*), the Complement slot by an adjective (*angry*) or noun, the Adverbial slot by an adverb (*contentedly*). More usually, rather than a single word, a slot is filled by a group of words based on a 'main' word: a phrase. Indeed the single word is often viewed as the minimal form of the phrase. So, the Verb slot is filled by a verb phrase (Unit B5), the Subject and Object slots by a noun phrase (Unit B5), the Complement slot by an adjective phrase (Sub/unit C5.3) or a noun phrase, and the Adverbial slot by an adverb phrase or a prepositional phrase (*very diligently, in the hall, to Budapest*).

All the slots apart from the Verb slot may also be filled by a subordinate clause (*because his engine blew up*). A subordinate clause (see Unit A6) has the basic structure of a sentence, but it mainly has a function within the slot of another sentence as Subject, Object, Complement or Adverbial, e.g.

Birds singing in the trees delighted the poet (Subject).
The protestors argued *that the new road was unnecessary* (Object).
Relaxation is *sitting by the river with a good book* (Complement).
I will tell you the news *when you get back* (Adverbial).

✪ Activity 5

Analyse the following sentences into their elements. Give a slot and a category label to each element.

1   The train has arrived.
2   The guests thanked their host most warmly.
3   You are looking very posh.
4   The forecasters have predicted that we shall have a hot summer.
5   We cannot come to your party because we are on holiday.

Commentary

The solutions are as follows:

1   *The train* (Subject: noun phrase) – *has arrived* (Verb: verb phrase).
2   *The guests* (Subject: noun phrase) – *thanked* (Verb: verb (phrase)) – *their host* (Object: noun phrase) – *most warmly* (Adverbial: adverb phrase).
3   *You* (Subject: pronoun) – *are looking* (Verb: verb phrase) – *very posh* (Complement: adjective phrase).
4   *The forecasters* (Subject: noun phrase) – *have predicted* (Verb: verb phrase) – *that . . . summer* (Object: clause).
5   *We* (Subject: pronoun) – *cannot come* (Verb: verb phrase) – *to your party* (Adverbial: prepositional phrase) – *because . . . holiday* (Adverbial: clause).

Clearly, the clauses could in turn be analysed in the same way (see Unit B6).

SENTENCE PATTERNS

In Unit A4 we established the types of element or slot that can make up the structure of English sentences. We also noted that, while Subject and Verb occur in most sentences, the occurrence of other slots is determined in part by the main verb word in the Verb slot, e.g. *catch* expects an Object slot. In this unit we shall examine the main patterns of sentence structure that result from the possible combinations of elements.

Activity 1
Identify and name the slots in the following sentences:

1   The marks have disappeared.
2   The children have gone into the garden.
3   Your hair is a mess.
4   The team has achieved a great victory.
5   I will tell you a story.
6   We consider her our star pupil.
7   The secretary will put a notice on the board.

Commentary
The first four of these sentences have structures that we have discussed already (in Unit A4), but the last three may have been more difficult to work out. The analysis is as follows:

1   *The marks* (Subject) – *have disappeared* (Verb).
2   *The children* (Subject) – *have gone* (Verb) – *into the garden* (Adverbial).
3   *Your hair* (Subject) – *is* (Verb) – *a mess* (Complement).
4   *The team* (Subject) – *has achieved* (Verb) – *a great victory* (Object).
5   *I* (Subject) – *will tell* (Verb) – *you* (Object) – *a story* (Object).
6   *We* (Subject) – *consider* (Verb) – *her* (Object) – *our star pupil* (Complement).
7   *The secretary* (Subject) – *will put* (Verb) – *a notice* (Object) – *on the board* (Adverbial).

You will notice that the pattern of each of these sentences is different. Arguably, each sentence is grammatically complete and makes sense; and, equally, if any element were omitted, the sentence would be grammatically incomplete, not make sense, or have a quite different meaning. These patterns are therefore 'basic' for the verbs that they contain. In fact, they are considered to be the seven basic patterns that underlie all the occurring sentences of English. They may vary according to context: elements may be omitted or rearranged. The sentences may be added to by further Adverbials. But, in the end, any sentence of English can be traced back structurally to one of these patterns.

Transitive and intransitive
Traditionally, a distinction is made between 'transitive' and 'intransitive' sentence structures, and by implication verbs. Dictionaries continue to label verbs as transitive (vt) and/or intransitive (vi). Transitive verbs are those that are followed by an Object

slot; so transitive sentences are those that contain an Object slot. Intransitive verbs and sentences do not. Thus, in the list above, Nos. 1 to 3 are 'intransitive' sentences, and Nos. 4 to 7 are transitive. Clearly, this is quite a crude distinction and does not do justice to the range of sentence patterns in English. The transitive/intransitive distinction does reflect one important syntactic process, however: it is by and large only transitive sentences that can be made passive (see Unit B1), because in transforming an active into a passive sentence, the Object of the active sentence is made the Subject of the passive.

We need a more extensive set of terms to talk about the sentence patterns of English outlined above. The genuinely 'intransitive' pattern is No. 1, with just a Subject and a Verb slot. No. 2 can also be called 'intransitive'; it has a more-or-less obligatory Adverbial (most frequently of 'place/direction') in addition to the Subject and Verb. The third sentence, with a Complement in addition to Subject and Verb, is termed an 'intensive' pattern, where the Complement reflects back (intensively) on the Subject, in contrast to the 'extensive' nature of the transitive patterns. No. 4 is the genuinely 'transitive' pattern, though to distinguish it from the others, it is termed 'mono-transitive', because it contains a single Object slot. No. 5 is, thus, 'di-transitive', because it contains two Objects. No. 6, with an Object and Complement slot, is termed 'complex-transitive'; here the Complement reflects back on the Object. And No. 7 relates to No.4 in the same way that No. 2 relates to No. 1, i.e. it is a mono-transitive pattern with a more-or-less obligatory Adverbial (again usually of 'place/direction').

Summary
The underlying sentence patterns of English are:

1   Subject – Verb (intransitive) [SV]
2   Subject – Verb – Adverbial (intransitive) [SVA]
3   Subject – Verb – Complement (intensive) [SVC]
4   Subject – Verb – Object (mono-transitive) [SVO]
5   Subject – Verb – Object – Object (di-transitive) [SVOO]
6   Subject – Verb – Object – Complement (complex-transitive) [SVOC]
7   Subject – Verb – Object – Adverbial (mono-transitive) [SVOA]

The conventional abbreviations (initial capital letters) are in square [] brackets.

Activity 2
Identify the sentence patterns underlying the following sentences (based on a BBC News Website report):

1   Burmese police stop Suu Kyi.
2   The 1991 Nobel Peace Prize laureate and other members of her party left Rangoon on Thursday morning.
3   Police halted them at the nearby town of Dala.
4   They have not returned home.
5   A plainclothes security official told reporters not to go to Dala.
6   Aung San Suu Kyi became leader of the pro-democracy movement in 1988.

7   The military placed Ms Suu Kyi under house arrest for six years.
8   Suu Kyi is the daughter of the late Burmese nationalist leader, General Aung San.
9   Some of her party's members have been jailed.

Commentary

1   This sentence (a headline) has a straightforward SVO pattern: *Burmese police* [S]
     – *stop* [V] – *Suu Kyi* [O].
2   This also has the SVO pattern, but with an added Adverbial (*on Thursday morn-
     ing*). The Subject is *The 1991 Nobel . . . of her party*; the Verb is *left*; and the Object
     is *Rangoon*. The Adverbial is arguably an optional element: the verb *leave* forms
     a complete sentence with a Subject (someone/something that leaves) and an Object
     (the thing/place that is left): *She left Rangoon*. The Adverbial (of time) is needed
     because a simple past tense verb (*left*) requires specification of the time when it
     happened (see Subunit C5.2); compare *She has left Rangoon*, where the (present
     perfect) verb does not require such specification. So, this is an underlying SVO
     pattern, rather than SVOA.
3   This sentence likewise has SVO and A: *Police* [S], *halted* [V], *them* [O] and *at
     the nearby town of Dala* [Adverbial of place]. Is this an SVO pattern or an SVOA
     pattern? Is the Adverbial slot obligatory with the verb *halt*? Arguably, in both its
     intransitive form (*They halted at Dala*) and, as here, in its transitive form, *halt*
     expects the specification of 'where' the halting happened. But it does not appear
     to be absolutely necessary: *Police halted them* is not unequivocally incomplete.
     Whether Adverbials (especially of place/direction) are obligatory or not is a mat-
     ter of degree, rather than being an either/or decision. So, whether this sentence
     has an underlying SVO pattern or SVOA is a matter of judgement.
4   The underlying pattern for this sentence is probably SVA: *They* [S], *have not returned*
     [V], *home* [A of place/direction]. Again, it is a matter of judgement whether the
     Adverbial is obligatory; but *They have not returned* assumes a place, i.e. where 'they'
     started out from.
5   The pattern that underlies this sentence is SVOO: *A plain clothes security official*
     [S], *told* [V], *reporters* [O], *not to go to Dala* [O].
6   This sentence has the intensive pattern SVC, with an additional Adverbial (of time):
     Aung San Suu Kyi [S], *became* [V], *leader of the pro-democracy movement* [C], *in
     1988* [A].
7   The pattern here is almost certainly SVOA, with the verb *place* (like *put*) having
     a very strong requirement for an Adverbial of place/direction. There is an addi-
     tional Adverbial of time: *The military* [S], *placed* [V], *Ms Suu Kyi* [O], *under house
     arrest* [A of place], *for six years* [A of time].
8   This sentence has only the three elements of the SVC pattern: *Suu Kyi* [S], *is* [V],
     the daughter of the late Burmese nationalist leader, General Aung San [C]. Here the
     pattern has its typical verb, *be*; in this case in an 'equational' pattern, where the
     Subject and Complement are in a relation of equivalence and are potentially
     reversible: *The daughter of the late Burmese nationalist leader is Suu Kyi*.
9   This last sentence has two elements: *Some of her party's members* [S], *have been
     jailed* [V], but the underlying pattern is not the intransitive SV structure. This

sentence is in the passive form, and is derived from the active transitive structure: *[Someone] jailed some of her party's members.* So, the underlying pattern is mono-transitive [SVO].

This exercise has shown that one of the main analytical problems in recognising an underlying pattern in an occurring sentence relates to the status of Adverbials of place/direction. We have, of course, been using written sentences for our examples. When we try to relate the material of spoken discourse to sentence patterns, there are a number of other analytical problems that confront us, e.g. omission of elements, rearrangement of elements, non-relevant items of speech (*um, er, you know,* etc.), items used to structure spoken language but which do not form part of underlying sentence patterns (many instances of *and* or *cos* (*because*?)). Nevertheless, the contention still stands that the seven patterns identified in this unit underlie the structure of all occurring sentences.

CLAUSES AND PHRASES

In Unit A4, we mentioned 'clauses' and 'phrases' as types of element that fill the slots of sentence structure. In Unit A1, we called 'sentence' and 'word' the basic elements of grammatical structure. In a hierarchy of grammatical elements, 'clause' and 'phrase' come between 'sentence' and 'word', in terms both of their usual size and of their place in the structure. A common convention in British linguistics is to recognise a clear hierarchy of grammatical units: sentence – clause – phrase – word. The units at any level are composed of units at the level next below and function in the structure of the units next above, with a certain amount of variation. This is the approach taken in 'Scale and Category' grammar, associated with the names of Michael Halliday and John Sinclair (e.g. Scott *et al.* 1968).

Thus a 'simple' sentence (A4, A5) is composed of one clause, and the terms 'clause' and 'sentence' are in effect interchangeable. 'Complex' sentences containing more than one clause are discussed in Unit B6.

Phrases are elements that fill the slots of clauses (A4). Most types of phrase contain a word that forms the core of the phrase. It is usually called the 'head' of the phrase, and it is the minimal form of the phrase.

Activity 1

Which is the 'head' word of the following phrases? Try removing elements from the phrase and determine which word cannot be removed without irretrievably altering the meaning of the phrase.

1   his cautious approach to the euro
2   has been proposed
3   very enthusiastic about the new currency
4   quite simply
5   a number of photographs of his family attending church
6   over the summer

Commentary

The headword in the first phrase is *approach*, which is a noun; so the phrase is a 'noun phrase', since phrases are termed after their headword. In the second, the headword is *proposed*, here the past participle of the verb *propose*; so the phrase is a 'verb phrase'. The third phrase has *enthusiastic* as the headword, which is an adjective; so this is an 'adjective phrase'. Of the two words in the fourth phrase, the head is *simply*, an adverb: it is an 'adverb phrase'. The fifth phrase is a noun phrase, like No. 1, and the head noun is *photographs*. All these phrases – noun, verb, adjective, adverb – are composed of the headword as the minimal element, and a number of possible 'modifiers'.

The phrase at No. 6 is rather different from the others. There is no single head-word: both *over* and *summer* need to be present for the phrase to make sense. *Over* is a preposition, and *summer* is a noun; the phrase is a 'prepositional phrase'. They are composed of an initial preposition followed usually by a noun phrase. Prepositional phrases are commonly occurring elements. They frequently fill the Adverbial slot, with information on place/direction (*in the hall, to the lighthouse*), on time (*on Monday, over the summer*), on manner (*with difficulty, by bus*), on cause/reason (*because of the rain*), and so on. The also function as modifiers of nouns (e.g. *to the euro* in No. 1 above, *of his family* in No. 5) and modifiers of adjectives (e.g. *about the new currency* in No. 3 above).

Let us return for a moment to the adverb phrase, illustrated at No. 4 above (*quite simply*). Adverb phrases also fill the Adverbial slot in sentence structure, most often as manner (*very carefully*) or time (*fairly soon*) Adverbials, or as some kind of comment (*quite frankly*). Their structure is very simple: the headword is an adverb, which may – though this is relatively infrequent – be modified by another adverb, usually from the set of so-called 'intensifying' adverbs (*very, quite, fairly, extremely*, etc.).

Summary

There are five types of phrase, as follows:

Noun Phrase (NP), composed of a head noun (or pronoun), with possible modifiers (see further Unit B5 and Subunit C5.1)

Verb Phrase (VP), composed of a head verb, with possible modifiers (see further Unit B5 and Subunit C5.2)

Adjective Phrase (AdjP), composed of a head adjective, with possible modifiers (see further Subunit C5.3)

Adverb Phrase (AdvP), composed of a head adverb, with a possible preceding modifying adverb

Prepositional Phrase (PrepP), composed of a preposition and a noun phrase

The first four types of phrase may contain a single word (the head), or more than one word (the head + modifier(s)).

Clauses

Clauses are the elements of sentence structure. A sentence may consist of a single clause, or a sentence may have two (or more) clauses, with one 'embedded' in the other. Here is an example:

The careers adviser told her that she needed further training.

This is a di-transitive sentence pattern (see Unit A5), containing two Object slots (see B4). The first is filled by the pronoun *her*; the second is filled by *that she needed further training*. If the initial *that* is omitted, what remains is a normal mono-transitive (SVO) sentence (A5): *she* (S) – *needed* (V) – *further training* (O). However, because it fills the Object slot in another sentence, it is an embedded clause with a 'subordinate' or 'dependent' structure, signalled by the introductory conjunction *that*.

Now consider this further example:

The careers adviser told her to gain some more experience.

The structural pattern is the same (SVOO), and the second Object slot is again filled by a clause: *to gain some more experience*. However, in this case, the mono-transitive structure of the clause is incomplete: *to gain* (V) – *some more experience* (O). The Subject slot is missing, and you will notice that the verb is in the infinitive form (*to gain*). In cases like this, the missing Subject can usually be supplied from elsewhere in the sentence, normally the nearest noun or pronoun to the left: *her* in this sentence. This is an example where a sentence structure has undergone some adaptation as a result of being used as a subordinate clause.

Activity 2

Identify the subordinate clauses in the following sentences and say whether the clause is a complex structure or has undergone an adaptation of its structure.

1   I'll ask if the train has arrived yet.
2   We cannot assume that it is running on time.
3   I don't know where the enquiry desk is.
4   What we need to know is its scheduled arrival time.
5   Waiting for trains can be tedious.
6   You requested me to check the timetable.
7   If the train is late, they'll miss their connection.
8   They're coming to Birmingham to see Twelfth Night at the theatre.
9   You mean the Repertory Theatre, which is on Broad Street.
10 It has a reputation extending back a long way.

Commentary

These sentences illustrate some of the variety of subordinate clauses that are found in English. Subordinate clauses both complicate the syntax of sentences and provide an important extension to the communicative resources of the language. A sentence may contain a number of clauses, and clauses may contain further clauses. Our example sentences, however, contain only one subordinate clause each.

1   The subordinate clause is *if the train has arrived yet*, which fills the Object slot. It has a complete sentence structure (SVA), with the addition of the introductory conjunction *if*. The conjunction *if* often functions as the introduction to a 'conditional' clause (e.g. in No. 7 above); here it introduces an indirect (or reported) yes/no interrogative (see Subunit C1.2) after the verb *ask*. In this context it has an alternative: *whether*.

2 The subordinate clause is *that it is running on time*, which fills the Object slot in the sentence. It has a complete sentence structure (SVA), with the addition of the introductory conjunction *that*. Such clauses are termed 'that-clauses', and they usually function as indirect statements or thoughts.

3 The subordinate clause is *where the enquiry desk is*, which fills the Object slot. It is introduced by a *wh*-word, and it has a complete sentence structure (ASV), with no additions: the *wh*-word (*where*) fills the Adverbial slot in the clause. Such clauses are termed 'wh-clauses', and their structure is similar to that of *wh*-interrogatives (see Subunit C1.2). They often function as indirect *wh*-questions.

4 The subordinate clause is *what we need to know*, which is also a *wh*-clause, though here filling the Subject slot. It has a complete sentence structure (OSV), with *what* filling the Object slot in the clause.

5 The subordinate clause is *waiting for trains*, which fills the Subject slot in the sentence. It is not a complete structure; it contains just a Verb (*waiting for*) and an Object (*trains*). The Subject is missing, and the verb is in the present participle form. The Subject cannot be recovered from the sentence; the Subject could be anybody; the focus is on the event of 'waiting'.

6 The subordinate clause is *to check the timetable*, which fills the second Object slot. It is again an incomplete structure, with just a Verb and Object. In this case, however, the Subject can be recovered: it is the same as the first Object (*me*). The verb is in the infinitive form.

7 The subordinate clause is *if the train is late*, which fills an Adverbial slot. The clause has a complete structure (SVC), with an introductory conjunction, *if*, indicating a 'condition'.

8 The subordinate clause is *to see Twelfth Night at the theatre*, which also fills an Adverbial slot. However, the clause is an incomplete structure: the verb is in the infinitive form, and the Subject is missing, though recoverable (*they*). As an Adverbial, an infinitive clause usually indicates a 'purpose' meaning.

9 The subordinate clause is *which is on Broad Street*. This clause has a rather different function from those previously considered. It does not fill a slot in sentence structure, but is a modifier within the Object noun phrase (*the Repertory Theatre, which is on Broad Street*). It has a complete structure (SVA); the Subject slot is filled by *which*, a 'relative pronoun'. And the clause is termed a 'relative clause' (see C6.2).

10 The subordinate clause is *extending back a long way*; it also functions as a modifier in a noun phrase (head noun *reputation*). But it does not have a complete structure, and the verb is in the present participle form (*extending*). The missing Subject is the head noun of the noun phrase.

What these examples illustrate is that subordinate clauses come in various forms:

a *if-/whether*-clause, *that*-clause, *wh*-clause, relative clause
b infinitive clause, *-ing*-clause (i.e. present participle)

The clauses at (a) are 'finite' clauses, with a complete sentence structure and a finite verb phrase (see Unit B5). Those at (b) are 'non-finite' clauses, with incomplete structure – usually a missing Subject – and a non-finite verb phrase.

Subordinate clauses also have various functions: as Subject, Object, Complement and Adverbial in sentence structure – particularly as Object; and as a modifier in noun phrases.

A7 GRAMMAR RULES

Activity 1
Write down the first two rules of grammar that come into your head.

Commentary
Unless we stop to think about it, along with most people, we have a strange notion of what constitutes a rule of grammar. Some people immediately think of grammar as being about the rules of writing, especially punctuation. I should not be surprised if many of you have written down statements such as the following: 'you must not end a sentence with a preposition' or 'you should never begin a sentence with "and" or "but"'. You may have a slightly more sophisticated rule, such as the one much loved by government ministers and constructors of the National Curriculum in the UK: '"subjects must agree with their verbs"; i.e. it's "you were", not "you was", silly!'

Rules expressed in this way focus on the 'dos' and 'donts' of, usually, writing, though some people will transfer such notions to speech. One of the reactions that you frequently get if you say that you are a teacher of English language is a confession of 'poor grammar', or 'I'll have to watch what I say.' But linguists do not consider themselves to be language police, because they do not believe that there are 'rules' that need to be enforced. That is not what is meant by 'grammar rules'. So, a preposition may be something that you end a sentence with. And, a conjunction is not always out of place at the beginning of a sentence.

Activity 2
Look back at Units A4 and A5. Is there any suggestion in those units of what linguists might regard as a 'grammar rule'?

Commentary
In A4, there are statements like, 'Subject-Verb-Object is the usual order of elements in English sentences', 'Subject and Verb are common to nearly all sentence structures'. In A5, we propose seven basic sentence patterns for English and state, 'any sentence of English can be traced back to one of these patterns'.

What statements like these imply is that sentences cannot be put together randomly. There are constraints on the structure of sentences and of their elements (phrases and clauses). There are limitations on which elements can occur together and on the order in which they may occur. There is a set of grammatical rules, according to which sentences, and their elements, are usually constructed. If such a set of rules did not exist, we would find it rather difficult to communicate.

The rules are codified in grammar books (e.g. Quirk *et al.* 1985, Biber *et al.* 1999), but we do not, in general, learn them, as we learn the Highway Code, for example, in order to become a proficient driver. The codified rules of a grammatical description are a (more or less accurate) reflection of what we have internalised in our brains as a result of the process of language acquisition. When we receive schooling in the rules of grammar, it is either to acquaint us with the dialect (usually the 'standard') that is used in education and with which we are not familiar from our pre-school experience, or to instruct us in aspects of the craft of writing, e.g. the formation of complex sentences or of textual structure.

Activity 3

Rules operate at many levels of grammatical structure. Formulate rules for the following in English:

1   the plurals of nouns
2   the comparative of adjectives
3   the use of *some*
4   the use of *who, whom* and *whose* as relative pronouns

Commentary

1 If you have written no other rule down for the plural of nouns, you will have specified that an 's' or 'es' is added to the end of the singular form of a noun. Unfortunately, and this is the case with most rules of grammar, the situation is rather more complicated than that. First of all, we need to note that such a rule refers to spelling, and not to pronunciation. Second, we need to specify under which circumstances 's' is added, and under which 'es' is added. Clearly, '-s' is the most usual plural suffix; '-es' is added when the singular form of the noun ends in 's' (*mosses*), 'z' (*waltzes*), 'sh' (*dishes*), 'o' (*tomatoes*), or 'y' (if it is preceded by a consonant letter) – which changes to 'i' (*ponies* but *boys*). Occasionally a single 's' or 'z' at the end of the singular may double when the plural suffix is added (*gasses, quizzes*).

This does not exhaust the rules for forming plurals. There are a number of 'irregular' plurals, which you may have remembered: *feet, geese, men, mice, teeth*, etc. There is a set of nouns ending in a single 'f' that change the 'f' to a 'v' and add '-es' to form the plural: *calves, dwarves, halves, leaves, shelves, wolves*, etc., but not *chiefs, griefs, gulfs, proofs, spoofs, waifs* and usually these days *hoofs* (rather than *hooves*) and *roofs* (rather than *rooves*). And then there are the 'foreign' plurals, some of which are beginning to be replaced by the regular '-(e)s' suffix: *cacti* or *cactuses, appendices* or *appendixes*; but still *alumni* (not *alumnuses*) and *loci* (rather than *locuses*); however, *focuses* (rather than *foci*) and *radiuses* (rather than *radii*). But things are changing in this area: you rarely hear *referenda*, only *referendums*; and something interesting has happened with *criterion/ criteria* – the singular *criterion* seems to have dropped out of use, and the old (Greek) plural *criteria* has become a singular, with a regular plural *criterias* (at least that is what seems to happen in students' essays – and not only there).

2 You may have thought that the rules for the comparative of adjectives were even simpler than those for the plural of nouns, and in some ways they are. The regular prefix is '-er', added to the 'base' form of the adjective: *greater, higher, shorter, slower, warmer*. There is a very small number of 'irregular' forms: *worse* (for *bad*), *better* (for *good*). That would seem to be it. However, there are two kinds of complication.

One is that the addition of the '-er' suffix may result in some spelling changes. If the adjective ends in an 'e', e.g. *wide – er*, only one 'e' is retained in the comparative form (*wider*). If the adjective ends in consonant + 'y', the 'y' may change to 'i': *drier, busier* but *slyer, spryer* and *wrier* or *wryer* (compare also: *fussier, soapier, worthier*). If an adjective comprising a single syllable with a short vowel ends in a consonant such as 'b', 'd', 'g', 'm', 'n', 'p', 't', the consonant normally doubles with the addition of '-er': *madder, bigger, thinner, hotter;* but *prouder, greener, deeper, stouter*.

The other complication is that the '-er' suffix applies only to single-syllable and some two-syllable adjectives. So, *abler, acuter, ampler, barrener, cleverer, commoner* are possible, as well as all two-syllable adjectives ending in '-y' (*angrier, clumsier, costlier, creepier, emptier*); but *absent, abrupt, brutal, callous, civil, content* cannot take the '-er' suffix. Like three-syllable and longer adjectives, they must form the comparative (periphrastically) with the word *more*.

3 The last two sets of rules have been morphological, specifically inflectional. With the third set, the use of *some*, we turn to syntactic rules. *Some* belongs to the word class of 'determiners' (see Unit A2), and to the subclass of 'indefinite quantifiers'. It is a word that accompanies nouns to indicate that an undefined quantity or amount of the noun is being referred to. It is used with 'countable' nouns (in the plural) to refer to usually three or more of the noun: *some boxes, some flowers, some states*. It is used with 'uncountable' (or 'mass') nouns (in the singular) to refer to a quantity of the noun: *some flour, some money, some water*.

However, *some* is used in such contexts only in positive, declarative sentences. Compare the following:

a   The filling station has *some* petrol.
b   The filling station doesn't have *any* petrol.
c   Does the filling station have *any* petrol?

In the 'negative' sentence (b) and the interrogative sentence (c), *some* has been replaced by *any*. In the interrogative sentence, the use of *some* is possible:

d   Does the filling station have *some* petrol?

but it sets up the expectation of a positive answer to the question, whereas (c) is neutral as to expected reply.

4 We stay with syntax for our fourth set of rules – for the relative pronouns, *who, whom* and *whose*. The function of relative pronouns is to introduce a relative clause (see Unit A6 and Subunit C6.2); a relative clause normally modifies a noun and comes after it; the relative pronoun stands for the noun within the relative clause. It is useful to have some examples, from which to work out the rules. Consider the following:

a   the person *who* has made the application
b   the member of your staff *whom* we saw yesterday
c   the adviser with *whom* we discussed the matter
d   the politician *whose* speeches impress me most
e   the beech tree, *whose* leaves do not fall until October

Leaving *whose* aside for the moment, the relative pronouns *who* and *whom* require a noun referring to a person as their 'antecedent'; the non-person alternative is *which*. The choice between *who* and *whom* is determined by the grammatical function of the relative pronoun within the relative clause. In (a), *who* is the Subject of *has made*, while in (b) *whom* is the Object of *saw*. In (c), *whom* follows the preposition *with*; and *with whom* is an Adverbial element in the clause – but that is not relevant to the case. We can conclude from this that *who* is used if the relative pronoun is personal and Subject of the relative clause, while *whom* is used if the relative pronoun is personal and either Object of the relative clause or follows a preposition. These rules reflect the evidence of the noun phrases in (a) to (c) above, but not necessarily the practice of most contemporary speakers of English. Would you really say (rather than write in a formal context) either (b) or (c)?

You would, I suspect, be more likely to say one of the following:

b1   the member of your staff who we saw yesterday
b2   the member of your staff that we saw yesterday
b3   the member of your staff we saw yesterday
c1   the adviser who we discussed the matter with
c2   the adviser we discussed the matter with

The fact is that *whom* is falling out of use, except when used directly after a preposition, or if the context is very formal indeed. The linguistically insecure, aware of a disputed usage, probably avoids having to make a choice – and a possible fool of themself – by going for (b2) or (b3), or (c2).

How about *whose*? This appears to be in the same set as *who/whom* and so requiring a person noun as antecedent, as in (d); but, increasingly, non-person nouns may also be followed by *whose*, as in (e), especially since the alternative – *of which* – sounds cumbersome and over-formal. *Whose* is the equivalent of 'of whom', and so is the 'genitive' (or possessive) form of the relative pronoun; *which* has no possessive form, just as it has no Object form (equivalent to *whom*), which perhaps accounts for the spread of *whose* to non-person nouns.

Final comment
What this discussion has shown is that grammatical rules do exist, as descriptions of the way in which sentences are put together and structured. Very often, the rules are not straightforward, and may involve a number of exceptions – it is amazing how much complexity and messiness in language our brains can cope with. What has also emerged is that the rules are not necessarily static – we observed changes with some plural forms, and with the use of *whom*. We look in B7 at how to bend the rules still further.

VOCABULARIES

You will need a largish dictionary to hand for this unit, e.g. *Collins English Dictionary*, *New Oxford Dictionary of English*.

We speculated in Unit A2 that the total word stock of English might amount, on a conservative estimate, to around one million words, but it could be double that if we were to include all the specialist terminology of science, technology, medicine, and so on. No one person knows anything like the one million words, not even 'passively', as vocabulary they might recognise in reading.

How many words do you know? That is a very difficult question to answer. First, we need to distinguish 'active' vocabulary – the words that you use in your own speech and writing – and 'passive' vocabulary – the words that you recognise and can make sense of in the speech and writing of other people. The latter is, of course, always greater than the former. The size of either will depend on a number of factors: your age, the level of education you have achieved, the subjects that you are studying, the hobbies and leisure pursuits that you engage in, how widely and often you read, and so on.

Activity 1

Take your dictionary and peruse 1 per cent of its pages, i.e. 20 pages of a 2000-page dictionary, or every hundredth page (you need to take a range of letters of the alphabet). Note down how many words: (a) you are confident that you would regularly use; (b) you would recognise and understand if you read or heard them. Be brutally honest with yourself! Then multiply your totals by 100, to give a first approximation of your likely active and passive vocabularies.

Commentary

David Crystal tried this experiment on (a) an office secretary, (b) a businesswoman who read a great deal, and (c) a lecturer; and he came up with the following figures (Crystal 1995: 123):

	Active	Passive
a	31,500	38,300
b	63,000	73,350
c	56,250	76,250

How do yours compare? It is interesting that the lecturer had a larger passive vocabulary than the businesswoman, but a smaller active one. That may be a reflection of the lecturer's area of specialism.

Activity 2

Take one of your leisure interests – ballet, cricket, ice skating, music, horse riding, or whatever – and make a list of the specialist vocabulary (terminology or jargon) of your pursuit. Think particularly of terms that you would not expect an 'outsider' to understand. Then compare what you have done with someone else's results for this activity.

Commentary

You will each have produced a list for a different leisure pursuit, so it is not possible to comment in detail. What you may well have found is that some of your words are exclusive to your pursuit, e.g. *innings* or *wicket keeper* in cricket, while other words are shared but have a special meaning in your leisure interest, e.g. *square* or *out* in cricket. In the *Concise Oxford Dictionary* (ninth edition), there are over 200 words or meanings of words that are marked with the specialist label 'cricket'.

The subject matter of an activity or pursuit, of an area of academic or scientific study, of a profession or trade, is just one dimension of language variation that gives rise to particular sets of terms, or specialist vocabularies. This is the dimension of variation that is sometimes called 'register' or 'occupation', or 'jargon' (see Unit B8). Another dimension of variation that has an important effect on vocabulary is geographical; this includes national varieties of English, e.g. the words special to New Zealand English or West African English or British English, as well as regional varieties (dialects) within a national boundary, e.g. Scots English, Tyneside dialect, West Midlands dialect.

Activity 3

List some of the words that you think are special either to the national variety of English that you speak, or to a local dialect.

Commentary

Here are some of the words that are marked 'NZ' (i.e. New Zealand) in the *Concise Oxford Dictionary* (ninth edition): *ashet* (a large plate or dish), *bowyang* (band or strap worn round the trouser leg below the knee), *cockabully* (a variety of freshwater fish), *fossick* (rummage around), *haere mai* (welcome – from Maori), *kai* (food – from Maori), *pakeha* (white person – as opposed to a Maori), *rimu* (a softwood tree native to NZ), *sheila* (girl, young woman), *stickybeak* (inquisitive person), *two-up* (a gambling game involving tossing coins), *wahine* (woman, wife).

Here are some words that are marked 'Northern English dialect' in *Collins English Dictionary*: *asket* (a shallow oval dish or large plate), *bield* (shelter, home), *brat* (apron, overall), *clarts* (lumps of mud, especially on shoes), *dub* (puddle, pool of water), *eatage* (grazing rights), *fleysome* (frightening), *ginnel* (narrow passageway between buildings), *lop* (flea), *oxter* (armpit), *snicket* (narrow passageway between walls or fences), *threap* (scold, contradict), *wuthering* (of wind, blowing strongly with a roaring sound), *yon* (that).

Activity 4

We have noted so far two ways in which words may be labelled in dictionaries for particular restrictions on their usage: subject matter and region. Look carefully at half a dozen pages from different parts of your dictionary, and note down any other labels that imply a restriction on the contexts in which a word, or a meaning of a word, may be used.

Commentary

You will, almost certainly, have found labels relating to levels of 'formality', such as 'informal' or 'colloquial', 'slang', and perhaps even 'formal' itself. These labels refer to the situational context in which it is appropriate to use such words. Related to these labels are those like 'vulgar', 'coarse slang' or 'taboo', usually applied to words referring to sexual and excretory functions; these are not so much 'formality' labels, rather labels of 'status' or 'propriety'.

Another set of labels includes items such as 'jocular'/'humorous', 'derogatory', 'euphemistic', which describe the 'effect' that a word may have when it is applied to someone or something. For example, *oldfangled*, meaning 'old-fashioned' is marked as 'derogatory' in *Collins English Dictionary*; *departure* is used euphemistically to mean 'death'.

A further set of labels, including 'literary' and 'poetic', refer to the use of a word or sense of a word in works of imaginative fiction or poetry. So, *nevermore* is marked as 'literary' in *Collins English Dictionary*, and *morrow* as 'poetic'. A related label is 'archaic', implying that a word has an old-fashioned ring to it. Some words in *Collins English Dictionary* that are marked 'poetic' are also marked 'archaic', including *morrow*, and *perchance*.

What this investigation suggests is that a large number of words are restricted in their contexts of use: by geography, by subject matter, by formality, by status, by effect, or by literariness. Any one of us will be competent in only a restricted number of sets of words relating to these dimensions of variation. Viewed in the round, we could say that it is more useful to talk about 'vocabularies' of English, rather than simply 'the vocabulary' of English.

Clearly, there are some words that may occur in any context. They belong to what has been called the 'common core' of the vocabulary (e.g. by the original editors of the *Oxford English Dictionary* – see Jackson and Zé Amvela 2000: 119). This is the bedrock of words that all of us need and use in order to speak and write English in the normal activities of our daily lives. Beyond that, there are vocabularies that we share with a limited number of other English speakers by virtue of being a member of various 'groups'; e.g. speakers of a regional dialect, a trade or profession, a religion, a sport (either as spectator or player), a hobby, an entertainment (theatre, music, cinema). Each of us has access to a particular combination of vocabularies that may be quite different from those of the next person. A Yorkshire plumber who is a Muslim and a cricket fanatic will have a quite different active and passive vocabulary from a Home Counties stockbroker who is a Buddhist and a stamp collector.

Activity 5

List the vocabularies that you have access to by virtue of your membership of various groups. Compare your list with those of a number of other students.

Activity 6

Look at the following sets of words and phrases. Determine which 'vocabulary' each of them belongs to.

1   equity, up, down, footsie, bid, blue chip, trading session, stocks, shares, profit, demerge, loss, first-half, dividend, exceptionals, turnover, market leader
2   production, season, stage, set, staging, stall, auditorium, director, act, scene, drama, heroine, repertory, performance
3   arpeggio, cadenza, diminuendo, fortissimo, larghetto, molto, obligato, passacaglia, pizzi-cato, rondo, scherzo, staccato, tempo, vibrato
4   ambulance chaser, anyplace, ballpark, boondocks, candy apple, condo, diaper, expressway, fry pan, hash browns, jelly roll, mailbox, preppy, redneck, streetcar
5   biddy, bimbo, commie, conchie, fat cat, gink, pinko, slaphead, stitch up, woofter

Commentary

1   The words in this set belong to the vocabulary of economics or finance, and specifically to that used to talk about the stock market.
2   These belong to another 'subject matter' vocabulary, concerned with the theatre.
3   This is a selection of the words belonging to the vocabulary of music, many of which derive from other languages; those given here are all of Italian origin.
4   The words here belong to a 'dialect' vocabulary, from North America, i.e. American English.
5   All the words in this set are marked both 'slang' and 'derogatory' in the *Concise Oxford Dictionary* (ninth edition); so, they belong both to a 'status' vocabulary and to an 'effect' vocabulary.

DEVELOPMENT

FURTHER CONCEPTS IN GRAMMAR AND VOCABULARY

TYPES OF SENTENCE

In Unit A1, we established that sentences have structure. In this unit, we distinguish a number of 'types' of sentence on the basis of their structure. In C1 we develop this by matching sentence structure with the functions of sentences in ongoing discourse.

Activity 1
Examine the following sentences and describe how they differ in structure:

1   The choir is singing Verdi's Requiem in the Symphony Hall tonight.
2   Is the choir singing Verdi's Requiem in the Symphony Hall tonight?
3   What is the choir singing in the Symphony Hall tonight?
4   Sing the Dies Irae!
5   How wonderfully the choir sang Verdi's Requiem in the Symphony Hall tonight!

Commentary
The first sentence is generally considered to represent the basic type of sentence. This example has five elements:

1   The choir (Subject)
2   is singing (Verb)
3   Verdi's Requiem (Object)
4   in the Symphony Hall (Adverbial of Place)
5   tonight (Adverbial of Time)

This sequence of elements – Subject, followed by Verb, followed by any Objects and other elements – is the most frequently occurring. Sentences with this order of elements are termed 'declarative' (C1.1). Their typical function is to make 'statements'.

The second sentence differs from the first only in the inversion of *is* and *the choir*. The word *is* is part of the Verb, forming the 'present progressive' (see C5.2) of the verb *sing*; it is a form of the verb *be*, which is here acting as an 'auxiliary' verb in the formation of the progressive. Sentence 2 differs from the declarative sentence in 1 by the inversion of the Subject and the auxiliary verb. This type of sentence is termed a 'polar interrogative'. It typically functions as a 'yes/no' question, i.e. a question that expects either the answer 'yes' or the answer 'no' (see C1.2).

Something more complex is happening in the third sentence. Clearly, it is a type of interrogative, with a question function. It begins with the word *what*, which is substituting for the Object (*Verdi's Requiem*), which is followed by the auxiliary verb (*is*), then the Subject, the main part of the Verb, and the remaining elements. The initial element is the interrogative word, sometimes called a *wh*-word, since they usually begin with 'wh' (the exception is *how*). Any of the elements, apart from the Verb, could become the interrogative word, and so be questioned:

1   Who is singing Verdi's Requiem in the Symphony Hall tonight?
2   What is the choir singing in the Symphony Hall tonight?
3   Where is the choir singing Verdi's Requiem tonight?
4   When is the choir singing Verdi's Requiem in the Symphony Hall?

In the first of these sentences, the interrogative word (*who*) substitutes for the Subject (*the choir*): in that case there is no Subject-auxiliary inversion. The order of elements for this '*wh*-interrogative' type of sentence is, then: *wh*-word + auxiliary + Subject (if *wh*-word is not itself the Subject) + rest of Verb + Object(s)/Adverbial(s) (except where one of these is the *wh*-word).

Taking now the fourth sentence from the original list under Activity 1, this contains only two elements:

1   Sing (Verb)
2   the Dies Irae (Object)

We have omitted the Adverbial elements, though they could have been included, but producing a rather unnatural sounding sentence, perhaps. The other missing element, and omitted by necessity, is the Subject. The first element is the Verb, and it consists of the base form of the main verb word (*sing*). This type of sentence is termed the 'imperative', and it typically functions for issuing 'commands' (C1.3).

The fifth and final sentence contains an additional element, which is placed initially (*how wonderfully*). It is an Adverbial of manner (*wonderfully*) preceded by the word *how*. Otherwise the elements in the sentence are in the declarative order. This type of sentence is termed the 'exclamative'. It has an alternative form, e.g.

What a wonderful performance the choir gave in the Symphony Hall tonight!

The exclamative word is now *what*, followed by a noun phrase (B5). In this example, it is the Object (*a wonderful performance*) that is being exclaimed about and so has been moved to the beginning of the sentence. Sentences of the exclamative type have the function, as may seem obvious, of making 'exclamations'. They begin with either *how* + adjective/adverb or *what* + noun phrase, and then follow the declarative order.

There is one further, unconnected, distinction of sentence structure that we need to mention at this stage.

Activity 2

Examine the following pair of sentences and describe the differences between them:

1   The band played some 1960s hits for the oldies.
2   Some 1960s hits were played by the band for the oldies.

Commentary

These two sentences contain the same four elements:

1   the band
2   played
3   some 1960s hits
4   for the oldies

However, *the band* is first (Subject) element in (1), while in (2) it comes after the Verb and is introduced by the preposition *by*. The element *some 1960s hits*, which is Object (positioned after the Verb) in (1), is promoted to initial (Subject) position in (2). And lastly, the form of the Verb is different: in (1), it is in the simple past tense (*played*); in (2), it has a form of the auxiliary verb *be* (*were*) followed by the past participle of the main verb (*played*).

The sentence in (1) is termed an 'active' sentence, that in (2) a 'passive' sentence. A passive sentence brings the Object of an active sentence into Subject position, has a passive form of the Verb, and puts the Subject of the active sentence into a *by*-phrase after the Verb, or indeed omits it altogether, e.g.

Some 1960s hits were played for the oldies.

A passive structure enables a speaker/writer to bring into initial position in the sentence the victim of an action. Subjects of active sentences with Objects are usually the (mostly human) instigators of actions, the 'agents'. In a passive sentence, the agent either comes near the end of the sentence or is omitted altogether. The passive construction is an important means that speakers/writers have for rearranging the elements in a sentence. However, not all active sentences can be made passive, largely only those that contain an Object.

Passive sentences are common in scientific writing and in certain kinds of newspaper reporting. Some style manuals recommend that they are used sparingly or not at all. They tend to be routinely highlighted by computer style checkers – or perhaps that should be: 'Computer style checkers routinely highlight them.'

NOUN AND VERB

As we noted in Unit A2, the noun and verb word classes are the largest, and they are the classes to which most new words are added. In that unit, we characterised nouns as the class of words whose members characteristically refer to 'things', take a plural inflection, and most importantly function as heads of noun phrases in Subject and Object slots in sentences. You were invited to provide a similar characterisation of the verb class. In this unit, we will expand on our discussion of the noun and provide some answers to Activity 5 from Unit A2.

All word classes contain a more or less heterogeneous set of items, but which have enough in common grammatically to justify them being lumped together in the same class. This is equally true of nouns.

Activity 1

To illustrate some of the diversity among nouns, consider the follow examples. Test whether they can be used with an indefinite article (*a/an*), with a definite article (*the*), with the quantifier *some*, and whether *some* triggers the plural form.

ant, Aristotle, advice, argument, anarchy, annunciation

Commentary

The first item, *ant*, is a straightforward 'countable common noun', referring to a 'concrete' object. It can be used with both the indefinite and the definite articles, in both singular and plural form with the latter, and *some* triggers the plural (*some ants*). With the singular of *ant*, *some* is no longer a quantifier, but an emphatic (*some ant!*). A large number of nouns are like *ant*.

Aristotle is a 'proper noun'. It refers to a unique person, the Greek philosopher. Its status as a proper noun is indicated by the initial capital letter. When denoting the Greek philosopher, *Aristotle* cannot be used with any of the determiners. However, the articles can be used, but with rather specific meanings. To say 'He's an Aristotle' implies that the person is something of a philosopher or acting as if they were. If you say 'Do you mean the Aristotle?', you are checking that the reference is to the famous Greek philosopher rather than to anyone else called *Aristotle*. Names of people, places and institutions constitute the subclass of 'proper nouns'.

The remaining nouns in the list are 'abstract' (as against 'concrete') nouns of various kinds. *Advice* is uncountable; it has no plural form, it cannot occur with the indefinite article, and *some* retains the singular form (*some advice*). To make *advice* countable, it must be prefaced by the quantity expression *a piece of*, which can be made plural (*some pieces of advice*). Many uncountable nouns, both abstract and concrete, may be made countable in this way.

Like *advice*, *argument* is an abstract noun derived from a verb; but it is usually a countable noun, when it operates in the same way as the concrete *ants*: it can be accompanied by both articles, occur in the plural with *the*, and *some* triggers the plural form. But *argument* may also be used as an uncountable noun, in contexts such as *without argument* or *for the sake of argument*.

Anarchy is an uncountable abstract noun, like *advice*; but it more restricted in the determiners that may accompany it. Neither the indefinite article nor the quantifier *some* may occur with it; only the definite article. Most usually, however, it occurs without any determiner.

The word *annunciation* is a special case. It occurs almost always in the form *the Annunciation*, to refer to the biblical episode (Luke 1: 26–38) when the angel Gabriel announced to Mary that she would be the mother of the Christ child, or to paintings of this event. So, it is a kind of proper noun. It derives from the same Latin root as underlies *announce*, and it is sometimes used (inappropriately?) instead of *announcement*, e.g. 'the drafting and annunciation through the UN of a comprehensive set of rules applying to the relationships between states' (from the *British National Corpus*, CHC899).

Summarising, nouns may be subcategorised according to whether they are 'proper' or 'common', 'abstract' or 'concrete', 'countable' or 'uncountable'.

We turn now to verbs. We make a distinction between 'main' verbs and 'auxiliary' verbs (B5). Both subclasses of verb function within a verb phrase, main verbs as head, and auxiliary verbs as pre-modifiers – which provides a syntactic definition of the verb class. 'Main' verbs give the main meaning of the verb phrase; 'auxiliary' verbs add meanings associated with tense, aspect, modality (C5.2) and passive (B1). Verbs used as auxiliaries include: *be, have, do; can, may, shall, will, must*. Let us look now at the morphology of verbs.

Activity 2

Give the present tense, past tense, and participle forms of the following verbs: for example, *speak*: present *speak, speaks* (form with 'third person singular' (*he, she, it*) Subjects); past *spoke*; participles *speaking* (present participle), *spoken* (past participle).

see, search, sing, tell, go, have, be, may

Commentary

The forms of these verbs are as follows:

Present tense	Past tense	Present participle	Past participle
see, sees	saw	seeing	seen
search, searches	searched	searching	searched
sing, sings	sang	singing	sung
tell, tells	told	telling	told
go, goes	went	going	gone
have, has	had	having	had
am, is, are	was, were	being	been
may	might		

The one anomaly in this list is *may*, which has no participle forms, and no third person singular present tense form. It shares these features with other 'modal' auxiliary verbs, which, along with the meanings that these verbs have, sets them apart as a special subclass of auxiliary verbs.

Otherwise, all the examples have the following five forms: present, third person singular present, past, present participle, past participle. The verb *be* additionally has a first person singular present tense form (*am*) and differentiates a singular (*was*) and a plural (*were*) past tense form. Some verbs have identical forms for past tense and past participle, including the 'regular' verb *search*.

From this evidence, we can see that the inflectional morphology of the verb provides a particularly sound and comprehensive definition of the class, with only a small number of exceptions to be accounted for.

Activity 3

Traditionally, verbs have been defined notionally as 'doing words', but this is probably an oversimplification. Which main verbs in the following sentences would you call 'doing words'? And if a verb is not about 'doing', what is it about?

1   Barry kicked the ball into touch.
2   Eva shouted encouragement from the sidelines.
3   Then the rain fell.
4   Both players and spectators got wet.
5   The pitch was already muddy.
6   The groundsman wondered about the state of his turf.

Commentary

The most obvious 'doing' verb among these is *kick* in No. 1, denoting a physical action. *Shout* in No. 2 probably also counts as a 'doing' verb, in this case a verbal action. The verbs in the remaining sentences can hardly be called 'doing words', however. In No. 3, *fall* is something that 'happens' rather than 'doing', and similarly with *get* in No. 4. In No. 5, the main verb is *be*, expressing the state something is in; and in No. 5, *wonder* could possibly be construed as 'doing', but also as a 'state of mind', or a mental process.

Arguably, verbs may refer to: actions (what someone (usually) does), events (what happens to someone or something), states (how someone or something is).

MAKING NEW WORDS

B3

In Unit A3, we took an analytical approach to the structure of words, identifying the various types of element (root and affix morphemes) of which they are composed. In this unit, we are taking a more synthetic approach, examining how new words are coined from existing language material, both native and foreign. New words are being created nearly every day, to give expression to new products, new ideas, new perceptions, new processes, new epithets. Most of them are nouns, but with a sprinkling of verbs and adjectives as well. In this unit we will outline the processes of word formation and in Subunits C3.1 and C3.2 we will look at the two main ones in more detail.

Compounding

A compound word is formed from the combination of two or more roots: *footbridge*, *footpath*, *footprint*. As with these examples, many compounds are written 'solid', as one orthographic word. Otherwise, compounds may be written with a hyphen between the elements (*foot-dragging*) or as separate words (*foot passenger*). The latter are known as 'open' compounds. Dictionaries may differ in their judgements about how compounds should be written. Longer compounds may combine more than one method, e.g. *blue-collar worker*, *whitewall tyre*, *red sandalwood*. Most compounds belong to the noun word class, but they are also found as verbs (*outsource*, *hot-wire*), adjectives (*struck*, *off-limits*), adverbs (*double quick*, *somewhere*), as well as, less productively, as pronouns (*anybody*, *herself*), prepositions (*into*, *on top of*), and conjunctions (*in order to*, *as if*). We will discuss compounds further in C3.1.

Derivation

The term 'derivation' refers to the process of forming new words by adding prefixes and suffixes to roots or other derived words. When in the 1990s building societies and insurance companies in the UK were beginning to cease to be 'mutual' institutions (owned by their members, rather than by shareholders), the term *demutualisation* was coined to denote the process of converting from a mutual society to a PLC ('public limited company'). This term has been formed in the following way: to the root adjective *mutual* is added, firstly, the 'undo' prefix *de-* together with the 'causative' suffix *-ise*, to make the verb *demutualise*; to this has then been added the 'nominalisation' suffix *-ation*, to make the noun *demutualisation*.

What this example illustrates is:

1 a root may take more than one affix; it is rare to find more than one prefix, but multiple suffixes are not uncommon;
2 derivation may involve the simultaneous application of more than one affix (*de-* and *-ise* to form *demutualise* – neither *demutual* nor *mutualise* occur on their own).

We will discuss derivation further in C3.2.

Conversion

Most suffixes, though only a few prefixes, change the word class of the root to which they are added. Conversion refers to the process by which a word changes word class, and becomes a new lexical item, without the addition of an affix. Typical examples are words like *bottle* and *skin*, which were originally nouns, but have taken on a verb meaning ('put in a bottle', 'remove the skin from'). Sometimes, conversion may make a small difference in pronunciation, usually as a consequence of a change in stress patterning: compare *progress* /ˈprəʊgrɛs/ (noun) and *progress* /prəˈgrɛs/ (verb).

Blending

We come now to the more minor processes of word formation, and first to blending, which takes, usually, the parts of two words and combines them. A classic example is *motel*, blended from *motor* and *hotel*. So, the beginning part of the first word is combined with the end part of the second word. A more recent example is *genome*, blended from *gene* and *chromosome*; or *edutainment*, from *education* and *entertainment*; or *ebonics*, blended from *ebony* and *phonics*, to denote what is more technically termed 'Black English Vernacular' or in the USA 'African-American Vernacular English'. Sometimes the blend takes the whole of one word, especially if it is quite short, and combines it with part of another word; e.g. *eyerobics*, from *eye* and *aerobics* ('exercises for the eyes'); or *docudrama*, from *documentary* and *drama*.

Acronyms and initialisms

There has been a growing trend, and nowhere more so than in IT terminology, to use the initial letters of an expression to make a convenient abbreviated word, usually spelt with capital letters. Sometimes, the result is pronounced as a word, e.g. MIDI /mɪdi/ (Musical Instrument Digital Interface), in which case we call it an 'acronym'. Alternatively, the letters are pronounced individually, e.g. OCR /əʊ si: ɑː/ (Optical Character Reader), in which case we call it an 'initialism'. One further type of acronym is formed not with initial letters but with the initial syllables of an expression, e.g. *biopic*, from 'biographical picture'. This is a 'syllabic acronym' and spelt with lower case letters. Well-established letter-based acronyms may also in due course lose their capital letters, e.g. *laser* (light amplification by stimulated emission of radiation) or *bios* (basic input/output system), and their acronym origin may become obscured.

Backformation

This process occurs when a word is coined in which a recognisable affix is removed to form a new word. A classic example is *babysit*: the compound noun *babysitter* was first formed, and then by the process of backformation the verb *babysit* was formed by the removal of the supposed 'agentive' *-er* suffix. Similarly, *burgle* was formed by backformation from *burglar*, *edit* from *editor*, *enthuse* from *enthusiasm*, *liaise* from *liaison*, *surreal* from *surrealism*, and *televise* from *television*.

Abbreviation or clipping

Strictly speaking, this process does not form a new word, merely a shorter, and often less formal, form of an existing word. The longer word may then gradually become obsolete or restricted to specialist or technical contexts. Clipping produced *pram* from *perambulator*, *fridge* from *refrigerator*, *bus* from *omnibus*, *budgie* from *budgerigar*, *fax* from *facsimile*, *gym* from *gymnasium*, and *maths* (US *math*) from *mathematics*.

Borrowing

This is not only a misnomer, it is not a word formation process either; though it is a very important means of adding new words to the vocabulary. Borrowing refers to the act of taking a word from another language and adding it to the native vocabulary, with or without adjustments of spelling and pronunciation to conceal its origin. The words thus 'borrowed' are called 'loanwords', but there is no intention to 'give back' the borrowed word in due course: the 'import' and 'export' of words might be a better metaphor. It has been estimated that around 80 per cent of modern English vocabulary has been 'borrowed' from other languages, particularly from French, after the Norman conquest of 1066, and from Latin, which has been a source of erudite vocabulary for many European languages. English is probably a net exporter of words these days, but it continues to import words also: think only of *karaoke, salsa, bhangra* and *fatwa*, for recent imports.

Activity

Visit Michael Quinion's 'World Wide Words' webpage <http://www.worldwidewords.org> and look in particular at the sections titled 'Turns of phrase' and 'Topical words'.

If you are interested in IT terminology, the 'Netlingo' website is a good one to explore: <http://www.netlingo.com>.

To get an impression of the range of languages that English has borrowed from, look at Crystal (1995: 126–7).

B4 SUBJECT AND OBJECT

This unit expands on the discussion of Subjects and Objects in A4. Read the following text – adapted from *The Princess and the Pea*, a Hans Andersen fairytale – and do the activities that follow. The numbers in the text mark the beginning of sentence structures and are used to refer to them.

---

[1] Once upon a time a prince wanted to marry a princess, [2] but she would have to be a real one. [3] He travelled around the whole world looking for her. [4] He met many princesses; [5] but he did not like any of them. [6] Something was always wrong; [7] they just weren't real princesses. [8] He returned home very sad and sorry. [9] He had set his heart on marrying a real princess.

[10] One evening a storm broke over the kingdom. [11] The lightning flashed, [12] the thunder roared, [13] and the rain came down in torrents. [14] In the midst of the storm, someone knocked on the city gate. [15] The king himself went down to open it.

[16] On the other side of the gate stood a princess. [17] She was very wet. [18] Water ran down her hair and her clothes. [19] It flowed in through the heels of her shoes and out through the toes. [20] But she told them that she was a real princess.

[21] 'We'll find that out soon enough,' thought the old queen, [22] but she didn't say a word to anyone. [23] She hurried to the guest room, [24] and she took all the bedclothes off the bed. [25] Then on the bare bedstead she put a pea. [26] on top of the pea she put twenty mattresses; [27] and on top of the mattresses she put twenty eiderdown quilts. [28] She gave the princess this bed on which to sleep.

[29] In the morning, someone asked the princess how she had slept. [30] She replied, 'Oh, just wretchedly! [31] I didn't close my eyes once the whole night through. [32] I don't know what was in that bed; [33] but it was something very hard, [34] and I am black and blue all over.'

[35] Now they knew that she was a real princess. [36] She had felt the pea through twenty mattresses and twenty quilts. [37] Only a real princess could be so sensitive! [38] The prince married her. [39] They exhibited the pea in the royal museum. [40] You can go there, [41] and see it, if it hasn't been stolen.

Activity 1

Make a list of the Subjects in the first twenty sentence structures of the text.

Commentary

You will have noticed how the dominant Subject changes between the paragraphs: the prince in the first paragraph, aspects of the storm in the second, and the princess in the third. In detail, the Subjects are as follows:

[1] *a prince*; [2] *she*; [3], [4] and [5] *he*; [6] *something*; [7] *they*; [8] and [9] *he*
[10] *a storm*; [11] *the lightning*; [12] *the thunder*; [13] *the rain*; [14] *someone*; [15] *the king himself*
[16] *a princess*; [17] *she*; [18] *water*; [19] *it*; [20] *she*

The Subjects are quite short: the noun phrases contain only a determiner (*a*, *the*) in addition to the noun (except for the emphatic *himself* in [15]). Otherwise the Subject slot is filled by a pronoun, substituing for a previous noun phrase, e.g. *he* for *a prince*, *it* for *water*, *she* for *a princess*. A Subject often makes a link with a previous sentence in a text.

If you examine the Verbs you will discover that the Subjects take on a number of different roles in relation to the meaning of the main verb word, e.g. 'doer' of an action ([3], [8], [14], [15], [20]), 'undergoer' of an event ([4], [10] to [13], [18]), 'experiencer' of a thought or emotion ([1], [5]), 'site' of a state ([7], [17]), 'positioner' of a stance ([16]).

Activity 2

Make a list of the Objects that occur in this text. Although every sentence structure will contain a Subject slot, not every one will contain an Object, only those that are 'transitive' (see Unit A5).

Commentary

The fillers of the Object slot are more variable in size, from a single pronoun to a whole clause, and some structures contain two Objects. Objects tend to be longer than Subjects; they convey much of the 'new information' in a sentence.

In detail, the Objects in this text are: [1] *to marry a princess*; [4] *many princesses*; [5] *any of them*; [9] *his heart*; [20] *them* and *that she was a real princess*; [21] *'We'll find that out soon enough'*; [22] *a word* and *to anyone*; [24] *all the bedclothes*; [25] *a pea*; [26] *twenty mattresses*; [27] *twenty eiderdown quilts*; [28] *the princess* and *this bed on which to sleep*; [29] *the princess* and *how she had slept*; [30] *'Oh, just wretchedly!'*; [31] *my eyes*; [32] *what was in the bed*; [35] *that she was a real princess*; [36] *the pea*; [38] *her*; [39] *the pea*; [41] *it*.

It is more difficult to identify Objects than it is to identify Subjects, especially to distinguish them from Complements and Adverbials. We confront that difficulty in Subunits C4.1 and C4.2.

An Object is sometimes simply the 'undergoer' of an action ([24] to [27]). An Object may also express what is said or thought, either as 'direct' speech or thought ([21], [30]), or as 'indirect' speech or thought ([20], [29], [32], [35]); the speech or thought is usually expressed by a complete clause (see A6, C6.1), though in [22] it is simply the noun phrase *a word*. An Object may also be the thing experienced ([1], [5], [36]).

Where a structure contains two Objects, a distinction is usually made between the 'direct' Object and the 'indirect' Object. The terms imply that one of the Objects is involved in the action of the sentence directly, and the other less so. In fact, the Direct Object usually expresses an 'undergoer', and the Indirect Object a person to whom or for whom the action is done. Look at [28] as an example: the main verb is *give*, which normally takes two Objects; *the princess* (Indirect) is the person to whom *this bed . . .* (Direct) is given. Similarly in [20], *them* is Indirect, and *that . . . princess* is Direct Object. It is normally the case that the Indirect Object precedes the Direct. However, with some verbs and as an alternative construction with others, the Indirect Object may follow the Direct, and then it is introduced by a preposition (*to* or *for*): [22] is an example – *a word* (Direct), *to anyone* (Indirect).

Subunits C4.1 and C4.2 continue the discussion of Objects, and Subunit C4.3 expands on what we have said about the Subject.

NOUN PHRASE AND VERB PHRASE

The Subject and Object slots in sentence structure (see Units A4, A5, B4) are most often filled by a noun phrase (see A6), while the Verb slot is always filled by a verb phrase. This unit will outline the basic structures of noun and verb phrases, with more detail provided in Subunits C5.1 and C5.2, respectively.

Let us begin with the noun phrase (which we will abbreviate to the conventional 'NP'). We noted in Unit A6 that most phrase types, including NP, are composed of a 'head' word, which gives the name to the phrase, and a number of 'modifiers'.

Activity 1

Identify the headword in each of the italicised noun phrases in the following sentences:

1   *Trees* are good for the planet.
2   We must cultivate *them*.
3   *The last three survivors* are home at last.
4   *The most famous battle of the last war* is the subject of this film.
5   *A lot of train passengers crossing the station concourse* did not notice the crater.
6   *Something awful* has happened.
7   *The most direct way there* takes you past the bus station.
8   They called her *'she who must be obeyed'*.
9   *All the king's men at the top of the hill* are waiting for the order to descend.
10 *The job application I posted last week* hasn't arrived yet.

Commentary

In the first two, there is only one word, so it must be the head. These two examples illustrate, first, that a noun phrase may consist of just a head, and second, that the head may be either a noun or a pronoun. The heads of the remaining NPs are: (3) *survivors* (4) *battle* (5) *passengers* (6) *something* (7) *way* (8) *she* (9) *men* (10) *application*. In some cases the head is obvious, if only because it is the sole noun in the phrase (as in 3 and 7); in others there seems to be a choice between competing nouns (e.g. in 5 or 9). Within the sentence context, however, the choice is usually clearer, because the noun will refer to the person(s) or thing(s) involved in the action, event or state denoted by the Verb.

Let me point out two rather unusual NPs among the examples: Nos. 6 and 8. The head of No. 6, *something*, is an 'indefinite pronoun' (see Subunit C2.1); it is modified by the adjective *awful*, which is positioned after the head, whereas with a noun it would precede the head (e.g. *an awful shock*). The head of No. 8 is the pronoun *she*; it is modified by a relative clause (see Subunit C6.2). Pronoun heads usually occur on their own, without any modifiers. If they are modified, then it is usually by a relative clause, as in No. 8.

Activity 2

The NPs in Activity 1 contain a variety of modifiers. Here is a further set of NPs specifically designed to illustrate the range of modifiers in NPs. Which modifiers usually precede the head, and which usually follow?

1   three blind mice
2   the farmer's wife
3   a carving knife
4   all their tails
5   some lovely strawberry tarts
6   the knave of hearts
7   the house that Jack built
8   a pieman going to the fair

Commentary

The heads in these NPs are all nouns. Preceding them, you should have found: articles (*a, the*), quantifiers (*three, all, some*), possessives (*the farmer's, their*), adjectives (*blind, lovely*), participles (*carving*), nouns used as modifiers (*strawberry*). Following the heads are an example each of: a prepositional phrase (*of hearts*), a relative clause (*that Jack built*), and a participle clause (*going to the fair*).

The modifiers preceding the head (pre-modifiers) are ordered: closest to the head come noun modifiers, then adjectives and participles, then most quantifiers, then possessives and articles, which may be preceded by a quantifier like *all* (as in No. 4). The modifiers following the head (post-modifiers) usually occur singly, and if more than one occurs ordering appears to be pragmatic, perhaps on the basis of the euphony of the phrase or sentence.

Summarising, an NP consists of:

article/possessive – quantifier – adjectives/participles – noun modifier – HEAD – prepositional phrase/relative clause/participle clause

This is not the whole story, but it is the basic structure. It is discussed further in Subunit C5.1.

Activity 3

We turn now to the verb phrase (conventionally abbreviated 'VP'). The head of a VP is a 'main verb', which is the verb that denotes the action, event or state that the sentence in which it occurs is about. Which is the main verb (head) in the following VPs:

1   saw
2   was
3   is enjoying
4   couldn't come
5   has been overlooked
6   might have been guessing
7   could be being processed
8   won't have been being interrogated

Commentary

In the first two, the head must be the *saw* and *was* respectively, as the sole items. These illustrate that a VP may consist solely of a head, and No. 2 shows that the verb *be* can operate as a main verb. The main verbs in the remaining examples are always the last items: *enjoy, come, overlook, guess, process, interrogate*. VPs have no postmodifiers, only pre-modifiers.

Activity 4

Now look at the modifiers in the above examples, and attempt to describe what kinds of word they are.

Commentary

Apart from the 'negative' word *not*, abbreviated to *n't* in No. 4 and No. 8, all the other modifying words are verbs, and a restricted set of verbs at that, known as 'auxiliary' verbs. The set of auxiliary verbs includes: *be*, which occurs as *is* in No. 3, *been* in Nos. 5, 6 and 8, *be* in No. 7, and *being* in Nos. 7 and 8 – so it may occur twice in the same VP (Nos. 7 and 8); *have*, which occurs as *has* in No. 5, and as *have* in Nos. 6 and 8; and the so-called 'modal' verbs, *could* in Nos. 4 and 7, *might* in No. 6, and *will* (in the form *wo + n't*) in No.8.

The full set of modal auxiliary verbs includes: *can, could, may, might, shall, should, will, would, must*, as well as less central members of the group, such as *ought to, have to, need, dare*.

Both *be* and *have* can also be used as main verbs, as can one further auxiliary verb not illustrated here: *do*, used in forming interrogative and negative sentences (see Unit B1 and Subunit C1.2).

Have as an auxiliary has one function in the VP, *be* has two: *have* marks the so-called 'perfective' aspect, and the following verb is in the past participle form; *be* marks the 'progressive' aspect when it is followed by a verb in the present participle form (Nos. 3 and 6), or the 'passive voice' (see Unit B1) when it is followed by a verb in the past participle form (No. 5). Aspect is further discussed in Subunit C5.2.

The premodifying auxiliary verbs are ordered as follows:

modal – *have* – progressive *be* – passive *be* – MAIN VERB

The negative word *not* is placed after the first auxiliary verb in a VP. In writing, its abbreviated form *n't* is then joined to the auxiliary (*isn't, hasn't, can't*).

MAIN AND SUBORDINATE

B6

We have defined a 'sentence' as a structure composed of at least a Verb slot, but only one, and usually a Subject slot, together with other obligatory or optional elements (see Units A4, A5). The obligatory elements in a sentence are determined by the (sense of) the main verb (Unit A5), and besides the Subject may include a Direct Object, either an Indirect Object or an Object Complement, and an Adverbial, though Adverbials are normally optional elements in a sentence. A sentence (i.e. a single clause) is a complete structure, and though it may have contextual links with other, especially preceding, sentences, it can be regarded as a syntactically independent structure.

Sentences may consist of clauses combined in two different ways: by co-ordination, and by subordination. Clauses are co-ordinated when they are joined by means of one of the co-ordinating conjunctions (A5), specifically *and, or, but*, or alternatively the 'correlative' conjunctions *both . . . and, either . . . or, not only . . . but also*.

Activity 1
Identify the individual clauses in each of the following examples (from Jane Austen's *Pride and Prejudice*). How have they been co-ordinated?

1   Mrs Long has just been here and she told me all about it.
2   He had either been deceived with regard to her fortune or been gratifying his vanity.
3   Miss Bennet he acknowledged to be pretty, but she smiled too much.
4   The world is blinded by his fortune and consequence, or frightened by his high and imposing manners.
5   I would keep a pack of foxhounds and drink a bottle of wine every day.
6   Elizabeth was surprised but agreed to it immediately.

Commentary
In No. 1, the clauses are either side of the *and*. The conjunction could be omitted and the two clauses stand separately as independent sentences. No. 2 has a correlative conjunction, *either . . . or*, and the two clauses are: 'He had been deceived with regard to her fortune', 'He had been gratifying his vanity.' Note that you have to supply *he had* to the second if it is to stand independently. In No. 3, the two clauses are either side of *but*. Here the conjunction adds rather more by way of meaning than does *and* in No. 1; omission of *but* does not allow the 'adversative' relation between the clauses to be so easily discerned. In No. 4, the clauses are either side of *or*, and *The world is* has to be supplied to the second one to complete the structure. Note that the two *ands* in this sentence merely join words. No. 5 has *and* to join the clauses, and *I would* needs to be added to the second for completeness. The conjunction in No. 6 is *but*, and *Elizabeth* is needed to complete the second clause.

You will have noticed that items are often omitted from the second clause in a co-ordinated pair. It is usually the Subject that is omitted, if it is shared by both clauses (e.g. *Elizabeth* in No. 6, though not *Mrs Long* in No. 1, which is replaced by *she* in the second sentence). Additionally the Verb, or part of the verb phrase, usually the first auxiliary, may be omitted (e.g. *had* as well as *he* in No. 2, *is* in No. 4, and *would* in No. 5. This phenomenon, which contributes to economy of expression, is termed 'ellipsis'. The omitted items can always be recovered from the preceding clause.

Co-ordinated clauses are considered to be 'main' clauses, because they can in principle stand as independent sentences. Co-ordination is not restricted to two sentences or a single type, e.g.

They attacked him in various ways; with barefaced questions, ingenious suppositions, and distant surmises; **but** he eluded the skill of them all; **and** they were at last obliged to accept the second-hand intelligence of their neighbour Lady Lucas.

We turn now to the second type of sentence combination: 'subordination', or 'embedding'. In this type, one clause functions as an element in another clause. The subordinate or embedded clause we are calling a 'subordinate clause' (see Unit A6). The clause that contains the subordinate clause is called the 'main' or 'matrix' clause. Look at the following two examples:

1   I knew that his conduct had not been always quite right.
2   They walked towards the Lucases, because Kitty wished to call upon Maria.

In No. 1, the matrix clause is 'I knew X'; 'X' is the Object slot, which is filled by the subordinate clause 'that his conduct . . .'. The matrix clause cannot stand on its own; *know* is a transitive verb that requires an Object. In No. 2, the matrix clause is 'They walked towards the Lucases', and the subordinate clause is 'because Kitty . . .'. Here the matrix clause is independent, because the subordinate clause fills an optional Adverbial slot.

Activity 2

In the following, all the subordinate clauses are in the Object slot of the matrix clause. Describe how the subordinate clauses differ in structure. You may find it useful to look back at Unit A6.

1   I do not suppose that it ultimately would have prevented the marriage.
2   She could not determine how her mother would take it.
3   I do not know what to say to you.
4   She resolved to give her the information herself.
5   I expected you to stay two months.
6   Mrs Bennet began scolding one of her daughters.
7   She heard somebody running up stairs in a violent hurry.

Commentary

The subordinate clause in No. 1 is introduced by the conjunction *that* and otherwise has the structure of an independent sentence. In No. 2, the subordinate clause is introduced by *how*, a *wh*-word, which fills an Adverbial slot in the structure of the subordinate clause. The structure is complete, but the *wh*-word stands for some missing Adverbial (of manner) information. It represents an interrogative sentence: 'How would her mother take it?' (see B1).

In No. 3, the subordinate clause is introduced by *what*, a *wh*-word. The clause contains an infinitive verb (*to say*) and no Subject. It is assumed to be identical with the Subject of the matrix clause. In this case the *wh*-word fills the Object slot within the subordinate clause.

Nos. 4 and 5 both have an infinitive clause as the subordinate clause: 'to give her . . .' and 'you to stay two months'. In No. 4 the Subject of the subordinate clause is identical with that of the matrix clause (*she*), but in No. 5 the Subjects are different, and *you* has been added to the subordinate clause as its Subject.

In Nos. 6 and 7, the subordinate clause is a present participle (*-ing*) clause: 'scolding one . . .', 'somebody running up . . .'. Again the difference is that in No. 6 the Subjects of subordinate and matrix clauses are identical, whereas in No. 7 they are not, and *somebody* has been added as a different Subject in the *-ing*-clause.

Summary
Subordinate clauses come in a number of structures:

that-clause (No. 1) and *wh*-clause (No. 2) are finite clauses with a complete structure;
infinitive clauses, with an infinitive verb phrase, may be without Subject (No. 4) or with Subject (No. 5), or a *wh*-infinitive (No. 3);
-ing-clauses, with a present participle verb phrase, may be without Subject (No. 6) or with Subject (No. 7).

The functions of subordinate clauses are further explored in C6.

BREAKING RULES B7

Activity 1
How might each of the following sentences be thought to 'break' a rule of modern standard English (i.e. the variety used in published written English)?

1 You ain't seen nothing yet.
2 And then I says to her: 'We never heard them!'
3 Go and get me them scissors.
4 That's the same story what he told me.
5 You don't think they was in on it?
6 She also gave that excuse to Lydia and I.
7 What say you to my proposal?
8 The young can sometimes be wiser than us.
9 None of the passengers were injured in the coach crash.
10 The media is very much a feature of contemporary life.

Commentary
I would not expect you all to react necessarily in the same way to these sentences. You may have found some of them to be perfectly acceptable as examples of modern standard English.

In No. 1, perhaps it was *ain't* that you reacted to, as a form of colloquial or informal English. The usage note on *ain't* in NODE comments that it is quite normal in informal or dialectal speech, but that 'it does not form part of standard English'. But there may be a further objection to No. 1: it contains a double negative (*not . . . nothing*), instead of 'You haven't seen anything yet.'

No. 2 could be part of an oral narrative, informal story telling in the present tense. There are two items here that may strike you as non-standard. The first is the form *says*, associated with third person Subjects (*he/she*) rather than first (*I*), although in some dialects (e.g. in the south-west of England) this form is possible with *I*. The second is the use of *never* as an emphatic negative particle instead of *not*, which is regarded as colloquial, though perhaps not as non-standard.

In No. 3, the use of *them* as a 'demonstrative determiner' (*them scissors*), instead of *that/those*, is non-standard. In No. 4, it is the use of *what* as a 'relative pronoun', instead of *which/that*, that is non-standard. No. 5 illustrates a classic non-standard agreement: *you was* instead of *you were*.

You may consider No. 6 to be quite standard, and you may be right. However, you may have thought that the *I* should be *me*, on the argument that after prepositions (*to* in this case) the Object form of the personal pronoun always occurs (see Subunit C2.1, Unit A4). But, if you are happy with *to Lydia and I*, then you have accepted the change that is happening in English, sometimes called the 'between you and I' phenomenon. It states that for the first person singular pronoun, if *it* is the second item in a co-ordinated structure (usually with *and*) after a preposition, it has the Subject form (*I*) rather than the Object form (*me*). This change seems not to be affecting other pronouns yet; I suspect that you would still say *to Lydia and him*, rather than *to Lydia and he*. Here is an example, then, where a rule 'broken' by enough people consistently causes a change in the grammar of the standard language.

No. 7 may sound a little odd to you, perhaps rather archaic, Shakespearean even; but you might be unlikely to think it non-standard. However, it does not conform to the usual rules for constructing interrogatives in modern English (see B1, C1.2), which specify the use of the auxiliary *do* in interrogatives with no other auxiliary in the verb phrase: *What do you say . . . ?*

No. 8 occurred in a Queen's Christmas Broadcast during the 1990s and was much criticised by language purists: the Queen was no longer speaking the Queen's English! I would expect that you cannot see anything wrong with the sentence. The dispute is about the use of *than*. Traditionally, *than* is a conjunction, and so followed by a clause. In this sentence, as is common practice, it is being used as a preposition and followed by a noun phrase/pronoun. According to the purists, the Queen should have said: 'The young can sometimes be wiser than we are.'

The sentence in No. 9 illustrates a further divergent practice. Again, you may not have had a problem with it. It is another agreement issue, specifically the use of plural *were* as against singular *was*. Strictly, the Subject of the sentence is *none*, which is singular, and so the verb should be singular *was*. But there seems to be a kind of 'nearest noun' rule operating, which says that the verb agrees with the nearest preceding noun, in this case plural *passengers*, and so *were* is acceptable. Whether you regard this as a rule violation depends on how much of a purist you are.

The sentence in No. 10 is taken from the *British National Corpus* (Text AN3 166), and it illustrates another agreement issue. Technically *media* is a plural noun, whose singular is *medium*; but when it has the sense of 'the mass media', it seems to be used as an uncountable and so followed by a singular verb form (in this case *is*). The *BNC* has instances of both singular and plural verbs after *media* (in the 'mass media' sense). It is, clearly, a form whose status is uncertain, and it is a matter of opinion whether a singular verb after *media* represents a rule violation.

What these examples illustrate is that 'rule breaking' depends on whose rules you are talking about. The earlier examples (Nos. 1 to 5) may be quite acceptable in informal, colloquial speech, but they are usually considered unacceptable in the standard form of the language that is used in writing for publication. The examples at Nos. 6, 8, 9 and 10 probably reflect changes that are taking place in the grammar of standard English, and so they are points of 'disputed usage'; their acceptability depends on whether you are resisting the change or participating in it.

Activity 2

Look up the following points of disputed usage in a good up-to-date dictionary:

1. the 'correct' preposition after *different* – *from*, *to* or *than*?
2. the use of *hopefully* to begin a sentence, like *mercifully*
3. singular or plural (present tense) verb after *the data* (*is* or *are*)?
4. is *fun* an adjective as well as a noun? Can you say *funner*?
5. *these kind of books*, *these kinds of books*, or *this kind of book*?
6. is the past participle of *prove* '*proved*' or '*proven*'?

'JARGON'   **B8**

As we noted in Unit A8, all walks of life, trades, professions, leisure pursuits, systems of belief, and so on, have their specialist vocabulary, which makes sense to an insider, but often not immediately or not at all to an outsider. Becoming a member of any group involves learning the jargon, or technical vocabulary, associated with the group's activities.

Activity 1

Examine the following pair of texts and identify the words that are special to the subject matter of each text, or any words that have special senses. Which type of 'jargon' does each text exhibit?

A

An adjournment debate is a short half-hour debate that is introduced by a backbencher at the end of each day's business in the House of Commons.

This technical procedure of debating a motion that the House should adjourn gives backbench members time to discuss issues of concern to them.

The Speaker holds a weekly ballot in order to decide which backbench members will get to choose the subject for each daily debate. Backbenchers normally use this as an opportunity to debate issues related to their constituency.

An all-day adjournment debate is normally held on the final day before each parliamentary recess begins. On these occasions MPs do not have to give advance notice of the subjects which they intend to raise.

The Leader of the House replies at the end of the debate to all of the issues raised.

B

When taking out your endowment policy, your adviser should have ensured that your mortgage was suitable for your needs.

The adviser should have:

- ❏ told you how your premiums would be invested, and warned of the risks involved.
- ❏ explained that an endowment was a long-term investment.
- ❏ checked you were comfortable with the risks involved in investing on financial markets.
- ❏ ensured you were likely to be able to maintain premiums.
- ❏ explained any fees and charges, and their implications for your policy.

You may be entitled to compensation if your adviser failed to inform you on all these points. A shortfall in the value of your endowment mortgage compared to the sum predicted is not on its own sufficient reason to warrant compensation. And compensation cannot be paid where there is no financial loss, even if your mortgage was missold. You may be able to make a complaint even if you have surrendered your policy.

Commentary

The text at A comes from an 'A-Z of Parliament' on the BBC News website and it deals with an aspect of parliamentary procedure. The vocabulary that is associated with this subject matter includes at least:

adjournment, backbencher/backbench member, constituency, debate, House of Commons/the House, Leader of the House, motion, MPs, parliament(ary), recess, Speaker

Some of these words are used exclusively or primarily in this jargon, e.g. *backbencher, Leader of the House*. Others are more general words but are used with a special sense in this jargon, e.g. *debate, motion, recess*.

The text at B comes from the business section and it deals with a financial services issue – 'endowment mortgages'. The vocabulary in this text that may constitute the jargon of the financial services industry includes at least:

endowment, fees and charges, (long-term) investment, (financial) markets, missell, mortgage, premium, sum predicted, surrender (a policy)

Most of these words occur either in the general vocabulary of English or in other jargons, but they have special senses in the financial services context.

Activity 2

Another professional group that uses words in ways peculiar to their sphere of activity are estate agents, in their choice of vocabulary for describing the houses that they have to sell or let. Here are some examples. Which words or uses of words strike you as typical of this variety of English? Note especially the adjectives that are used to describe houses or their features.

---

[1] Superb modern detached in immaculate decorative order offering excellent family accommodation. The property comprises enclosed porch, entrance to reception hall, delightful lounge, modernised and refurbished kitchen, superb conservatory, four bedrooms, refurbished bathroom with shower fitment, UPVC d/g and gas c/h, foregarden with parking facility, garage, delightful rear garden.

[2] Conveniently located traditional semi-detached residence which forms part of a popular and well-regarded locality. The property offers enclosed porch entrance to reception hall, delightful through lounge, modern kitchen, garage with excellent sized utility area, three bedrooms, bathroom on the first floor, has double glazing installed, gas-fired central heating system, fore garden and most delightful and generous sized rear garden.

[3] Close to open countryside this delightful well-presented 'Bryants' built modern semi-detached home has a lovely landscaped garden and ideal family accommodation centrally heated and double glazed with a terrific 22ft through living room, excellent fitted kitchen, 3 good sized bedrooms, smart bathroom and integral garage.

[4] Set in this sought after location you will be surprised at the accommodation offered having a double-glazed entrance porch to an inviting hall, a bright spacious 23ft through living room, very smart extended 16ft fitted kitchen, three good sized bedrooms and a fully tiled bathroom, enclosed patio style rear garden and all well presented.

[5] Excellent extended modern detached residence comprising . . .

[6] Well-presented annexe flat forming part of a timber-framed property comprising . . .

[7] Spacious well-maintained purpose built flat comprising . . .

[8] Presentable modern two-bedroomed ground floor flat within pleasant cul-de-sac location consisting of . . .

[9] Substantial semi-detached residence comprising . . .

Commentary

Let us begin with the adjectives (C2.2), which are, understandably, uniformly positive in tone, but perhaps tend in the direction of exaggeration: *superb* [1], *immaculate* [1], *delightful* [1, 2, 3], *lovely* [3], *excellent* [1, 2, 3], *terrific* [3], *smart* [3, 4], *presentable* [8], *substantial* [9]. The intensifying adverb *well* is characteristic: *well-presented* [3, 4, 6], *well-maintained* [7].

The house is called a *property* [1, 2, 6], *residence* [2, 5, 9], *home* [3]. Note the use of the verb *offer*, with *property*, etc., as the Subject: 'Superb modern detached . . . offering . . .' [1], 'The property offers . . .' [2], '. . . surprised at the accommodation offered . . .' [4]. An alternative verb is *comprise*, usually in its present participle form (*comprising*), as in [5, 6, 7, 9].

There are a number of 'formal', even 'pompous', terms: *foregarden* [1] or *fore garden* [2] for 'front garden'; *rear garden* [2, 4] for 'back garden'; *parking facility* [1] for 'parking space'; *located* [2] or *location* [4, 8] for 'place'.

Lastly, note a number of typical phrases or collocations that tend towards cliché: *immaculate decorative order* [1], *conveniently located* [2], *excellent/ideal family accommodation* [1, 3], *good sized bedrooms* [3, 4], *sought after location* [4], *inviting hall* [4].

You may like to compare these examples with your local property advertising. Do you find the same words and phrases occurring?

EXPLORATION

ASPECTS OF INVESTIGATION

SENTENCE TYPES IN USE

Declaratives

The majority of our language use involves using declarative sentences (B1). We also use interrogatives (C1.2), as well as imperatives (C1.3) and occasionally exclamatives. We use declaratives because we want to comment on some situation, or because we want to inform someone about some topic, or in response to a question that we have been asked. A declarative may be functioning as a greeting, an apology, a reply, an excuse, a warning, a complaint, a prediction, a pleasantry, a piece of news, a compliment and so on. As with any sentence, a declarative is usually part of an ongoing and developing discourse or text, a spoken interaction or a spoken or written monologue, and so its function will be interpreted by a hearer or reader within its context.

Activity 1

For each of the following declaratives, suggest a context and a function:

1　The president has resigned, on this day of all days.
2　I'm afraid that I forgot the time.
3　You haven't done the washing up.
4　You're looking very summery today.
5　The elements of a word are called 'morphemes'.
6　I hope you have a good journey.
7　A tree has fallen across the road.
8　You could win a prize if you return the voucher.
9　You have forgotten to sign your cheque.
10　Applicants must complete the form in black ink.

Declaratives are typically used for making 'statements' of various kinds. But you might note that the first of these declarative sentences comes close to an exclamation, and the last one would normally be construed as a command.

In Unit B1, we noted that declarative sentences typically consist of the Subject + Verb + Object/Adverbial order of elements. All the sentences in Activity 1 are of this type.

Activity 2
Identify the Subject of each of the sentences in Activity 1. If you need more information about Subjects, please refer to Unit B4.

Commentary
The Subject is, in each case, the first element in the sentence: (1) *The president* (2) *I* (3) *You* (4) *You* (5). The elements of a word, (6) *I* (7) *A tree* (8) *You* (9) *You* (10) *Applicants*.

   The Subject is the point of departure for this basic type of declarative sentence. Then the sentence says what the Subject 'is', or 'does', or what 'happens' to it – in the Verb. And the sentence is then completed with other elements representing people or things also involved in some way, or with circumstances (time, place, etc.) attendant on the statement. This is the most usual, and the 'neutral', order of elements in a declarative sentence. However, declaratives do not always have this neutral order of elements.

Activity 3
Which is the first element in the following sentences, and where is the Subject positioned?

1   His first wife he poisoned.
2   To her housekeeper she left all her jewellery.
3   There goes the last bus home.
4   Into the room came a tall, elegant woman.
5   This afternoon we will visit the castle.
6   Very cautiously she approached the bend in the road.
7   It is difficult to find good staff nowadays.
8   Seldom have I witnessed such a display of jealousy.

Commentary
In all of these sentences the first element is <u>not</u> the Subject. They do not, therefore, follow the usual declarative order, even though they are declarative sentences. In detail, the order of elements is in each case as follows:

1   Object (*his first wife*) + Subject (*he*) + Verb (*poisoned*)
2   Indirect Object (*to her housekeeper*) + Subject (*she*) + Verb (*left*) + Direct Object (*all her jewellery*)
3   Adverbial (*there*) + Verb (*goes*) + Subject (*the last bus home*)
4   Adverbial (*into the room*) + Verb (*came*) + Subject (*a tall, elegant woman*)
5   Adverbial (*this afternoon*) + Subject (*we*) + Verb (*will visit*) + Object (*the castle*)
6   Adverbial (*very cautiously*) + Subject (*she*) + Verb (*approached*) + Object (*the bend in the road*)
7   'It' + Verb (*is*) + Adjective Complement (*difficult*) + Subject (*to find good staff nowadays*)
8   Adverbial (*seldom*) + Auxiliary verb (*have*) + Subject (*I*) + Main verb (*witnessed*) + Object (*such a display of jealousy*)

In the first two sentences, an Object has been moved to initial position in the sentence; otherwise the order is unchanged. In (3) and (4), an Adverbial takes up initial position, and Subject and Verb have inverted. Sentences (5) and (6) also have an initial Adverbial, but they are like (1) and (2) in not otherwise having any change in the order of elements. In (7) the Subject is a whole clause and it has been postponed to the end, with its initial position taken by 'it', which acts as a 'place-holder' for the Subject. In (8) the initial adverb, *seldom*, is one of a small number of such adverbs, which when positioned initially, trigger Subject-Auxiliary Verb inversion.

What reasons are there for disrupting the 'normal' order of elements in a declarative sentence? We have mentioned already that sentences do not usually occur in isolation, but as part of ongoing text or discourse. The initial element in a sentence often makes a connection with the sentence(s) that have gone before in the text/discourse. It announces the starting point, or 'topic', for the sentence. So, there may be good reason for positioning a particular element initially in order to provide the connection with previous text or to topicalise an item. We considered the passive construction in B1 as a means of bringing an Object into initial position; the sentences in Activity 3 illustrate further ways in which this can be achieved. It may also be achieved by selecting an alternative verb; compare

I'll <u>give</u> that man a piece of my mind.
That man will <u>get</u> a piece of my mind.
There <u>is</u> a fly in my soup.
My soup <u>has</u> a fly in it.

Activity 4

Now describe what has happened to the elements in the following declarative sentences:

1   It was Susan who had surprised her.
2   It was Jennifer that Susan had surprised.
3   It was in the tennis match that Susan had surprised Jennifer.
4   What Susan did was surprise Jennifer.

Commentary

Here is another set of manipulations of the declarative order. The first three have the structure: 'It' + *was* + Element in Focus + *who/that* + Rest of Sentence. This construction, more common in writing than in speech, enables a writer to draw a contrast by focusing on a particular element, the one occurring after the 'It was'. This type of structure will often be used to contradict or correct what a writer/speaker thinks the reader/hearer believes about a situation. It is called a 'cleft' construction, because the sentence is 'cleaved', or split, in two, in order to extract an element to focus on. The fourth sentence is a 'pseudo-cleft' construction, with the structure: 'What X did/What happened + *was* + Rest of Sentence. It enables the writer to draw the reader's attention to the action performed or the event that happened.

In speech, some of the same effect can be achieved by the stress and intonation resources of the human voice; a speaker can emphasise a particular element for contrastive purposes without altering its position in the sentence:

SUSAN surprised Jennifer.
Susan SURPRISED Jennifer.
Susan surprised JENNIFER.

Activity 5

Provide as many rearrangements of the following declarative sentences as you can, using the passive construction, the examples from Activity 3, and the cleft constructions. Make sure that your sentences sound natural. Consider the contexts in which such rearrangements might be appropriate, e.g. to contradict what someone has just said, to draw attention a particular topic.

1   This successful entrepreneur has donated large sums to party funds.
2   The press have been hounding this poor politician for days.
3   We're meeting our friends on the bridge at midnight.

C1.2 Interrogatives

In Unit B1, we identified the interrogative sentence type as the one typically used for asking questions. Here are some further examples of that sentence type:

1   Have you locked the door?
2   Did you shut down the computer?
3   Who was on the telephone?
4   Who are you meeting this evening?
5   Which CD have you bought?
6   When will her train arrive?
7   Where have you put the biscuits?
8   Why did you interrupt me?

The first two of these are polar interrogatives, expecting the answer 'yes' or 'no'; the others are *wh*-interrogatives, asking for some item of information.

Activity 1

Suggest possible answers to the interrogatives above. Your answers should follow as exactly as possible the structure of the interrogative, so that you can see the declarative sentence from which the interrogative is derived. For example, the answer to No. 4 might be: 'I am meeting Lydia this evening' – which preserves the same elements and the same (progressive) verb form as the question.

Commentary

The answer to the yes/no interrogative in (1) is straightforward: 'I have locked the door.' In the case of (2) you could answer: 'I did shut down the computer', with the inclusion of the auxiliary verb *did*, which makes the answer sound rather petulant. Alternatively, you could specify a time when you did it, e.g. 'I shut down the computer before I left/at 5 o'clock.' This illustrates the point that, when a declarative sentence contains no auxiliary verb (*be*, *have*, or a modal), then to make an interrogative we have to supply the auxiliary *do*.

In the case of the *wh*-interrogatives, you have to supply the required piece of information for the appropriate element:

3   My mother was on the telephone (Subject).
4   I am meeting Lydia this evening (Object).
5   I have bought the new Mozart CD (modifier of Object noun).
6   Her train will arrive at 8:15 (Time Adverbial).
7   I have put the biscuits on the top shelf (Place Adverbial).
8   I interrupted you because you were rambling on (Reason Adverbial).

Note the use of the *do* auxiliary in the interrogative form of No. 8, because the Verb of the declarative contains no auxiliary.

What do we use interrogatives for? We clearly use them to check that something has been done (Nos. 1 and 2 above). We also use them in order to find out items of information that we need to know or that we are curious about (Nos. 3 to 8 above). While these may be the obvious and perhaps major uses of interrogatives, they are not all that we use them for.

Activity 2
What might the speaker of the following interrogatives be seeking to achieve in each case? You may like to think in terms of what the possible answers could be.

1   Could you open the door for me, please?
2   May I interrupt you for a moment?
3   Can you leave the documents with my secretary?
4   Shall I carry those for you?
5   Where do you think you're going?
6   What's the meaning of this?
7   Is that so?
8   How do you do?

Commentary
Although these sentences have an interrogative form (initial auxiliary or *wh*-word and Subject-auxiliary inversion), their purpose is not really one of asking a question. The auxiliary in the first four examples is a 'modal' auxiliary (*could, may, can, shall*: see C5.2), which has an influence on the meaning or function of the interrogative sentence. The form of these sentences is that of a polar interrogative, but a simple 'yes/no' answer would in most instances either be inappropriate or not enough: they expect some other kind of response, either verbal or non-verbal.

Specifically, No. 1 is a 'request' for someone to perform an action (opening the door); the modal auxiliary *could* adds a measure of politeness, as does the addition of *please*. No. 2 is similarly a polite request, but in this case the speaker is seeking 'permission', by using the modal *may*, for him/herself to perform a verbal action (of interrupting). No. 3 is a more direct version of No. 1 (note the use of *can* rather than *could*), so that it comes over as an 'instruction' and not simply as a request. No. 4, with the modal auxiliary *shall*, has the function of an 'offer' by the speaker to perform an action for the person addressed. Summarising, *may* (or *can*) with a first person Subject (*I, we*) asks for permission; *shall* (or *can*) with *I/we* makes an offer; *can* with a second person Subject (*you*) gives an instruction; and *could* with *you* makes a request.

Returning to the list of interrogatives in Activity 2, the last four are all types of conventional phrase, which are readily associated with specific situations. While it may require an answer including a place Adverbial, No. 5 primarily issues a 'challenge' to someone whose presence is expected to be elsewhere. Similarly, No. 6 may result in a response that could be construed as an answer to the question, but it is essentially an 'accusation', requiring an apology or an excuse. You would expect No. 7 to be uttered by the current 'hearer' in a spoken dialogue, to register interest and express surprise at the news or the story that the 'speaker' is telling: it does not expect an answer. No. 8 is a conventional formal greeting when two unacquainted persons are introduced to each other: the response to it is the same formula. There is a similar, more colloquial, exchange in the West Midlands region of England: *Alright?* has as its response, *Alright?*

Activity 3

Now examine the following sentences and work out why they are interrogatives and how they are formed.

1   You have posted my letter, haven't you?
2   They are coming to the party, aren't they?
3   We can't help her, can we?
4   She hasn't explained her absence, has she?
5   The judge sent him to prison, didn't he?
6   The crew will be rescued, won't they?

Commentary

These sentences function as questions but they are composed of a declarative followed by a 'tag' interrogative, which asks for the confirmation of the declarative. If the declarative is positive (Nos. 1,2,5,6), confirmation is sought by a negative tag; if the declarative is negative (Nos. 3,4), confirmation is sought by a positive tag. The tag is formed by repeating the auxiliary verb of the declarative followed by an appropriate pronoun, e.g. *has* and *she* in No. 4, *will* (+ *not* = *won't*) and *they* (for *the crew*) in No. 6. Notice that when there is no auxiliary verb in the declarative, *do* is used as the auxiliary in the tag (No. 5), just as in other types of interrogative.

We have seen that the interrogative is the typical structure for asking questions, usually involving Subject-auxiliary inversion and, in the case of information-seeking questions, an initial *wh*-word. In writing, a question conventionally ends with a question mark (?), and in speech some form of rising intonation contour often accompanies a question, though not always for *wh*-questions. It is, though, possible to ask a question using the declarative form of a sentence, signalled in writing by a question mark and in speech by rising intonation, e.g.

You'll be at the meeting?
Julia's coming to dinner?

Such questions are usually used either to seek confirmation of information already given, or as an expression of surprise:

You're going to see Henry?
He was wearing a what?

Activity 4

Interrogatives perform a number of very important functions in our use of language. To follow up on this topic, take particular note for a day of how people around you, and in the broadcast media, use interrogatives to seek information, make requests, get other people to do things, seek confirmation, express surprise. You could do this by jotting down examples in a notebook.

Imperatives

C1.3

In Unit B1, we noted the 'imperative' sentence (*Sing the Dies Irae*) as the type used typically for issuing commands.

Activity 1

As a recap, look at the following imperative sentences and identify the elements in each case:

1   Turn to page 5.
2   Take your books back to the library.
3   Please reply by return.
4   Lydia, look at this specimen.
5   Kindly switch off the light as you leave.
6   Stop!

Commentary

All these sentences have the basic imperative structure, with a 'base form' of the verb (*turn, take, reply, look at, switch off, stop*), and omitting a Subject. As with imperatives generally, they are addressed directly to 'you'. The other elements follow the verb: *to page 5* – Adverbial of place (No. 1); *your books* – Object, *back to the library* – Adverbial of place (No. 2); *by return* – Adverbial of time (No. 3); *this specimen* – Object (No. 4); *the light* – Object, *as you leave* – Adverbial of time (No. 5). Two of the sentences are fronted by politeness markers (*please* – No. 3, *kindly* – No. 5), and one (No. 4) has a 'vocative' element, the name *Lydia*. Note that *Lydia* is not a Subject here: it is conventionally set off from the rest of the sentence by a comma. It functions as a 'nomination', identifying a particular person to respond to the command.

The imperative sentence is not the only type that is used to issue commands. Indeed, the imperative can come across in English as rather abrupt and too direct, even when mitigated by a politeness marker. We noted in C1.2 that an interrogative sentence containing the modal auxiliary *can* may have the force of a command (*Can you leave the documents with my secretary?*), and it is only a short step from here to the use of interrogatives to make requests, again usually with a modal auxiliary (*Could you open the door for me, please?*).

Activity 2

Here are some sentences that are not of the imperative type. What is it in each case that gives the sentence the force of a command?

1   Passengers must cross the line by the bridge.
2   You should remove your shoes before entering.
3   Customers are requested to deposit their coats in the cloakroom.
4   You are required to submit the return by the end of January.
5   Smoking is not permitted in the auditorium.
6   No mobile phones!
7   Inside, quick!
8   Access to frontages only.

Commentary

The first five of these examples are sentences with the declarative structure, which we have associated with making statements (C1.1). The last three are types of 'minor' sentence: they contain no Verb element. None of these examples is of the imperative type, or of the interrogative 'request' type. You will agree, though, that they would all be interpreted as a command by a hearer or reader. There must be some other way in which the command is being communicated.

In Nos. 1 and 2, the sentence is understood to be a command because of the inclusion of a modal auxiliary verb of 'obligation': *must* in No. 1, and *should* in No. 2. These two modals, as well as *ought to* and, to a lesser extent *have to* and *need to*, have the force of an obligation laid by the speaker on the hearer. The modal auxiliary *shall* is used with a similar force, but only in quasi-legal contexts, e.g. 'The lessee shall keep the property in good decorative order.'

In Nos. 3 and 4, it is the main verbs *request* and *require* that give the sentences the force of a command. Note that the sentences have a passive structure (see B1), which enables the persons addressed (*customers* in No. 3, *you* in No. 4) to be in initial, Subject position. In No. 5, by contrast, the initial Subject position is taken by the activity that 'you', the addressee, are commanded not to do. No. 5 represents a 'prohibition', and it could have been expressed by the verb *be prohibited*: prohibition is the counterpart to 'permission'. We saw in C1.2 that permission may be sought and granted by means of the modal auxiliaries *may* and *can*, e.g.

May/can I interrupt you?
You may/can leave now.

A negative sentence with *may/can* implies a prohibition:

You may not leave during the first hour of the examination.

In all these cases the giving or withholding of permission is achieved by means of the declarative sentence type.

Now let us turn to the last three sentences in our list. In No. 6, it is the word *No* that expresses a prohibition; this form of command is typical of public notices that prohibit some activity ('No smoking', 'No ball games'). No. 7 consists of two adverbs: a place adverbial, in this case *Inside*, where it refers to a change of place or direction, can have the force of a command to move (*Over the fence! Upstairs!*). Clearly, it needs to be spoken with the appropriate intonation. The roadworks notice in No. 8 is usually accompanied by a 'Road closed' notice; the word *only* puts a limitation on somebody contemplating driving past the notice, effectively acting as a prohibition.

Commands are usually addressed to 'you', either directly (in imperatives or with a 'you' Subject of a declarative) or indirectly (in declaratives, with a Subject noun – *passengers, customers* – that 'you' identify with and feel addressed by). It is also possible for the speaker to include themselves in those that are addressed, e.g.

Let us pray. (Priest to a church congregation)
Let's take a break. (Overseer to a group of work colleagues)

As you can see, the formula includes the opener *Let us* or *Let's*, followed by the base form of the main verb. In these two examples, the function is that of a command: the addressees would be expected to comply. Sometimes this formula has more of a 'suggestion' function than a command, e.g.

Let's go to the cinema tonight.
Let's meet after work.

The difference between a command and a suggestion in these cases is determined by the 'power' relationship between speaker and hearer(s): you have to be in a position to be obeyed (vicar, overseer) for your 'suggestion' to be taken as a 'command'. A *let's* between equals will always be a suggestion.

Activity 3

Instructions and prohibitions are everywhere in our world. Look out for them on notices, note them down and analyse the form that they have. Is there some relationship between the form of the instruction/prohibition and the context in which it is found? For example, where would you (expect to) find each of the following?

No mobile phones!
Please respect others' privacy. Switch off your mobile phone.
All mobile phones must be switched off.
Patrons are requested to switch off their mobile phones.

C2 CLASSES OF WORDS

C2.1 Nouns and pronouns

We introduced the word class of nouns in Unit A2, using it as an exemplar for testing the criteria relevant to establishing a class of words. We explored the class of nouns further in Unit B2, looking in particular at the variety of words included within the class. In this unit, we are considering nouns in relation to the pronouns that may substitute for them.

Activity 1

We begin with a text (taken from the start of the traditional fairy tale, *Snow White*). The sentences have been numbered for easy reference. Identify the pronouns in the text, and say which noun each of them substitutes for. (Note: in A2, we counted *my, our, your*, etc., as determiners, specifically 'possessive identifiers', and not as pronouns.)

---

[1] Once upon a time, in the middle of winter, when the snowflakes were falling like feathers on the earth, a Queen sat at a window framed in black ebony and sewed. [2] And as she sewed and gazed out on the white landscape, she pricked her finger, and three drops of blood fell on the snow outside.

[3] Because the red showed up so well against the white, the Queen said to herself, 'Oh, what I would give to have a child as white as snow, as red as blood and as black as ebony!'

[4] And her wish was granted, for not long afterwards a little daughter was born to her, with a skin as white as snow, lips and cheeks as red as blood and hair as black as ebony. [5] They called her Snow White, and after her birth the Queen died.

[6] After a year, the King married again. [7] His new wife was a beautiful woman, but so proud that she could not stand any rival to her beauty. [8] The new Queen possessed a magic mirror, and when she stood before it, she asked:

Mirror, mirror, on the wall,
Who is the fairest of us all?

and it always replied: *Thou, Queen, art the fairest of all.*

. . .

[9] At last she could endure Snow White's presence no longer. [10] She called a huntsman to her and said: 'Take the child out into the wood and never let me see her face again. [11] You must kill her and bring me back her lungs and heart, so that I may know for certain she is dead.' [12] The huntsman did as he was told and led Snow White out into the wood, but as he was in the act of drawing out his knife to slay her, she said: 'Oh, dear huntsman, spare my life. [13] I promise you that I will disappear into the forest and never return home again.'

Commentary

The pronouns in this text are as follows, given by sentence, together with the nouns for which they substitute, if any:

[2] *she* (twice) – Queen
[3] *herself* – Queen, *what, I* – Queen
[4] *her* (second one, after *to*) – Queen
[5] *they* – ?, *her* – daughter
[7] *she* – wife
[8] *she* – Queen, *it* – mirror, *she* – Queen, *who, us* – Queen + others, *it* – mirror, *thou* – Queen
[9] *she* – Queen
[10] *she* – Queen, *her* – Queen, *me* – Queen
[11] *you* – huntsman, *her* – child, *me* – Queen, *I* – Queen, *she* – child
[12] *he* – huntsman, *he* – huntsman, *her* – Snow White, *she* – Snow White, *I* – Snow White, *you* – huntsman, *I* – Snow White
(Note: where *her* is followed by a noun, as in *her finger* [2] or *her face* [10], it is a possessive identifier and not a pronoun.)

Most of the pronouns in this text belong to the subclass of 'personal' pronouns. This group of pronouns manifests a number of category distinctions, reflected in their forms, which are not all shared by the nouns for which they substitute. Pronouns vary:

1   according to who is speaking and about whom or what: compare *I, you, she.*
2   between singular and plural: compare *she, they*; *I, us.*
3   according to whether the referent is female, male, or neither: compare *she, he, it.*
4   according to the syntactic function of the pronoun: compare *I, me*; *she, her, herself.*

The relevant categories are: (1) person (2) number (3) gender (4) case. The forms of nouns vary for number (*snowflakes, drops, cheeks*), but not for any of the other categories. These distinctions are found only in the personal pronouns (and their related possessive identifiers). The forms in full are as follows:

Table C2.1

Person/ gender	Singular				Plural			
	Subject	Object	Posses- sive	Reflexive	Subject	Object	Posses- sive	Reflexive
First	I	me	mine	myself	we	us	ours	ourselves
Second	you	you	yours	yourself	you	you	yours	yourselves
Third/ masc	he	him	his	himself				
Third/ fem	she	her	hers	herself	they	them	theirs	themselves
Third/ neuter	it	it	its	itself				

First person pronouns are used by the speaker(s) to self-refer; second person pronouns refer to the addressee(s); third person pronouns to any 'third party/ies' being talked about. First and third person pronouns show clear distinctions of form for number, but the second person pronoun shows a singular/plural distinction only for the reflexive.

The category of gender applies only to the third person singular pronouns; it is based on 'natural' gender. 'Masculine' pronouns substitute for nouns referring to male animates, 'feminine' to females, and 'neuter' to others. There are some exceptions: names of countries, ships, mountains and some machines are often substituted by a feminine pronoun; and where the gender, of say a child or animal, is not known, the neuter pronoun may often be used. Much debate has taken place in recent years about the third person singular pronoun that should be used to substitute for a noun (e.g. *student*) that could refer to either a male or female. Which is your 'gender-neutral' pronoun – *s/he, he/she, they*?

Under 'case', pronouns share a 'possessive' form with nouns (*child's, children's*; *girl's, girls'*), though possessive case nouns are more often substituted by possessive identifiers, e.g. 'the *child's* lungs' – '*her* lungs'. Possessive pronouns are used in contexts such as: 'The fault is *mine*', where *mine* substitutes for 'my fault'. The basic case distinction between 'subject' and 'object' reflects the syntactic functions of Subject and Object (A4, B4): 'subject' pronouns are used in Subject slots, 'object' pronouns are used in Object slots and after prepositions (*to us, to her, to them*). Second person pronouns do not show this case distinction, although in older English, reflected in the mirror's answer to the queen in the text, a distinction was made as follows:

Table C2.2

	Singular		Plural	
Subject	Object		Subject	Object
thou	thee		ye	you

However, this was more than a simple number distinction; as in many modern European languages, the distinction was also used to express relative 'status' and 'familiarity', with, for example, higher status individuals using *thou/thee* to lower status persons but expecting *ye/you* in return. Such distinctions are reflected, for example, in how characters of differing social positions address each other in the plays of Shakespeare.

The 'reflexive' pronouns have also been included under 'case', though reflexiveness is not strictly speaking a 'case'. Reflexive pronouns are used in Object position, where the reference is the same as that of the Subject, e.g. 'Lydia has hurt herself', and they are also used together with another noun or pronoun for emphasis, 'She made it herself', 'You'll have to answer to the president himself.'

Activity 2

We have not yet mentioned the pronouns *who* and *what* from the text in Activity 1. We shall incorporate them in the following activity, which asks you to identify and classify, as far as you can, the pronouns (expect the personal pronouns) in the following sentences.

1   Who likes ice-cream?
2   Nobody here does, it seems.
3   Look at this!
4   What is it?
5   Did you find a nice one?
6   That is their final offer.
7   Can you smell anything?
8   It's raining again.

Commentary

Who and *what* appear in Nos. 1 and 4 as 'interrogative' pronouns; they ask for a specific piece of information in the form of a noun (phrase) and so substitute for a noun that has yet to be revealed. *Nobody* in No. 2 and *anything* in No. 7 belong to a group of 'indefinite' pronouns, which includes *someone, nothing, anybody*, etc., and which substitute for an unknown (indefinite) noun. *This* in No. 3 and *that* in No. 6 are 'demonstrative' pronouns, with corresponding plural forms *these* and *those*; they show a distinction between 'proximate' (*this/these*) and 'distant' (*that/those*). The pronoun in No. 5 is *one*, used to substitute for a noun in a previous sentence (e.g. 'I've been looking for a new jacket'): it is the ultimate 'pro-noun'.

Finally, the *it* in No. 2 and in No. 8 look as if they are third person singular neuter pronouns, but though they share the same form, they are not personal pronouns here. In neither case does *it* substitute for a noun. The use in No. 8 is sometimes called 'meteorological *it*', because of its use in reference to the weather. In No. 2, however, *it* merely fills Subject position because there is no other item to do so, and in all sentences, apart from imperatives, English requires the Subject slot to be filled. We could refer to this use as 'dummy *it*'; there is a similar use in the 'extraposition' construction (C6.1).

Summary

Pronouns are an interesting class of words, showing category distinctions that have been largely lost to nouns. The major subclass is that of the personal pronouns, with a number of other subclasses, including indefinite, interrogative and demonstrative, as well as relative pronouns, which are discussed in detail in C5.1 and C6.2.

Adjectives   C2.2

The word class of adjectives was briefly mentioned in Unit A2, where a distinction was made between 'gradable' and 'non-gradable' adjectives. Adjectives are also mentioned in relation to the modification of nouns, in B5 and C5.1; the structure and functions of the adjective phrase are discussed in C5.3. In this unit, we shall develop the comments made in A2, concentrating on the class of adjectives itself, on the gradable/non-gradable distinction and its implications for sentence structure, and on the semantic compatibilities of adjectives in relation to nouns.

The adjective class is one of the large, open classes of words. There are over 20,000 adjectives entered in *The New Oxford Dictionary of English* (1998). Many adjectives are derived from nouns and verbs by the addition of a suffix.

Activity 1

Which are the adjectives in the following headlines (from the *South China Morning Post* <www.scmp.com>). Are there any other types of word that have a similar, 'modifying', function to that of adjectives?

1   China welcomes US regrets but presses for full apology
2   Japan delays economic rescue package
3   State plan for stocks brings little cheer
4   Detained scholar's wife still in dark over arrest
5   Device opens computers to paralysed users
6   China seen as global trend-setter
7   Fate of Bush tax cuts uncertain
8   Barefoot doctors heal sick and health-care system
9   Expert's lasting legacy
10   Slick triads take gullible investors to the cleaners
11   Sinking city highlights water crisis
12   China's Samurai debts prove double-edged sword

Commentary

The words in these headlines that clearly belong to the class of adjectives are: *full* (1), *economic* (2), *little* (3), *global* (6), *uncertain* (7), *barefoot* (8), *slick* (10), *gullible* (10). Additionally, there are some participle forms of verbs used as adjectives: *detained* (4), *paralysed* (5), *lasting* (9), *sinking* (11). A past participle look-alike is *double-edged* (12), with its -*ed* suffix, but this is a different formation: the compounding of an adjective (*double*) and a noun (*edge*) with the addition of the -*ed* suffix (compare *blue-eyed, clear-headed, tender-hearted*, and see Gram-Andersen 1992).

Typical of headlines is the extensive use of nouns with an adjectival ('modifying') function: *US* (1), *rescue* (2), *state* (3), *Bush* and *tax* (7), *health-care* (8), *water* (11), *Samurai* (12). Note that *health-care* is hyphenated to indicate its adjectival use. Proper names, like *US* and *Bush* and perhaps *State*, would in other types of writing be possessives, like *China's* (12), and *Expert's* (9).

Gradable/Non-gradable

Adjectives fall into these two subclasses according to two criteria: (1) whether the adjective can have a 'comparative' and a 'superlative' form; (2) whether the adjective can be modified by an intensifying adverb (e.g. *very*). For example, *big* is a gradable adjective: it can form a comparative (*bigger*) and a superlative (*biggest*); and it can be modified by an intensifier (*very big*). On the other hand, the adjective *wooden* (i.e. 'made of wood') is non-gradable; it fulfils none of the criteria.

Activity 2

Apply the 'gradable' criteria to the following adjectives. Which of them pass, and which fail?

baroque, bitter, cold, communal, explicit, extinct, grumpy, heavy, laid-back, lateral, optimum, permanent, proficient, respectable, thin, unique, woolly

Commentary
The following adjectives are clearly gradable, passing the tests: *bitter, cold, explicit, grumpy, heavy, laid-back, proficient, respectable, thin*.

The following are clearly non-gradable in any context: *baroque, communal, extinct, lateral, optimum*. Either an entity is this quality, or it is not; it cannot be more or less. For example, either the dodo is *extinct*, or it is not *extinct*; it cannot be more or less *extinct* than another creature.

This leaves us with the following adjectives from the list: *permanent, unique, woolly*. *Permanent* stands in contrast to *temporary*, and we might argue that it is in an either/or relation: if something is *permanent*, it is not *temporary*, and vice versa. However, in reality, we comment on the relative 'permanence' of things, e.g. 'this structure is more permanent than that one is'. We may conclude, then, that *permanent* is essentially a non-gradable adjective, but it may also be used as a gradable one. *Unique* is a rather different case: by virtue of its meaning, 'without equal', 'sole', it must be a non-gradable adjective. If you call something *unique*, there is nothing to compare it with. However, people do use *unique* as if it were gradable: 'She is very unique', 'This is the most unique vase I've ever seen.' We must conclude either that such speakers are making an error in their use of English, or that *unique* has developed a use that allows it at least to be intensified – we might baulk at a comparison ('This vase is more unique than that one'). In the case of *woolly*, we need to distinguish between its literal ('made of wool') meaning and its figurative ('confused') meaning. In its literal meaning, as with all 'material' adjectives, *woolly* is non-gradable, like its related word *woollen*. In its figurative meaning, however, *woolly* is gradable: 'His thinking is very woolly', 'This is a woollier proposal than yours.'

From these examples, we may conclude that the gradable/non-gradable distinction may not always be clear-cut. In particular, essentially non-gradable adjectives may, in certain contexts, become gradable by virtue of how speakers choose to use them.

Activity 3
Gradable adjectives form their comparative and superlative forms in one of two ways: either (1) by the addition of the *-er* and *-est* suffixes (*bigger, biggest*), or (2) by placing the adverbs *more* and *most* before the adjective (*more significant, most significant*). How do the following adjectives form their comparatives and superlatives? Is there a pattern to it?

angry, bright, capable, certain, clever, common, corrupt, curious, delicious, eloquent, faithful, famous, genuine, horrid, lavish, late, lucid, magnificent, modern, nimble, obscure, remote, shallow, thirsty

Commentary
The adjectives from the list that, without any doubt, take the *-er/-est* suffixes are: *angry, bright, clever, common, late, nimble, shallow, thirsty*. Those that can clearly form comparative and superlative only with *more/most* are: *capable, certain, curious,*

delicious, eloquent, faithful, famous, genuine, lavish, lucid, magnificent. Those of you familiar with Lewis Carroll's stories of Alice will know that he puts the word *curiouser* into Alice's mouth, and comments on its oddness. Adjectives from the list that you may have been uncertain about, or that you thought could possibly be formed in either way, may have been among those remaining: *corrupt, horrid, modern, obscure, remote.*

Before we examine these adjectives, note that, in general, the adjectives taking *more/most* are longer, in terms of the number of syllables they contain, than those taking the suffixes. All the one-syllable adjectives are in the suffix list, and all the three-syllable or longer adjectives are in the *more/most* list. The two-syllable adjectives are divided between the two lists, and our residue consists of two-syllable adjectives. The two-syllable adjectives in the suffix list show the following characteristics: either simple, underived adjectives (*clever, common, nimble, shallow*), or formed with the *-y* suffix (*angry, thirsty*). Those in the *more/most* list are mostly derived (*faithful, famous, lavish, lucid*); the exception is *certain.* For those in the residue list, it is perhaps euphony in context (how it sounds to the speaker) that determines whether a suffix or an adverb is used: 'a corrupter government' or 'a more corrupt government'; 'an obscurer point' or 'a more obscure point'; 'the remotest military station' or 'the most remote military station' (as in the caption to a photograph on the front page of the *Guardian* (4.1.01). Generally, we probably favour the *more/most* construction as more euphonious.

Activity 4

The use of a comparative or superlative usually has implications for the structure of the sentence in which it occurs, since it implies a comparison between two or more entities. For example, 'The stream is shallower' is incomplete; we need to be told what it is 'shallower than'. Construct sentences containing the following fragments (the items do not necessarily have to be next to each other):

brighter than, the commonest, a most eloquent, more famous than, a more lavish, the most magnificent, nimbler than, the sweetest

Commentary

Here are some possible sentences, to illustrate the syntactic effects of comparative and superlative constructions:

1   It's a brighter day than we've had for a long time.
2   The magpie has become one of the commonest birds in the English garden.
3   She gave a most eloquent speech.
4   The Beatles are more famous than Beethoven.
5   I have not seen a more lavish entertainment.
6   This is the most magnificent view that I have ever seen.
7   You are much nimbler than I was at your age.
8   The sweetest wine was the Tokay.

Sometimes no additional element is required (Nos. 3 and 5). For comparatives, the following *than* may introduce either a noun phrase (No. 4) or a clause (Nos. 1 and

7), i.e. it may act either as a preposition or as a conjunction (though see the discussion in B7). Only around a quarter of comparative adjectives are followed by *than*; more usually the comparison is with something mentioned in a previous sentence, and in this way comparison contributes to the cohesion of a text. For superlatives, a preposition phrase may follow (No. 2), or a clause introduced by *that* (No. 6), or it may occur in the SVC construction of No. 8.

Activity 5
Finally, we concentrate on a single adjective, *heavy*, to examine its meanings, the kinds of noun it associates with, and its position in the sentence. Look at the following examples (extracted from *Collins COBUILD English Dictionary* 1995). For each example, say whether the meaning is 'literal' or 'figurative', and whether it would be more usual to find the adjective before the noun (*the heavy load*) or in predicative position (*the load was heavy*) or in both equally.

1   That was a heavy bag.
2   He worried about her heavy drinking.
3   Put the sugar and water in a heavy pan and heat slowly.
4   He had been feeling drowsy, the effect of an unusually heavy meal.
5   Her breathing became slow and heavy.
6   The plane made a heavy landing.
7   The outside air was heavy, moist and sultry.
8   Mr Maddison handed over his resignation letter with a heavy heart.

Commentary
No. 1 illustrates the most usual literal meaning of *heavy* ('of great weight') and it can be used in both positions (*The bag was heavy*). No. 3 similarly has the literal meaning, but with *pan* also implies thickness and protection of the contents of the pan from the direct heat source; *the pan is heavy* does not have that implication, only the straightforward 'weight' meaning.

In No. 2, *heavy*, in association with *drinking*, has the meaning of 'excessive'; it is not usual for *heavy* to occur in predicative position with *drinking*, the adverb would be expected, as in *She drinks heavily*. A 'heavy meal' (No. 4) may well be weighty (for a meal), but it is the fact that it takes time to digest that is in focus; *the meal was heavy* is possible, but probably less usual.

In No. 5, *heavy*, in relation to *breathing*, means 'laboured' or 'deep'; the adjective could equally well occur before the noun (*heavy breathing*).

Heavy in relation to *landing* (No. 6) refers to the nature of the touchdown, as if the plane fell like a dead weight out of the sky, rather than with a smooth and gentle approach. The predicative position (*the landing was heavy*) is possible, though probably less usual.

Heavy in relation to *air* (No. 7) refers to the feeling of sultriness, as if the air weighs on you. The predicative position, as in this example, is probably more usual. Similarly in No. 8, the heaviness is figurative, a feeling of weight; *with a heavy heart* is almost an idiom, but it is possible to say *His heart was heavy as he handed in his resignation letter*.

C2.3 **Adverbs and prepositions**

The classes of adverb and preposition gain a mention in Unit A2, and in the discussion of Adverbials in C4.2. Prepositions, or rather prepositional phrases, also make an appearance in C4.1 and in C5.1. But we have otherwise said little of substance about either class of words.

 Activity 1

As indicated in A2, the adverb class contains a number of subclasses, some of which have a limited membership. Examine the following sets of adverbs and determine what is common to each set.

1   accurately, badly, calmly, easily, gloriously, joyfully, magnificently, patiently, resolutely, slowly, smoothly, typically, visibly, wildly

2   again, always, ever, just, never, now, often, once, seldom, soon, then, yet

3   close, far, hence, here, near, thence, there, yonder

4   afterwards, backwards, downwards, earthwards, forwards, homewards, inwards, outwards, upwards

5   furthermore, however, meanwhile, moreover, nevertheless, notwithstanding, therefore, thus

6   downright, enough, just, most, pretty, quite, rather, so, very

7   certainly, leastways, maybe, perhaps, possibly, probably, surely

8   away, back, far, forth, out; before, behind, below, between, down, in, off, on, over, past, round, through, up

Commentary

The set of adverbs at No. 1 all end in -*ly*. They are derived from adjectives by the addition of this suffix; they mostly have a 'manner' meaning (see C4.2); and they form the largest subclass of adverbs – around 75 per cent of the adverbs entered in the *Cambridge International Dictionary of English* (2000) are -*ly* adverbs.

The set at No. 2 consists of 'time' adverbs; they are mostly simple, i.e. underived words, mainly of Old English origin. The adverbs at No. 3 are a corresponding set of 'place' adverbs. All the adverbs at No. 4 are formed by the addition of the Old English suffix -*ward(s)*; all have a 'direction' meaning, apart from *afterwards*, which is an oddity in this set with its predominantly 'time' meaning. Its parallel among 'time' adverbs is *beforehand*. However, *afterwards* can also be used in a 'position' sense, and, in that sense, it had a, now obsolete, correspondence in *aforeward*.

The adverbs at No. 5 are quite unconnected with any of those in the previous sets. Their function is to provide links between sentences, and they are known as 'conjunctive adverbs'. These adverbs normally come towards the beginning of a sentence, are set off by commas in writing, and provide an 'additive' (e.g. *furthermore*, *moreover*), 'contrastive' (e.g. *however, nevertheless*), or 'resultative' (e.g. *therefore*) link with the previous sentence. For example:

European capitals, especially Paris, have been champions of the municipal firework display for decades. Only last year did London compete with excessive millennium pyrotechnics. *However*, according to Britain's biggest firework producer, British families, pubs and local authorities have adopted a new year's eve firework tradition which will grow over the next few years. (The *Guardian*, 4.1.01, p.17)

Conjunctive adverbs are among an array of 'cohesive' devices that English uses to make links in texts (Halliday and Hasan 1976).

The set of adverbs at No. 6 is different again. These are the 'intensifying' adverbs that are used to modify adjectives (see C5.3) and other adverbs. Their range of meaning extends from positive emphasis (*downright, very*) to mitigation of emphasis (*quite, rather*).

The words in the set at No. 7 are the 'modal' adverbs, expressing the same kinds of 'modality' meanings as the modal auxiliary verbs (see C5.2): possibility (*maybe, perhaps*), probability (*probably*) and certainty (*certainly, surely*).

Finally, at No. 8 is the set of 'adverb particles'. They have various kinds of 'place' meaning; they are used with verbs of 'motion' to indicate direction ('Come *round* this evening', 'Please go *through*', 'Can I stay *behind* for a moment?'). They are also used to form 'phrasal verbs' (see C3.3), many of which have a figurative meaning, e.g. *pig out* ('eat excessively'), *take off* ('imitate'), *put down* ('humiliate'), *carry on* ('continue'). The adverb particles in the list after the semi-colon can also function as prepositions (see below).

This activity has illustrated the range of words that are conventionally included in the adverb class. It is usually included among the open, lexical word classes (see A5), but all the sets apart from No. 1 (the *-ly* adverbs) are restricted in membership and tend more towards the closed, grammatical classes.

Activity 2

The word class of preposition, to which we now turn, does have a restricted membership (The *Concise Oxford Dictionary*, ninth edition, lists around 130) and is considered to be a grammatical class (A2). Examine the sets of prepositions listed below and determine what is common to each set, especially in terms of meaning.

1 above, across, against, among, behind, below, beyond, down, into, near, off, onto, round, towards, under, up
2 during, for, till
3 after, at, before, between, by, from, in, on, over, through, to, until
4 about, as, by, despite, except, for, like, of, with

Commentary

The prepositions in the first set have exclusively, or predominantly, 'locative' (place and direction) meanings. Those in the second set have just 'temporal' (time) meanings. Those in the third set may have both 'locative' and 'temporal' meanings, according to context. The fourth set contains a miscellany of prepositions, with a variety of meanings that are neither 'locative' nor 'temporal'.

This is by no means a comprehensive analysis of the prepositions. You will notice that some prepositions have been entered more than once. In fact, quite a number of prepositions have multiple meanings, and just their main meanings have been taken account of in these listings. For example, the *Cambridge International Dictionary of English* (2000) lists fourteen meanings for *from*: 'place' (*from Berlin*), 'time' (*from tomorrow*), 'distance' (*miles from home*), 'origin' (*spices from the East*), 'material' (*made from pure wool*), 'level' (*from £4.99*), 'change' (*from villain to hero*), 'cause' (*die from malnutrition*), 'consider' (*from the evidence*), 'remove' (*five from forty*), 'difference' (*different from the others*), 'position' (*from this vantage point*), 'protection' (*shelter from the storm*), 'prevention' (*banned from driving*).

Activity 3

The *Concise Oxford Dictionary* (ninth edition (COD9)) lists ten meanings for the preposition *after*, illustrated by the following expressions. What labels would you give to distinguish each of these meanings?

1   after six months
2   after your behaviour tonight . . .
3   after all my efforts . . .
4   shut the door after you
5   hanker after it
6   enquire after her
7   named him William after the prince
8   a painting after Rubens
9   the best book on the subject after mine
10 after a fashion

Commentary

Here is the relevant part of the entry for *after* from COD9:

1   (a) following in time; later than (*after six months; after midnight; day after day*).
    (b) *N.Amer.* in specifying time (*a quarter after eight*)
2   (with causal force) in view of (something that happened shortly before) (*after your behaviour tonight what do you expect?*)
3   (with concessive force) in spite of (*after all my efforts I'm no better off*)
4   behind (*shut the door after you*)
5   in pursuit or quest of (*run after them; enquire after him; hanker after it; is after a job*)
6   about, concerning (*asked after her; asked after her health*)
7   in allusion to (*named him William after the prince*)
8   in imitation of (a person, word, etc.) (*a painting after Rubens; 'aesthete' is formed after 'athlete'*)
9   next in importance to (*the best book on the subject after mine*)
10 according to (*after a fashion*)

Activity 4

While prepositions may be used to introduce prepositional phrases functioning as Adverbials of 'time', 'place', 'manner' and so on (C4.2) or as postmodifiers in noun phrases (C5.1) with their more or less literal meanings, they are also used with verbs, to form 'prepositional verbs' (e.g. *belong to, look after*), and with certain adjectives to form their complements (e.g. *afraid of, different from/to*). Which prepositions would you use after the following verbs and adjectives? If there is a choice, does it represent a difference in meaning?

Verbs: attend, believe, collaborate, dissuade, fulminate, jam, marvel, presume, puzzle, stumble, veer, wheedle

Adjectives: absent, certain, conducive, eligible, exempt, fraught, impatient, keen, oblivious, proficient, sorry, worthy

Commentary

For the verbs, the appropriate prepositions are as follows: attend *to*, believe *in*, collaborate *with*, dissuade *from*, fulminate *about* or more specifically *against*, jam *into*, marvel *at*, presume *on*, puzzle *over*, stumble *on* (something unexpected) or *over* (e.g. words), veer *off* (a course) or *to* (a direction), wheedle *into* (persuade to do) or *out of* (obtain from).

For the adjectives, the appropriate prepositions are: absent *from*, certain *of*, conducive *to*, eligible *for*, exempt *from*, fraught *with*, impatient *with* (someone or a situation) or *for* (something to happen), keen *on*, oblivious *of/to*, proficient *at/in*, sorry *about* (a situation) or *for* (someone), worthy *of*.

In some cases, the preposition bears a clear relation to its literal meaning (*fulminate against, absent from*); in others the choice of preposition seems arbitrary and to contribute no relevant meaning (*presume on, fraught with*).

TYPES OF WORD STRUCTURE

C3

Compounds

C3.1

We briefly introduced the word formation process of compounding in Unit B3. In this subunit, we are going to examine compound words in English in more detail. Compounds are composed of two or more root morphemes and may be written 'solid', 'hyphenated', or 'open': *lifeboat, life-giving, life jacket*. However compounds are written, they constitute a single lexeme. The evidence for this lies in their pronunciation, grammar and meaning.

Activity 1

Compare the pronunciation of the items in the list on the left with those on the right. How does it differ? And which list contains the compound words?

checklist	check T-shirt
fire drill	fire pottery
honeycomb	honey taste
long distance (call)	long road
narrow-minded	narrow path
slug pellet	slug slime
teaching hospital	teaching students
wedding ring	wedding invitation

Commentary

You will have guessed quite easily that the list on the left contains the compound words, if only from the fact that some of them are written solid or hyphenated. But more importantly, the compounds on the left are pronounced as a single word, while the expressions on the right have a phrasal pronunciation. What this means is that the compounds have a single main stress – usually on the first element ('checklist), though not always (narrow-'minded) – while the expressions have potentially a main stress for each element ('check 'T-shirt, 'narrow 'path).

Compounds are also lexically single words. They are coined to name an object, idea, process, characteristic, etc., because that entity is new or has become significant enough to warrant denoting by a single lexeme. Compounding is the process most often used to coin a new 'name' for something.

Compounds are also grammatically single words. A compound operates as an indivisible unit in syntax; even if written open, it cannot be interrupted. It also belongs as a whole to a single word class, even if the parts belong to different word classes, e.g. *check* (verb) + *list* (noun) = *checklist* (noun), *six* (numeral) + *figure* (noun) = *six-figure* (adjective), *plea* (noun) + *bargaining* (verb, present participle) = *plea-bargaining* (noun).

Activity 2

Where a compound has more than two roots, the relation between the roots may not be simply additive; two of the roots may form a compound which then combines with a third root, e.g. *drop-in centre* – the hyphen shows that *drop* and *in* belong together and are an element that then combines with *centre*. Now identify the relations between the elements of the following compounds.

1   dual carriageway
2   disk operating system
3   Dutch elm disease
4   fair-weather friend
5   fine-tooth comb
6   local area network
7   optical character recognition
8   repetitive strain injury

Commentary

In some of these compounds, the written form suggests what the structure is intended to be: in No. 1, *dual* clearly relates to the already compounded *carriageway*; in Nos. 4 and 5, the hyphenated first two roots relate as a whole to the final element. In the completely open compounds the structure may not be so obvious. In No. 2, *operating* and *system* combine first, and then with *disk*; while in No. 3, *Dutch* and *elm* together combine with *disease*; so *disk (operating system)* but *(Dutch elm) disease*. For the remainder, No. 7 is fairly obviously *optical (character recognition)* and No. 8 is probably *(repetitive strain) injury*; but is No. 6 *local (area network)* or *(local area) network* (compare *wide area network*)?

Activity 3

Now consider how the following compounds are formed:

1   filling station
2   radio-controlled
3   windsurfing
4   hair's breadth
5   absent-minded

Commentary

All these compounds involve the combination of an inflected with an uninflected root: in No. 1 a present participle (*filling*), in No. 2 a past participle (*controlled*), in No. 3 a present participle (*surfing*) – though, interestingly, the verb *windsurf* is a back-formation from *windsurfing* – and in No. 4 a possessive noun (*hair's*). No. 5, however, is odd; it looks like No. 2, with the *-ed* past participle inflection. However, the root to which it has been added is not a verb, but a noun (*mind*), though the resulting compound (*absent-minded*) is an adjective, looking like a past participle, just as *radio-controlled* is. Compounds of the *absent-minded* type are quite numerous (see Gram-Andersen 1992), e.g. *blue-eyed, round-shouldered, soft-hearted, three-legged, wrong-headed*.

In Unit A3, we mentioned the type of compound called 'neo-classical compound', so called because they are formed from roots in the classical languages (Greek and Latin), combined in new ways in modern English to form words unknown to the ancients. Here are some further examples: *astronaut, autocracy, demography, dermatology, regicide, isochronous, neurogenesis*. Each of these is formed from a first part (*astro-, auto-, demo-*, etc.) and a second part (*-naut, -cracy, -graphy*, etc.), known as 'combining forms'. Some combining forms are always first parts of neo-classical compounds, others always second parts.

Activity 4

Now look at the following compounds, which are hybrids, in that they are composed of only one combining form, together with something else. Which is the combining form, and which the other element?

1   meritocracy
2   pesticide
3   neurosurgery
4   Francophile
5   technophobia
6   television

Commentary

The combining forms are in each case: (1) *-cracy* 'rule' (2) *-cide* 'killing' (3) *neuro-* 'nerve' (4) *-phile* 'fond of' (5) *-phobia* 'fear' (6) *tele-* 'distant'. In the case of the first three, the combining form has been added to a free root (*merit, pest, surgery*); in Nos. 4 and 5, a lookalike combining form has been coined, *Franco-* from *France*, and *techno-* from *technical*. In No. 6, a Greek first part (*tele-*) has been added to a Latinate second part (*vision* – from *visionis* 'seeing').

Our discussions so far in this subunit have concentrated on the structure of compounds and the formal relations between their parts. We are now going to consider the meaning relations between the parts of a compound. In most compounds, one element can be regarded as the 'head' of the compound and the other element as the 'modifier'. For example, in *moonlight*, the head is *light* and *moon* is the modifier: *moonlight* denotes the 'light reflected from the moon'. In *harvest moon*, the head is now *moon* and *harvest* is the modifier. This order reflects the modifier + head relation found in noun phrases (Unit B5). What is variable however is the relation of meaning that is found between modifiers and heads in compounds, e.g.

harvest festival 'festival to celebrate harvest'
harvest moon 'moon appearing around harvest time'
harvest mouse 'mouse that nests among cereal plants (which are harvested)'

Activity 5

Express the meaning relation between the parts of the following compound words:

1   pinhead, pinhole, pin money, pinprick
2   screenplay, screen test, screenwriter
3   fast food, fast track, fast worker

Commentary

If you are not sure of the meanings of these lexemes, then look them up in a dictionary. You should notice that the meaning relations represented in this small number of compound words is very varied. It is in the nature of the compounding process that the bringing together of two roots fixes the meaning relation to one of a number of possible meanings, because the compound is coined to fulfil exactly that need for a name. This is how compounds differ from the looser meaning relations of collocations, where two (or more) words occur together as a regular pattern, but without the specialisation of meaning associated with compounds (e.g. *pin a notice on a board, a cinema with twelve screens, my watch/clock is fast*).

Activity 6

Now look at the following compounds and attempt to describe the meaning relation between the elements.

1   bookworm
2   brainbox
3   egghead
4   highbrow
5   mastermind

Commentary

The meaning relation is not describable in the same terms for these compounds, as for those in Activity 5, because the meaning of the whole is other than the sum of the parts. The modifier + head relation does not operate in these compounds; they have a figurative or idiomatic meaning. All these words happen to refer to people who are considered intellectually superior, indeed to refer to them in a disparaging way.

A distinction is made between compounds like *pinhole*, where the modifier + head relation does operate, and those like *egghead*, where it does not, by the terms 'endocentric' and 'exocentric'. In endocentric constructions, like *pinhole* and most phrases in English, the head element stands for the whole construction. In exocentric constructions, like *egghead* and clauses in English, there is no head element to represent the whole; both, or more, elements are necessary for the construction to have meaning.

Activity 7
Compounds are pervasive in both the popular and the technical vocabulary of contemporary English. Look out for them. Here are a few to get you going: *dotcom, online, netsavvyness, techno-jitters, zip drive.*

Derivations

C3.2

We introduced the word formation process of derivation in Unit B3. It is the process for coining new words by adding an affix to a root or to an already derived word. Derivational affixes need to be distinguished from inflectional suffixes, which indicate different grammatical functions of a particular word class, e.g. plurals of nouns, past tense of verbs (see A2). In the composition of a word, an inflectional suffix is added after all the derivational suffixes have been applied, e.g. *class -ifi -cation -s*, where the final *-s* represents the PLURAL morpheme. Inflectional morphemes (suffixes) do not create new words, only grammatical variants. Derivational morphemes (prefixes and suffixes) have the function of creating new words, whose meaning may in time develop away from that of the roots from which they are derived.

Activity 1
Compare the meanings of the following pairs of roots and derived words. Can you detect a shift in the meaning of the derived word away from that of the root?

1 act – enact
2 centre – central
3 home – homely
4 nest – nestle
5 pure – purely

Commentary
The practice of most modern dictionaries is to give a derived lexeme a separate entry if its meaning cannot be easily deduced from the root word and so it needs its own definition. All these derived words have separate entries. You can look them up, but as an example, *homely* is defined as 'simple', 'plain', 'unpretentious' in British English and 'unattractive', 'ugly' in American English, which is straying quite a way from the meaning of *home*.

In considering derivation in more detail, we will begin with prefixes. It is unusual to find more than one prefix in any derivation, and unlike suffixes, prefixes for the most part do not change the word class of the item to which they are added, though a small number do.

Activity 2
In the following derived words, what is the meaning or function of the prefix? Do any of them change the word class of the root they are added to?

1   anticlimax
2   befriend
3   contraflow
4   dishonest
5   enslave
6   ex-president
7   hyperactive
8   improper
9   mislead
10 post-date
11 pro-life
12 reabsorb

Commentary
The meanings of the prefixes in these words are as follows: *anti-* 'opposite' (*anti-* can also mean 'against': *antiwar*); *be-* 'treat as' (*be-* has other meanings, e.g. in *besmear*, *belabour*); *contra-* 'against', 'opposite'; *dis-* 'not' (*dis-* can also mean 'reverse': *disengage*); *en-* 'bring into a condition of' (*en-/em-* can also mean 'put into': *embed*); *ex-* 'former', 'previous'; *hyper-* 'exceeedingly', 'excessively'; *in-/im-* 'not' (or, when added to nouns, *in-/im-* means 'without': *inability*); *mis-* 'wrongly'; *post-* 'after'; *pro-* 'in favour of' (the opposite of *anti-*); *re-* 'again'.

The only two of these prefixes that change the word class of the item to which they are added are: *be-*, *en-*. Both these prefixes are verb-forming: *be-* is added to nouns mainly (*befriend*), though also to some adjectives (e.g. *befoul*), as well as to verbs (e.g. *besmirch*), in which case it does not change the word class; *en-* is added mainly to nouns (*enslave*), but also to adjectives (*enable*), and to verbs, with the meaning of 'in(to)' (*enfold*).

Let us turn now to suffixes, which are more numerous, may occur together in a derivation, and usually change the word class of the item to which they are added.

Activity 3
Identify the suffixes in the following derived words; there may be more than one. Say what the meaning/function of each suffix is, including any word class change it triggers. Note that, as explained in Unit A3, the spelling of a morpheme may change when it is combined with another morpheme.

1   corrosive
2   forgetfulness

3 freedom
4 hesitation
5 homewards
6 musically
7 presidency
8 purity
9 sterilisation
10 wreckage

Commentary

1 The suffix -*ive* 'tending to' is added to the verb root *corrode* to form a related adjective.
2 The suffix -*ful* 'apt to' is added to the verb *forget* to form the adjective *forgetful*, to which is added the suffix -*ness* 'condition or instance of' to form the noun.
3 The suffix -*dom* 'state', 'condition' is added to the adjective *free* to form a related noun.
4 The suffix -*ion* 'action of', which has a number of variants, is added to the verb *hesitate* to form a related noun.
5 The suffix -*ward(s)* 'direction of' is added to the noun *home* to form a related adverb.
6 The suffix -*al* 'relating to' is added to the noun *music* to form the adjective *musical*, to which is added the suffix -*ly* 'manner' to form the related adverb.
7 The suffix -*ent* 'agent' is added to the verb *preside* to form the noun *president*, to which is added the suffix -*cy* 'status' to form a related abstract noun (no word class change here as such, only from person to abstract noun).
8 The suffix -*ity* 'quality', 'condition' is added to the adjective *pure* to form a related noun.
9 The suffix -*ise* 'cause to become' is added to the adjective *sterile* to form the verb *sterilise*, to which is added the suffix -*ation* (a variant of -*ion*) to form the related noun.
10 The suffix -*age* 'result of action' is added to the verb *wreck* to form a related noun.

You will notice that only one of the suffixes used did not cause a change of word class: -*cy* in *presidency*. Another example of this is the suffix -*ist* in words like *violin-ist, defeat-ist, perfect-ion-ist*, which is added to a noun to form an 'agent' noun.

Some affixes are still used regularly to form new words. For example, the *re-* prefix can be added to a large number of verbs to express a repeated action, or the -*ness* suffix can be used to form new abstract nouns from adjectives. On the other hand, some affixes are rarely if ever used nowadays to form new words: the 'diminutive' suffix -*kin*, as in *manikin*, or the 'feminine' equivalent of -*er/-or*, i.e. -*trix*, as in *negotiatrix* 'female negotiator'. We talk about the 'productivity' of an affix: a productive affix is one that is still used to derive new words. There are degrees of productivity; some affixes, like *re-* or -*ness* are still highly productive; others less so, such as the 'diminutive' -*let* (*booklet, piglet*), though they are not totally unproductive like -*trix*.

Activity 4

Another possibility is that new affixes may be formed. Look at the following sets of words and determine what process is being used to coin them.

1   chocoholic, shopaholic, workaholic
2   e-commerce, e-finance, e-mail
3   Eurocheque, Euro-election, Eurosceptic
4   Contragate, Irangate, Whitewatergate

Commentary

From the examples in set 1, we may conclude that a new suffix -*aholic*/-*oholic* has been formed, based on the word *alcoholic*, to mean 'a person addicted to'. Alternatively, these may be regarded as 'blends' (see B3), e.g. of *chocolate* and *alcoholic*. However, blends are usually one-off formations, so that if more words are coined on this basis, we shall have to recognise a new suffix. These three examples have already made it into dictionaries.

The examples in set 2 are perhaps rather newer, a product of the rapidly developing IT sector. The *e-* prefix stands for *electronic*, and this will spawn many new e-words as the computer revolution proceeds apace. The examples in set 3 arise from developments in the European Union and are well established (recorded in dictionaries); but there are still more Euro-words that have been coined but not yet codified.

Set 4 are coined from 'Watergate', the scandal in 1972 that led to the resignation of Richard Nixon from the US presidency. The 'gate' part of the name (of a building) has been taken to mean 'scandal involving covert operations or a coverup' and applied to other situations: the covert sale of arms to Iran, the proceeds of which financed arming the Nicaraguan 'Contras', the Whitewater property scandal during Clinton's presidency. (See the entry for '-gate' in Tulloch (1991).)

Derivation is an important and highly productive word formation process in English. Like compounding, it takes existing material (morphemes) from the language and creates new lexemes, so that we can talk about new things and experiences or discuss them in different and more detailed ways.

Activity 5

Take a (quality) daily newspaper and look in particular at the features pages (arts, education, business, IT, etc.) for examples of newly coined words. Determine how they have been formed – by compounding, derivation, or some combination; or perhaps by some other means. Look them up in a recent dictionary to see if they have been recorded yet.

C3.3   Multi-word items

You may not have come across the expression *hammer and tongs* before; it is not much used nowadays. It is used to indicate the enthusiasm and vigour with which someone goes about a task: 'She went at it hammer and tongs.' It occurs as a fixed expression; it cannot be reversed ('tongs and hammer'); and it has the grammatical function of an adverb, even though it is composed of two nouns joined by the conjunction *and*. It could be substituted by a single-word adverb such as *vigorously* or *energetically*. To all intents and purposes, it is a single lexeme, though made up of three orthographic words. This subunit is going to explore a number of such types of lexeme.

Activity 1

The first type of multi-word lexeme under consideration is a verb, made up usually of two, sometimes three, elements. Here are some examples. For each of them, can you think of a single-word equivalent?

1   catch up (someone)
2   come back
3   give up
4   go about (something)
5   hold back
6   let (someone) down
7   look out on
8   make out
9   pick up (someone)
10   point out
11   put up with
12   take (someone) off

Commentary

These verbs are composed of a (common) verb word and an adverb 'particle' (or two) (C2.3), which changes the meaning of the verb word, often introducing a figurative meaning; e.g. *put off* can denote a physical action ('remove'), but it can also have the meaning of 'postpone'. So these 'phrasal verbs', as they are called, have a unitary meaning, illustrated by their single-word synonyms:

1 reach 2 return, 3 relinquish 4 approach 5 retain, reserve 6 disappoint 7 face
8 perceive, distinguish 9 collect 10 indicate 11 tolerate 12 imitate

You will notice that the phrasal verbs, which are numerous in English, are generally more colloquial in tone than their single-word equivalents, which means that they are more usually found in spoken language and informal writing (e.g. letters, journalism, popular fiction). They represent quite a challenge for learners of English as a second or foreign language. In dictionaries, they are generally listed under the verb headword.

Activity 2

Now consider the following expressions. What is common about them? Do they have a literal meaning or a figurative meaning?

1   be-all and end-all
2   dribs and drabs
3   flotsam and jetsam
4   hard and fast

5   milk and honey
6   odds and ends
7   pros and cons
8   rank and file
9   spick and span
10   to and fro

Commentary

These are further examples of the *hammer and tongs* expression that we started this subunit with. They are known as 'binomial' (i.e. two name) expressions. They are fixed; the two terms cannot be reversed; they sometimes retain obsolete or archaic elements (*spick and span, kith and kin*) or include dialect items (*dribs and drabs*). They are sometimes pairings of near-synonyms (*odds and ends*) or of opposites (*pros and cons, to and fro*). Their meaning tends towards the figurative, or at least they are applied in a non-literal way. They add some colour to language, and they possess a certain rhythm.

Besides a fair number of binomial expressions, English also has a few trinomials, e.g. *hook, line and sinker; hop, skip and jump; lock, stock and barrel.*

Activity 3

The third type of multi-word lexeme we have already mentioned in C3.1: it is the 'open compound'. Many compounds begin life written as separate orthographic words, before becoming more accepted and regarded as regular members of the vocabulary – a process called 'lexicalisation' (see D3). Look up the following newish open compounds in a modern dictionary to see if they are yet recorded as lexemes in English.

1   anti-lock braking system
2   glass ceiling
3   grey literature
4   hot desking
5   information fatigue (syndrome)
6   performance poetry
7   road rage
8   Third Way
9   voice mail
10   wireless application protocol (WAP /wɒp/)

Commentary

At the time of writing (Spring 2000), one of the most up-to-date dictionaries is *The New Oxford Dictionary of English* (1998). The following items from the list above are already included in NODE: *glass ceiling, hot desking* (in fact, spelt with a hyphen), *performance poetry, road rage* (but not *air rage*, the counterpart in aeroplanes), *voice mail* (already written as a solid compound).

Whether included in NODE or not, all the items listed are arguably compound words, and so to be regarded as single, though multi-word, lexemes. A large number of open compounds have been coined in recent years, particularly in areas like computing and information technology, popular music, business and finance. Often they are regular collocations that develop into fixed expressions because they fill a perceived gap in the vocabulary of English.

Activity 4

Our last type of multi-word item is the most complex. The following are some examples. How many of these expressions are you familiar with? Try and give a paraphrase of each one. Look up those that you do not know.

1   buy a pig in a poke
2   the boot is on the other foot
3   bury the hatchet
4   spill the beans
5   between a rock and a hard place
6   the straw that broke the camel's back
7   on tenterhooks
8   shoot the breeze

Commentary

We are dealing here with expressions that are called 'idioms'. Every language has usually an extensive range of idioms, which are used largely in colloquial speech and more informal writing in order to add colour to the language. Perhaps, though, idioms are less frequently used than they used to be, especially by the younger generation. You may not have ever heard or seen one or more of the idioms given above. Idioms have two characteristics in greater or lesser measure: (1) their meaning is figurative and not literal, though an idiom may have a literal meaning as a phrase; (2) their composition is fixed, apart from verb forms and other minor variations. These two characteristics mean that idioms belong to the category of 'fixed expression' or 'multi-word item', though the term 'lexeme' might not be appropriate. However, idioms are entered in dictionaries, under one of the main words in the expression, though not usually as headwords.

The meanings of idioms can be expressed less colourfully by more literal expressions, e.g. for the list above, (1) buy something unseen; (2) a situation is now reversed; (3) make peace, be reconciled; (4) reveal a secret (also 'let the cat out of the bag'); (5) in an impossible situation (also 'between the devil and the deep blue sea'); (6) something that leads to a final disaster or breakdown; (7) waiting anxiously and impatiently; (8) chat casually about trivial things (an idiom better known in the USA than in the UK).

The origins of idioms are often obscure or relate to practices that are no longer current. *On tenterhooks*, for example, comes from cloth-making, when, after being woven, the cloth would be stretched (or 'tentered') on hooks. *Brewer's Dictionary of Phrase and Fable* (available in many editions) can usually suggest a plausible explanation for the origin of an idiom, though they need to be treated sometimes with a certain amount of caution.

Idioms continue to be coined, but it probably takes a long time before a new idiom is recognised as such. A relatively recent idiom would seem to be *a fly on the wall*, the first date for which is 1949 in the *Oxford English Dictionary* (1989); and the film-making technique ('fly-on-the-wall documentary') would appear to date from the 1980s. Although we often do not recognise them as such, idioms are pervasive in ordinary conversation, as well as in the broadcast media; if you listen out for them, you will hear them.

Activity 5

Perhaps the following are candidates for new idioms. Do you recognise them, and can you think of a meaning for them?

all-singing all-dancing	get a life
back to basics	in your (yer) face
a bad hair day	a level playing field
been there done that	move the goalposts
clear blue water	push the envelope
double whammy	the West Lothian question

All these expressions can be found explained in the *Oxford Dictionary of New Words* (1997).

C4   TYPES OF SLOT

C4.1   Object and Complement

In Unit A4, we identified the sentence slots of Object and Complement, and in Unit A5 we elaborated on their place in the structure of sentence patterns. In Unit B4 we drew a distinction between Direct and Indirect Objects and noted that, while a Complement could occur in the same sentence structure as a Direct Object, Indirect Objects and Complements are incompatible. In this subunit, we shall explore further the distinction between Object and Complement, as well as consider the range of fillers that these two slots may contain.

Activity 1

As a recap, identify the Objects and Complements in the following sentences:

1   Mark washed up the dishes.
2   Mildred had cooked him an excellent dinner.
3   They seem fond of each other.
4   She finds him good company.
5   Mark has asked her the vital question.
6   She will make him a good wife.

Commentary

No. 1 has a SVO pattern (Unit A5), with a phrasal verb (*wash up*) in the Verb slot; the Object is, thus, *the dishes*. No. 2 has a SVOO pattern, with *him* as the Indirect

Object and *an excellent dinner* as the Direct Object. No. 3 has a SVC pattern, with the adjective *fond* and its accompanying prepositional phrase (*of each other*) as the Complement. No. 4 has a SVOC pattern: *him* is the Object, and *good company* the Complement noun phrase. No. 5 is another SVOO pattern: *her* is the Indirect, and *the vital question* the Direct Object.

No. 6 has four elements. *She* is clearly the Subject, and *will make* the Verb. On the analogy of No. 2, *him* could then be Indirect Object and *a good wife* Direct Object; but that does not seem to accord with the sense. Perhaps the analogy should be No. 4, and so *him* is Direct Object and *a good wife* Complement. But that does not work either, because in a SVOC pattern the Complement relates to the Object, whereas in No. 6 *a good wife* relates to the Subject (*she*). The sentence *She will make a good wife*, where *be* could substitute for *make*, is clearly a SVC pattern. All that the addition of *him* does to the sentence is add a 'beneficiary', one of the roles of the Indirect Object (as in No. 2), and can be paraphrased by a *for* prepositional phrase (*for him*). So, is No. 6 an exception to the 'rule' that Indirect Object and Complement are incompatible? Perhaps so: 'make someone a good wife/husband' would appear to be the only instance of this pattern. Another oddity, however, is the relation of the Complement and Subject, rather than Complement and Object as in other SVOC patterns. Perhaps, then, we should regard it as an instance of the SVC pattern, with *him* in this case as a type of Adverbial. This would have the benefit of preserving the integrity of our patterns and the incompatibility rule. Grammatical explanations are not always neat and satisfactory!

Activity 2

What kinds of element fill the Object slots? Make a list of them from the following sentences:

1   Did she give him it?
2   She gave it to the sales assistant.
3   She gave him the faulty kettle that she had bought the previous day.
4   She told whoever would listen that she was free at last.
5   I'll ask the woman behind the desk if the last bus has gone already.
6   I'll ask her when the last bus goes.
7   You can guess how they spent the afternoon.
8   I hate to disappoint you.
9   I expect you to respond immediately.
10 We can't decide who to invite to the reception.
11 He admitted taking drugs in his youth.
12 He cannot stand anyone behaving like that.

Commentary

The Indirect Object slot, where it occurs in these sentences, is filled by:

a pronoun: *him* (Nos. 1 and 3), *her* (No. 6)
a noun phrase: *the woman behind the desk* (No. 5)
a prepositional phrase: *to the sales assistant* (No. 2)
a *wh*-clause: *whoever would listen* (No. 4)

The Direct Object slot is filled by:

a pronoun: *it* (Nos. 1 and 2)
a noun phrase: *the faulty . . . previous day* (No. 3)
a *that*-clause: *that she . . . at last* (No. 4)
an *if/whether*-clause (indirect yes/no question): *if the . . . gone already* (No. 5)
a *wh*-clause (indirect *wh*-question): *when the . . . goes* (No. 6)
a *wh*-clause: *how they spent the afternoon* (No. 7)
a *to*-infinitive clause: *to disappoint you* (No. 8)
a noun/pronoun + *to*-inf clause: *you to respond immediately* (No. 9)
a *wh-to*-inf clause: *who to invite to the reception* (No. 10)
an *-ing*-clause: *taking drugs in his youth* (No. 11)
a noun/pronoun + *-ing*-clause: *anyone behaving like that* (No. 12)

The range of elements possible in the Indirect Object slot is limited. Most commonly a pronoun or noun (phrase) occurs when the Indirect precedes the Direct Object. If the Indirect Object is more extensive than the Direct Object, then it tends to be placed afterwards, in which case it is a prepositional phrase introduced by *to* (for a 'recipient') or *for* (for a 'beneficiary'). The only clause that is possible is illustrated in No. 4: a *wh*-clause with *who(m)ever, whichever,* etc.

The Direct Object slot is the one that can take the widest range of elements, with a number of variations, including noun phrases, finite clauses (e.g. *that*-clause, *wh*-clause) and non-finite clauses (*to*-infinitive clause, *-ing*-clause) with or without a preceding noun or pronoun. Where the restriction comes is in the fillers that are possible after specific verbs. For example, the verb *request* may have the following types of Direct Object, but no others:

noun phrase: *She requested a room with a sea view.*
that-clause: *She requested that she should not be awoken before 8 o'clock.*
noun/pronoun + *to*-inf clause: *She requested the concierge to wake her at 8.*

A full account of possible sentence patterns and the verbs that may enter them can be found in *Collins COBUILD Grammar Patterns 1: Verbs* (1996).

Activity 3

Now let us investigate the types of filler that may be found in the Complement slot. Make a list of the Complements in the following sentences.

1 This road seems quite narrow.
2 Rachel is a mechanical engineer.
3 The water has gone cloudy.
4 Lydia has become a vegetarian.
5 She felt undermined by all the gossip.
6 I find his mannerisms rather offputting.
7 She thought him a true gentleman.
8 They consider the project to be too expensive.

9   You'll turn my hair grey.
10 He treats her as his unpaid servant.
11 You should fold the paper into a square.

Commentary

The Complement enters two kinds of sentence pattern (see Unit A5): SVC and SVOC. The first five sentences are examples of the SVC pattern, and the remaining six have the SVOC pattern. In most cases, the Complement slot is filled by either an adjective (phrase), a noun (phrase), or a prepositional phrase:

AdjP: *quite narrow* (No. 1), *cloudy* (No. 3), *rather offputting* (No. 6), *grey* (No. 9)
NP: *a mechanical engineer* (No. 2), *a vegetarian* (No. 4), *a true gentleman* (No. 7)
PrepP: *as his unpaid servant* (No. 10), *into a square* (No. 11).

The two sentences not included in this listing are Nos. 5 and 8. The Complement in No. 5 is 'undermined by all the gossip'. If *undermined* had occurred on its own, this past participle could have been regarded as an adjective; but it is followed by a further element (*by all the gossip*), which suggests a sentence-like structure and that the whole, therefore, be analysed as a past participle (*-ed*) clause. This type of Complement occurs with only a limited number of verbs.

The Complement in No. 8 is a *to*-infinitive clause, but it consists of the verb *to be* followed, in this case, by an adjective phrase (*too expensive*). It could also be followed by a noun phrase (e.g. *to be a white elephant*). With certain verbs, the adjective or noun phrase Complement may be preceded by *to be*.

Complements always relate to another element in the sentence, either the Subject in the case of SVC sentences, or the Object in SVOC sentences. They describe either the state some entity is in – *be*-type Complements (Nos. 1,2,5,6,7,8,10); or the state that something ends up in – *become*-type Complements (Nos. 3,4,9,11). This is the essential characteristic that distinguishes Complements from Objects: Objects denote different entities from other sentence elements; they do not have the descriptive relationship with another element that Complements have.

Activity 4

What types of Object/Complement may the following verbs take?

check, forget, grow, offer, reveal, watch

You can consult a grammar book or learner's dictionary to compare your answers.

Object and adverbial

C4.2

In Unit A4, we identified an Adverbial slot in sentence structure, typically containing elements relating to 'place', 'time', etc. In this subunit, we shall first distinguish Adverbials from Objects and then explore the nature of Adverbials in more detail.

Activity 1

Which elements in the following sentences are Objects and which are Adverbials? Are there any ways in which they clearly differ?

1   I'm attending a conference in Birmingham this week.
2   The conference lasts four days.
3   I shall travel to Birmingham by train.
4   The train reaches Birmingham at 11 o'clock.
5   I'm hoping for an interesting and instructive time.

Commentary

On the least controversial analysis, the following would count as Objects in the above sentences:

a conference (No. 1), *Birmingham* (No. 4), *an interesting and instructive time* (No. 5).

The remaining elements to the right of the Verb are, then, Adverbials, namely:

in Birmingham (No. 1), *this week* (No. 1), *four days* (No. 2), *to Birmingham* (No. 3), *by train* (No. 3), *at 11 o'clock* (No. 4).

What distinguishes Objects from Adverbials on the basis of these examples? First, you will notice that all the Objects are noun phrases, whereas the Adverbials are predominantly prepositional phrases. On this analysis, we assign the preposition *for* in No. 5 to the Verb (*hope for* as a prepositional verb) rather than to the Object. The noun phrase Adverbials both relate to time, either 'when' (*this week*) or 'how long' (*four days*). This brings us to the second point: Objects are generally identified by asking the question 'Who?' or 'What?', whereas Adverbials answer questions such as 'Where?', 'Where to/from?', 'When?', 'How?', 'Why?', 'How long/often/far/much?'. This criterion confirms *an interesting . . . time* in No. 5 as an Object, in answer to the question, 'What am I hoping for?' It confirms *this week* in No. 1 as an Adverbial, answering the question, 'When am I attending a conference in Birmingham?' But it makes problematical *Birmingham* in No. 4, which we have identified as an Object (because it is a noun phrase): is the question 'What did the train reach at 11 o'clock?' or 'Where did the train reach at 11 o'clock?' The answer is a matter of judgement.

In summary, Objects refer to people, objects, ideas, entities involved in the situation the sentence is about, while Adverbials refer to the accompanying circumstances of the situation in terms of 'place', 'time', 'manner', 'reason', and so on. As we have noted before, Objects are obligatory elements where a verb requires one, whereas Adverbials are generally more-or-less optional elements, except where required by verbs in SVA and SVOA patterns (A5).

Activity 2

Let us explore now the range of meanings that Adverbials can express, or the range of circumstances that we wish to include in our communication. Say what the general meaning is of each of the Adverbials in the following (e.g. 'place', 'direction', 'time', etc.).

1   They held the meeting in a remote village.
2   We travelled for miles from the main railway station up the valley.
3   The meeting began on Friday morning and lasted until Saturday evening.
4   There was a break every two hours.
5   The programme ran smoothly and with few revisions.

6   One session had to be cancelled because the speaker was ill.
7   The talks were planned for entertainment as well as to provide information.
8   You learn more efficiently if you are engaged by the speaker.
9   Despite the difficulties of reaching the venue, participants enjoyed the programme.

Commentary

The Adverbials in Nos. 1 and 2 are concerned with various aspects of 'place': 'in a remote village' refers to place proper, i.e. place 'where'; 'for miles' refers to 'distance', place 'how far'; 'from the main railway station' refers to 'direction – source', place 'where from'; and 'up the valley' refers to 'direction – path', place 'where by'. If we had added 'to the end', that would have been a 'direction – goal', place 'where to', Adverbial.

The Adverbials in Nos. 3 and 4 are concerned with various aspects of 'time': 'on Friday morning' refers to time proper, i.e. time 'when'; 'until Saturday evening' refers to 'duration', time 'how long'; 'every two hours' refers to 'frequency', time 'how often'. As with 'direction' in place, 'duration' in time can be viewed as having three aspects: duration 'from' ('since this morning'), duration 'to' ('until Saturday evening'), and duration 'general' ('for two days').

In No. 5, there are two 'manner' Adverbials: 'smoothly' and 'with few revisions'. 'Manner' includes a range of meanings associated with 'how' something happened or was done, e.g. 'means' ('We travelled *by train*'), 'instrument' ('He loosened the nut *with a wrench*'), 'accompaniment' ('The participants came *with their spouses*').

No. 6 contains a 'reason' Adverbial: 'because the speaker was ill'. No. 7 contains two 'purpose' Adverbials: 'for entertainment' and 'to provide information'. No. 8 has a 'conditional' Adverbial: 'if you are engaged by the speaker'. No. 9 has a 'concession' Adverbial: 'despite the difficulties of reaching the venue'.

This does not exhaust the range of Adverbial meanings available in English, but it presents the main ones. We shall now look at the types of grammatical element that can fill the Adverbial slot (see A4).

Activity 3

Examine the Adverbials again in the sentences in Activity 2. For each meaning, what types of element are used (prepositional phrase, adverbial clause, etc.)? Can you think of any further types of element that are not illustrated in these sentences?

Commentary

The 'place' Adverbials in Nos. 1 and 2 are all prepositional phrases (*in . . . , for . . . , from . . . , up . . .*), which is the most usual type of element for this Adverbial. A 'distance' Adverbial, in common with most Adverbials expressing quantity or amount, may be a noun phrase, e.g. 'a long way', 'six kilometres'. An adverbial clause occurs rarely as a place Adverbial, and then only introduced by *where*, e.g. 'You'll find it *where you left it*'. A small number of adverbs have a place meaning: *here, there, somewhere, anywhere*.

The 'time' Adverbials in No. 3 are prepositional phrases (*on . . . , until . . .*), and the 'frequency' Adverbial in No. 4 is a noun phrase (*every two hours*). Duration and frequency are routinely expressed by noun phrases (*all day, each day*), but frequency may also be expressed by an adverb (*often, regularly, daily*). Time 'when' is typically represented by a prepositional phrase, and many prepositions may have both a time and a place meaning, e.g. *in* ('in the morning', 'in the house'), *on* ('on Monday', 'on the shelf').

Time Adverbials are more regularly expressed by a clause than are place Adverbials. Consider the following examples:

1   We'll have tea when the children come home.
2   Before they arrive, we can get things ready.
3   While we're eating, they can tell us about their day.
4   They watched a film after they had done the washing-up.
5   Before going to bed, they brushed their teeth.
6   'Good night,' she whispered, turning out the light.

In the first four there are adverbial clauses (with a complete sentence structure) introduced by the conjunctions *when* (No. 1), *before* (No. 2), *while* (No. 3), *after* (No. 4), which have the effect of sequencing two events in time. One of the events is subordinated, in the adverbial clause, to the other in the matrix sentence. The last two sentences illustrate the use of a present participle (*-ing*) clause to express a time Adverbial, in No. 5 introduced by the conjunction *before* (to sequence the two events), and in No. 6 without a conjunction (to indicate simultaneous events).

Returning to the sentences in Activity 2, the 'manner' Adverbials in No. 5 have the form of an adverb (*smoothly*) and a prepositional phrase (*with . . .*). These forms are typical of Adverbials of manner: most adverbs formed from adjectives by the addition of the *-ly* suffix have a 'manner' meaning (*boldly, slowly, carefully, jokingly*, etc.). The most common preposition in prepositional phrases with a manner meaning is *with*, to express 'manner' itself (*with courtesy*), as well as 'instrument' (*with a stick*). Manner is also expressed by *in a . . . way/manner*, e.g. *in a joking way*. The preposition for 'means' is more usually *by* (*by train*). Clauses with a 'manner' meaning include those introduced by *as if* or *as though* (e.g. *as if no one else existed*) or *by* + present participle (e.g. *by removing the cause of the infection*).

The 'reason' Adverbial in No. 6 is expressed by an adverbial clause, introduced by the conjunction *because*. There is a corresponding prepositional phrase, with the preposition *because of*, e.g. 'because of the speaker's illness'.

The 'purpose' Adverbials in No. 7 comprise a prepositional phrase (*for . . .*) and an infinitive clause (*to provide . . .*). Whenever an infinitive clause fills the Adverbial slot, it has a 'purpose' (or 'result') meaning; it is sometimes preceded by *in order* ('in order to provide information'). A finite clause (with a complete structure) with a purpose meaning is introduced by *in order that* or *so that*, though the latter may also express the related 'result' meaning ('You should arrive by 10.00, so that we can start promptly' – purpose; 'They arrived by 10.00, so that we were able to start promptly' – result).

In No. 8, the 'conditional' Adverbial is an adverbial clause introduced by the conjunction *if*, which is the usual way of expressing a condition, unless the condition has an 'excluding' meaning, in which case the adverbial clause is introduced by *unless* ('Unless you are engaged, you will not learn.').

C

The Adverbial in No. 9 expresses a 'concessive' meaning, with the prepositional phrase (*despite . . .*). Concessives are more usually expressed by an adverbial clause introduced by *though* or *although* ('Although it was difficult to reach the venue, we enjoyed the conference.').

Adverbials express a wide range of circumstantial meanings and are expressed by a wide range of structures: adverb, prepositional phrase, noun phrase, *-ing*-clause, *to*-infinitive clause, finite adverbial clauses with a variety of introductory conjunctions.

More on subjects

C4.3

In Units A4 and A5, we noted that the Subject slot occurs in all the most usual types of sentence structure. The exception is the imperative sentence type (see B1, C1.3). In Unit B4 we saw that the element filling the Subject slot may have a number of different roles in relation to the Verb, e.g. doer of an action, undergoer of an event. In this subunit, we are going to examine the nature of Subjects and their relation to the other sentence elements in more detail.

Activity 1

⭐

Examine the following text (from the *Guardian*, 21.11.00, p.26). Identify the Subject of each numbered structure. Say what role the Subject has in relation to the Verb. What type of element (noun phrase, pronoun, etc.) fills the Subject slot?

---

[1] Cyberspace is proving tricky to navigate for the young entrepreneurs [2] who dreamed of making millions from the Internet. [3] Yesterday saw another high-profile US dot.com pull its flotation. [4] In Britain the picture is just as bleak. [5] One of Unilever's forays into the web recently ended [6] when Wowgo, a site aimed at teenage girls, folded [7] and the financial news site TheStreet closed its Clerkenwell offices on Friday. [8] Shopping advice site Ready2shop is also scaling back its ambitions.

[9] Webmergers, a US-based investment site, said at least 130 internet companies have shut down worldwide since the beginning of this year. [10] Nearly 100 of those companies focused primarily on a consumer rather than a business audience. [11] The rate of closure has accelerated in November, according to Webmergers.com.

[12] Few of Britain's more high-profile launches have survived. [13] Boo.com, [14] which lost an estimated £80m in about seven months, and Clickmango, fronted by Joanna Lumley, both failed in their original forms.

[15] This gloomy picture has not discouraged everyone, however. [16] It has just emerged that Henry Lane Fox has left Lastminute.com.

Commentary

You were asked to say three things about the Subjects in the structures of this text. You will have found that the answers are not always very straightforward, particularly in respect of the relation between the Subject and the Verb. Here are the answers, together with some discussion of this more tricky area.

[1] *Cyberspace* is the Subject. The Verb *prove* is behaving rather like *be*; it is followed by the adjective *tricky*; so the structure is SVC, with the Subject as the 'site' of the 'attribute' *tricky*. The Subject is a noun (phrase).

[2] In this relative clause (C6.2), the Subject is *who*. To determine the role of the Subject, we need to decide whether the Verb *dream* is a mental 'action' or 'event', something that the Subject instigates or something that just happens to them. If *dream* is an 'action', then the Subject has the role of 'doer'; if a mental event, then of 'experiencer'. In this context an 'action' interpretation would seem more plausible, as some deliberate 'dreaming' is suggested on the part of the 'young entrepreneurs'. The Subject is a relative pronoun, standing for *the young entrepreneurs* in the main sentence.

[3] The Subject is *yesterday*. This is a strange structure, with an expression of time together with the Verb *see*, as if *yesterday* was being regarded as a person. If we take it as such, then the Subject has the 'experiencer' role in relation to the 'perception' Verb *see*. *Yesterday* is here a noun; it sometimes behaves as an adverb (e.g. in 'I spoke to her yesterday').

[4] The Subject is *the picture*. It is related to the Verb *be* as the 'site' of the 'attribute' *bleak*. And it is a noun phrase.

[5] The Subject is *one of Unilever's forays into the web*. It is related to the Verb *end* as the 'undergoer' of an 'event'. *End* can be used either as an 'action', when 'someone ends something', or, as here, as an 'event', when 'something ends'. The Subject is a quite complex noun phrase, with the head noun *forays*.

[6] In this subordinate *when*-clause, the Subject is *Wowgo, a site aimed at teenage girls*. It has the role of 'undergoer' in relation to the 'event' Verb *fold*. It is composed of two noun phrases in apposition: the proper noun *Wowgo*, and the elaborating phrase *a site . . . girls*.

[7] This structure is part of the *when*-clause started in [6]: the Subject is *the financial news site TheStreet*. It has the role of 'doer' in relation to the 'action' verb *close*. It has the same composition as the Subject in [6], except in reverse: the explanatory phrase comes first (*the financial news site*) and the proper noun (*TheStreet*) second.

[8] The Subject is *Shopping advice site Ready2shop*. It has the role of 'doer' in relation to the 'action' Verb *scale back*. And it has the same apposition structure as the Subject in [7]: the noun phrase *shopping advice site* and the proper noun *Ready2shop*.

[9] The Subject is *Webmergers, a US-based investment site*. It has the role of 'doer' in relation to the verbal 'action' Verb *say*. It has the same composition as the Subject in [6]: proper noun *Webmergers* and elaborating noun phrase *a US-based investment site*.

[10] The Subject is *Nearly 100 of those companies*. It has the role of 'doer' in relation to the action verb *focus*. It is a noun phrase, whose head could be regarded either as the noun *companies* or as the numeral *100* (when *of those companies* would be a postmodifying prepositional phrase).

[11] The Subject is *The rate of closure*. It has the role of 'undergoer' in relation to the 'event' Verb *accelerate*. It is a noun phrase, with *rate* as the head noun.

[12] The Subject is the bulk of this sentence: *Few of . . . launches*. It has the role of 'undergoer' in relation to the 'event' Verb *survive*. It is a noun phrase, whose head is the final noun *launches*.

[13] The Subject in this sentence is especially long: in essence it is the two, co-ordinated, proper nouns *Boo.com and Clickmango*, together with each of their postmodifications. Because of their length, they are picked up by the word *both* immediately before the Verb. The Subject has the role of 'undergoer' in relation to the 'event' Verb *fail*. The Subject consists of a pair of co-ordinated noun phrases: the first, with the proper noun *Boo.com* as head, is postmodified by a relative clause (*which . . . months*); the second, with the proper noun *Clickmango* as head, is postmodified by an *-ed* (past participle) clause (*fronted . . . Lumley*).

[14] This picks up the relative clause from [13]; so the Subject is *which*. It has the role of 'undergoer' in relation to the 'event' Verb *lose*. It is a relative pronoun.

[15] The Subject is *This gloomy picture*. The Verb that it relates to (*discourage*) is an 'action' verb, but 'doers' of 'actions' are normally human instigators: *this gloomy picture* is not. In order to preserve the notion of a 'doer' as human, linguists have proposed alternative labels for items such as the Subject in this sentence; e.g. 'instrument', where the Subject expresses the means by which something is done (*A computer solved the problem*, related to *Someone solved the problem with a computer*), or 'external causer', where the Subject expresses a natural phenomenon (*An earthquake destroyed the village*). Neither of these quite fit the Subject here, and for the sake of simplicity it is probably best to extend the label 'doer' to cover such non-human cases. The Subject is a simple noun phrase, with head noun *picture*.

[16] In this sentence, the Verb is the 'event' *emerge*. The Subject looks as if it is the preceding pronoun *it*, but this pronoun is holding the place for the real, postponed Subject: *that Henry Lane Fox has left Lastminute.com*. It is common for clausal Subjects to be postponed (or extraposed) in this way (as in this sentence! – see C6.1). The Subject has the role of 'undergoer', because *emerge* is an 'event'. It consists of a *that*-clause.

Summary

Subjects normally precede their Verb elements, except where extraposition operates. Their role is determined by the meaning of the Verb: 'doer' with 'action', 'undergoer' with 'event', 'experiencer' with 'thought/emotion/perception', 'site' with a state. Their composition varies enormously, from a single word (pronoun, proper noun), through a variety of noun phrase structures (including apposition and co-ordination), to a clause (e.g. *that*-clause).

C5 | **COMPONENTS OF PHRASES**

C5.1 | **Modifying nouns**

In Unit B5, we established the basic structure of noun phrases. You may like to look back at that unit to refresh your memory. In this subunit, we are going to extend our discussion of noun phrases and consider a broader range of examples. We shall begin with the following text, in which the sentences are numbered.

---

[1] Driving ban cut for rail 'victim' (the *Guardian*, 16 December 2000, p.9)

[2] Judge offers sympathy over commuter's 'nightmare'.

[3] While most commuters fume about the state of the railways, Cliff Newman must secretly be rubbing his hands. [4] A judge yesterday cut the engineer's driving ban after hearing that he could not get to work on time because the train services were so appalling. [5] Mr Newman, 38, received a three-month ban in October after being caught speeding on his motorcycle at 101mph. [6] It was his third offence.

[7] He was obliged to make the 40-mile trip to work by train instead, but due to delayed and cancelled services found it took him over four hours to make a journey that previously took 45 minutes. [8] Worried that he would lose his job because of his continual lateness, he launched a legal appeal. [9] At Swindon crown court, Judge Tom Longbotham cut his ban by three weeks, telling him: 'Your driving record is atrocious. [10] But taking into account the problems you have had arriving late at work and your tiredness, I will uphold the appeal.'

[11] The ruling came as official figures revealed that train punctuality performance was declining even before the Hatfield crash. [12] Just one of the 25 train companies improved its punctuality in the six months ending just before the mid-October derailment compared with the same period in 1999.

[13] Mr Newman said yesterday: 'It was a nightmare every day. I never once arrived on time and when I finally got home at night, I was exhausted.' [14] He commutes from his home in Swindon, Wiltshire to his job in Pangbourne, Berkshire. [15] In his Vauxhall Nova it was a 45-minute drive, while on his 1,100cc Honda motorcycle it could take as little as 30 minutes. [16] His new journey, which involved changing at Didcot, cost him £65 a week in fares. [17] To arrive in time for a 5.45 am shift he had to leave home as early as 2 am, around the same time he could expect to arrive home if working an evening shift.

Activity 1

Excluding pronouns and proper nouns (names and titles), identify the noun phrases in the text that consist of only a head noun. Do they have anything else in common, apart from being a single-word NP?

Commentary

In [2] *sympathy* is a noun phrase, as part of the common expression 'offer sympathy'. The noun *work* occurs three times on its own, twice after the preposition *to* [4, 7], and once after *at* [10]. The noun *time* occurs three times, twice after *on* [4, 13], and once after *in* [17]. Three other nouns occur on their own after prepositions: (*by*) *train* [7], (*in*) *fares* [16] and (*at*) *night* [17]. The expressions with *work, time, night* and *train* are common collocations, on the way to becoming almost fixed expressions (e.g. *on time, at night*). This seems to be a common characteristic of these single-word noun phrases. The only other single-word noun phrase in this text is *home* [13, 17 (twice)], and often *home* seems more like an adverb than a noun, e.g. *got home* in [13], *arrive home* in [17].

Activity 2

Identify the two-word noun phrases in the text that do not contain an article (*a, the*) or a possessive identifier (*his,* etc.).

Commentary

The first three two-word noun phrases occur in the headlines [1, 2]. In [1], both noun phrases (*driving ban, rail victim*) comprise a noun modifier + head noun. The NP in [2] (*commuter's nightmare*) has a possessive noun + head noun. Both structures accord with the compressed syntax of headline language. Most of the other two-word NPs consist of a numeral or quantifier + head noun: *most commuters* [3], *45 minutes* [7], *three weeks* [9], *every day* [13]. That leaves just the adjective + noun collocation *official figures* [11], and possibly *delayed and cancelled services* [7], which is not strictly a two-word NP, though it is a two-element NP: (participle + participle) (head noun).

Activity 3

Identify the three-word noun phrases in the text. Is the first item always a determiner (article or possessive)?

Commentary

There are several patterns of three-word NPs manifested in this text, and most have a determiner as their first element. A number consist of 'determiner + quantity + noun': *a three-month ban* [5], *his third offence* [6], *a 45-minute drive* [15]. Others have the classic 'determiner + adjective + noun' structure: *his continual lateness* [8], *a legal appeal* [8]; or, more frequently in this text, with a noun modifier in the place of the adjective: *the train services* [4], *your driving record* [9], *the Hatfield crash* [11], *the mid-October derailment* [12], *his Vauxhall Nova* [15], *a 5.45 am shift* [17], *an evening shift* [17]. That leaves three NPs without an initial determiner: two are strings of nouns with different patterns of modification – (*Swindon*) (*crown court*) [9], (*train punctuality*) (*performance*) [11]; the other is *over four hours* [7], where the adverb *over* modifies the numeral *four* and together they modify the head noun *hours*.

One other noun phrase might fit here: *the engineer's driving ban* [4]. While containing four words, it has only three elements: *the engineer's* is a possessive element (genitive NP), which as a unit modifies the head noun *ban*. It is equivalent to a possessive identifier (*his*).

Activity 4

Identify the noun phrases containing postmodifiers, and say, in each case, what type of postmodifier it is.

Commentary

All three major types of postmodifier occur in this text. The commonly found post-modifying prepositional phrase (A6) occurs in: *the state (of the railways)* [3], *the 40-mile trip (to work)* [7], *his home (in Swindon, Wiltshire)* and its parallel *his job (in Pangbourne, Berkshire)* [14].

Relative clauses (C.6.2) occur in [7] (*a journey that* . . .), [10] (*the problems (that) you* . . .), [16] (*his new journey, which* . . .), [17] (*the same time (that) he* . . .). Let us examine each of these in turn. In [7], the relative clause begins with *that* as the relative pronoun. When *that* occurs as a relative pronoun, it signals that the relative clause is 'defining' or 'restrictive': the relative clause restricts/defines which of a number of possible referents are being talked about, in this case the '45-minute journey', rather than any other 'journey'. The relative pronoun *that* in [7] functions as the Subject of the relative clause (*that* . . . *took* . . .). In [10], the relative pronoun has been omitted: we could supply *that*, since the relative clause is defining 'problems'. In contrast to *that* in [7], it is here the Object of the relative clause (*you have had* . . . *that*, i.e. *prob-lems*). It is because *that* functions as Object that allows it to be omitted. Similarly in [17], the relative pronoun (*that* or possibly *when*) is the Object of *arrive* in the rela-tive clause. The example in [16] is different: here the relative pronoun is *which*, func-tioning as Subject in the relative clause (*which involved* . . .). The relative clause is set off from the noun by means of a comma, which, together with the use of *which*, suggests a 'non-defining' relative clause: the noun *journey* is already 'defined' by the adjective *new*. As sentence-type structures, relative clauses are already complex post-modifiers; their complexity is further enhanced by the possible functions that relative pronouns may have within the relative clause, as well as the types of relative pronoun that may occur, e.g. *who/whom/whose* as against *which* or *that*, besides *where* with loca-tive nouns, *when* with temporal nouns, and *why* with nouns like *reason*.

The third major type of postmodifier is the non-finite clause (C6.2), of which there is one example in this text: *the six months (ending just before the mid-October derail-ment)* [12]. Non-finite clauses can be regarded as reduced forms of relative clauses. This example could be rewritten as: *the six months that ended* . . . Non-finite postmodifiers beginning with a present participle (*-ing*) form of the verb are reduced forms of active clauses; those with a past participle (*-ed*) form of the verb are reduced forms of pas-sive clauses, e.g. *the weapons amnesty declared by the chief of police*, reduced from *the weapons amnesty that was declared* . . . As in this text, the full relative clause occurs more frequently than does a non-finite clause equivalent. Relative clauses and non-finite clauses are taken up again in Subunit C6.2.

Tense, aspect and modality

In the second half of Unit B5, we outlined the structure of the verb phrase (VP), in terms of auxiliary and main verbs and the order in which they occur. In this subunit, we shall explore further the functions and meanings associated with particular auxiliary verbs and the structures they generate.

Activity 1

What do the initial verbs in the VPs at 1 to 4 below share in common, which is different from the initial verbs in 5 to 8?

1 speaks
2 is talking
3 has mentioned
4 are quoted
5 thought
6 was wondering
7 had decided
8 were considered

Commentary

The difference between the initial verbs in 1 to 4 above and those in 5 to 8 is one of 'tense': the verbs in 1 to 4 are in the 'present tense', those in 5 to 8 are in the 'past tense'. Tense is merely a matter of form: the inflection of the verb word (see B5), and in English 'present' and 'past' are the only tenses formally marked in the verb. However, the terms 'present' and 'past' have real-world meanings in relation to our concept of time. We divide time conventionally into three periods: 'present' (now), 'past' (before now), and 'future' (after now). The interesting question is how the categories of real-world time relate to the grammatical categories of tense. One obvious mismatch is in the number of categories: there is no 'future tense' in the grammar of English – though this does not mean that English speakers are unable to talk about the future! We shall also find that, even for present and past, tense does not match neatly with time.

Activity 2

All the VPs in the following sentences have a main verb in the 'simple' present tense. What time period do they refer to?

1 The drug causes short term memory loss.
2 MPs vote today on the government's proposals.
3 Shy singer arrives in Scotland for low-key wedding.
4 The memo raises new questions about the government's role.
5 He steps down from the chairmanship in June 2001.

Commentary

The simple present tense is more variable than the past in respect of the time periods it may refer to. It is used to express 'timeless' states of affairs, as in No. 1. It can refer to future time, either the immediate future, as in No. 2, or a more distant future, as in No. 5. In newspaper headlines, of which No. 3 is an example, the simple present tense is used to refer to past time; the article then usually continues in the past tense. Written documents, which have been composed in past time, can nevertheless be said to 'say' things in the present, as in No. 4. So, the simple present tense can, according to context, refer to past, present or future time, though, ironically, rarely to the present moment as such.

Activity 3

The present moment is most usually referred to by a verb phrase in the present progressive form. Most of the VPs in the following sentences have progressive verb forms. There are many subtleties of meaning associated with progressive aspect. What difference does the progressive make to the meaning of these sentences?

1   The South Korean police are investigating a spate of web-assisted suicides.
2   If I am working a late shift, I don't get home until 10 pm.
3   The Post Office is hoping to use the network for its universal bank.
4   His political comeback was fizzling out last night.
5   I was queuing behind a lady last week in Sainsbury's, who wanted to buy an iron.
6   I was playing with the kids in the garden.

Commentary

The first three sentences contain verb phrases in the present progressive; the last three have verb phrases in the past progressive. No. 1 illustrates the classic use of the present progressive: to refer to an action or event that spans the present moment of speaking: it may have started in the past and may continue into the future, but it is happening as we speak, the true present moment. In No. 2, either simple present (*If I work a late shift . . .*) or present progressive would be possible: the progressive adds a dimension of extended time, emphasising the length of a shift. In No. 3 likewise, a simple present could have been used (*The Post Office hopes . . .*): the effect here is to add a nuance of tentativeness; the simple present gives a more certain hope than the progressive.

In the case of the past progressive sentences, No. 4 is the classic case, where the progressive indicates an action or event 'in progress', rather than completed, as the simple past would have indicated (*His comeback fizzled out last night*). In No. 5, the simple past would be possible (*I queued behind a lady last week . . .*): what the progressive does is to provide a framework within which another event intervenes (*I was queuing . . . , when . . .*); the text goes on to relate a series of events that then happened. No. 6 likewise uses the progressive to indicate an action or event in progress, and we would expect it to be followed by another action/event going on at the same time, or intervening.

Activity 4

The other 'aspect' mentioned in Unit B5 was the 'perfective', formed with auxiliary *have* and the past participle, e.g. present perfective *has slept*, past perfective *had slept*. What meanings do the perfective verb phrases give to the following sentences?

1 They have developed some neat little tricks.
2 She has been playing the piano since the age of six.
3 They have just been officially declared cities.
4 He has seen the aftermath of the offences.
5 They had already received a 12% increase the previous year, and last year they received a further 8%.
6 He composed it in memory of his son, who had died that year.

Commentary

The first four sentences contain examples of the present perfective, the last two of the past perfective. The perfective verb phrase refers to past time. In the case of the present perfective, there is also usually some connection with the present. This may be because there are some effects in the present, as in No. 1 (the 'neat little tricks' now exist as a consequence of their development in the past), or because a situation begun in the past continues up to the present, as in No. 2. Alternatively, the present perfective may act as a 'pre-present' tense, to indicate an action/event that has 'just' happened, as in No. 3. Another possibility, illustrated by No. 4, is that the present perfective acts as an 'indefinite past', where the time when something happened is left vague and unspecific: if the verb in No. 4 was in the simple past (*He saw the aftermath . . .*), then we would expect some specification of the time when it took place.

The past perfective, as illustrated by Nos. 5 and 6, has the effect of placing one situation further back in past time in relation to another. It has been termed a 'past in the past'.

Summarising so far: 'tense' helps to situate an action, event or state in time; 'aspect' tends to show how that action, event or state is distributed in time – either in progress for the 'progressive', or up to a point in time for the 'perfective'.

Activity 5

We turn now to the third topic of this unit, modality, which relates to the meanings associated with the modal verbs identified in B5. The following are a number of sentences whose verb phrases include a modal verb. Describe the meaning that the modal verb gives to the sentence.

1 The newspaper must name the source who leaked the contents of a confidential diary.
2 This area of confidentiality should be safeguarded in democratic societies.
3 They could distract attention from their own failures.
4 Heavy rain may return late in the day.
5 You can go to a secondary modern and still become famous.
6 Licences might be obtainable under existing UK law.
7 No one could be that good again.
8 You can draw your own conclusions.

Commentary

In the first two sentences, the modal auxiliaries (*must, should*) are concerned with 'obligation', with *must* expressing a stronger degree than *should*. The modal auxiliary *could* in No. 3 expresses 'ability'; it may be paraphrased by *were able to*. The meanings of the modals in Nos. 4 to 7 are of a different order from those in the first three sentences: they express different degrees of possibility that the proposition expressed by the sentence is the case. No. 4 has *may* and No. 6 its past *might*: the latter expresses a more tentative possibility than *may*. No. 5 has *can* and No. 7 its past *could*: the latter expresses a more remote possibility than *can*. In all these four cases, the paraphrase is: *It is possible that* . . . The last example, with *can*, is ambiguous between an 'ability' interpretation (*You are able to draw* . . .) and a 'possibility' interpretation (*It is possible for you to draw* . . .). These are just a selection of modal meanings; it is an area full of indeterminacy and ambiguity: see Coates (1983) for a full treatment.

Activity 6

Finally, let us return to the question of future time. Here are some sentences that refer to the future, but use different means to do so. Can you discern any differences in the future meaning that they convey?

1 Rain will arrive in the west later.
2 We will return them as soon as possible.
3. There is going to be massive overcrowding.
4 He returns next month.
5 We will be writing to the manufacturers in the new year.
6 The government is to introduce new controls over the performance-enhancing drug nandrolone.

Commentary

The first two sentences express the future by means of the modal verb *will*, the most common means of referring to the future in written English: in No. 2 the meaning is quite neutral; in No. 1 there is an overtone of 'prediction', which sometimes accompanies *will*. No. 3 illustrates the use of *be going to* as the marker of future time; it is the most common form in spoken English. In No. 4 the simple present tense is used, together with an adverbial of time with future reference (*next month*): this is sometimes called the 'timetable' future; it has a sense of certainty. No. 5 has *will* together with progressive aspect, reinforcing the underlying 'intention' meaning that *will* sometimes has (e.g. perhaps in No. 2). Finally, No. 6 has the *be to* construction to express the future, indicating a sense of certainty and firm intention. Thus most expressions of the future – and these examples do not exhaust the possibilities – have some further overtone, indicating perhaps that we have less confidence in talking about the future than we have in reporting the past.

C5.3 Adjective phrase

In Unit A6, we identify five types of phrase in English, among them the adjective phrase. Unlike the noun phrase and verb phrase, considered in B5, the adjective phrase has a relatively simple structure. We consider that structure in this subunit. Like NPs and VPs, the adjective phrase (AdjP) is a headed phrase: its head is an adjective word. Adjectives as such are discussed in C2.2; here we look at how they are modified and how they operate in the structure of sentences.

Activity 1

Identify the adjectives in the following sentences. Do they all occur in the same kind of position in the sentence structure?

1   The majority were in serious financial difficulties.
2   Prospective students are being deterred from applying.
3   University was a worthwhile experience.
4   They are afraid of being saddled with debt.
5   Student hardship is widespread.
6   Gemma is keen to take a master's degree.
7   George is now confirmed as the president elect.
8   It will be a rather cloudy day but it will be mostly dry, although a few spots of drizzle are possible.

Commentary

The first three sentences illustrate the adjective used as a modifier of nouns in NPs, the so-called 'attributive' position of adjectives: *serious* and *financial* modifying *difficulties* in No. 1, *prospective* modifying *students* in No. 2, and *worthwhile* modifying *experience* in No. 3. The next three sentences illustrate adjectives in the 'predicative' position, as a Complement after a verb like *be*: *afraid* in No. 4, *widespread* in No. 5, and *keen* in No. 6. You may have noted that *afraid* and *keen* have a following associated element, which we will discuss below. In No. 7, the adjective (*elect*) follows the noun it modifies (*president*): the 'postpositive' position. No. 8 has an attributive adjective *cloudy* and two predicative adjectives, *dry* and *possible*. You may have noted that *cloudy* is itself modified by *rather*.

Adjectives may, then, occur in any of three positions in the structure of sentences: attributive (as pre-modifiers in noun phrases), predicative (as a Complement – A4, C4.1), and postpositive (as postmodifier in a noun phrase). But not all adjectives can occur in all three positions.

Activity 2

Construct sentences with the following adjectives, attempting to use them in all three positions. Is there any position in which the adjective in each case cannot be used?

alleged, alone, deficient, emeritus, galore, happy, idle, inaugural, next, principal, rampant, rightful, tantamount, triumphant, upset

Commentary

Most adjectives can be used in both attributive and predicative positions, though there are some that are restricted to one or other. Few adjectives can be used postpositively; they are mostly adjectives that derive from French or Latin and used either in the jargon of heraldry (*three lions passant guardant*) or of cooking (*lobster bordelaise*) or in fairly fixed phrases (*blood royal, decree nisi, knight errant*). However, indefinite pronouns (e.g. *someone, nobody, anything*) are always modified by a postpositive adjective, e.g. *something unpleasant, nothing important*.

The following are the possibilities for the adjectives listed above:

alleged: attributive only (*the alleged thief*)

alone: predicative only (*she is alone*), in common with most adjectives with the
            a- prefix

deficient: mainly predicative (*your diet is deficient in vitamins*)

emeritus: attributive (*an emeritus professor*) or postpositive (*a director emeritus*)

galore: postpositive only (*sweets galore*)

happy: attributive (*a happy smile*) or predicative (*she is happy*)

idle: attributive (*an idle moment*) or predicative (*he is just idle*)

inaugural: attributive only (*their inaugural performance*)

next: attributive (*the next train*) or, occasionally, predicative (*Who is next?*)

principal: attributive only (*the principal argument*)

rampant: attributive (*rampant inflation*), predicative (*the disease is rampant*), and, in
            heraldry, postpositve (*two lions rampant*)

rightful: attributive only (*the rightful owner*)

tantamount: predicative only (*his refusal is tantamount to treason*)

triumphant: attributive (*her triumphant success*), predicative (*her smile was
            triumphant*), and postpositive (*a story of common sense triumphant*)

upset: usually predicative (*you look upset*), but also attributive (*an upset stomach*)

We turn now to the types of modification that may occur in an adjective phrase. Most of our examples so far have consisted of a simple adjective (head) without modification. We had a *rather* modifying *cloudy* in No. 8 of Activity 1, but nothing else. The most common modifier is *very*, which is a more positive 'emphasiser' than *rather*. You should note that not all adjectives can be modified, only those that allow some variation or gradation (see C2.2): *inaugural* or *emeritus*, for example, cannot be modified by *very* or *rather*.

Activity 3

Examine the modifiers in the following adjective phrases. Do they form any obvious sets, using the meaning of the modifier as a criterion?

1   an amazingly intelligent answer
2   a completely inadequate reason
3   a deceptively shrewd proposal
4   an entirely understandable mistake
5   a disappointingly low attendance
6   an extremely well-informed audience
7   a pretty dull lecture
8   an incredibly penetrating observation
9   a clearly flawed argument
10 an encouragingly positive response

Commentary

We can perhaps identify three sets of modifiers here, with one of them having a range of related meanings. First, there is a set that includes *amazingly* (No. 1), *disappoint-*

ingly (No. 5), *incredibly* (No. 8), and *encouragingly* (No. 10), which expresses an emotional reaction to the quality denoted by the adjective. Second, there is a set that includes *deceptively* (No. 3) and *clearly* (No. 9), which expresses the speaker's assessment of the obviousness or otherwise of the quality denoted by the adjective. Third, there is a set that includes *completely* (No. 2), *entirely* (No. 4), *extremely* (No. 6), *pretty* (No. 7), as well as the *rather* of No. 8 in Activity 1. This is the set of 'intensifiers', which ranges from the positively asserted (*completely, entirely, utterly*) to the tentative and deflating (*pretty, rather, fairly, quite*). These modifiers of adjectives are usually regarded as belonging to the class of adverbs, and they may equally modify adverbs (*incredibly slowly, quite simply*).

Activity 4

There are some modifiers which are tied almost exclusively to particular adjectives. For example, *sopping* is invariably followed by *wet*. Which adjectives would you associate with the following modifying adverbs?

critically, eminently, hideously, hysterically, mutually, radically, strategically, unbearably, vitally, woefully

Commentary

You may well have come up with the following: critically ill, eminently suitable, hideously expensive, hysterically funny, mutually exclusive, radically different, strategically placed, unbearably hot, vitally important, woefully inadequate. Some of these collocations are approaching the status of cliché, e.g. *vitally important, radically different*.

Activity 5

Preceding adverbs are not the only type of modifier in adjective phrases. Some adjectives may also be followed by a 'modifier', but it is only adjectives used predicatively that can be modified in this way. Examine the following sentences and say what kind of modifier follows the adjective in each case.

1   You have no need to be ashamed of your outburst.
2   This type of account is exempt from tax.
3   We're sorry that you have been inconvenienced.
4   Our children are keen to make your acquaintance.
5   This game is suitable for young children.
6   The value of your property is liable to fluctuate.
7   You are quite certain that she didn't telephone.
8   Bureaucrats are adept at fending off criticism.

Commentary

Let us first establish which are the adjectives: (1) ashamed (2) exempt (3) sorry (4) keen (5) suitable (6) liable (7) certain (8) adept.

Some of these adjectives are followed by a prepositional phrase: ashamed of . . . , exempt from . . . , suitable for . . . , adept at . . . In the last of these the preposition introduces an -*ing*-clause (*fending off criticism*), instead of a noun phrase, as is more usual in prepositional phrases (see A6). Other adjectives are followed by a clause, either a *that*-clause (sorry that . . . , certain that . . .) or a *to*-infinitive clause (keen to . . . , liable to . . .).

Such items are not universally possible even with adjectives used predicatively. For example, *exempt* may be followed by a prepositional phrase introduced by *from*, but not by any other kind of element, or indeed by any other preposition. On the other hand, *eager* may be followed by a *for* prepositional phrase or a *to*-inf clause; *certain* may be followed by an *of* prepositional phrase, or by a *that*-clause, or by a *to*-inf clause. Because the elements following an adjective are special to that adjective, in the same way that sentence elements are determined by the main verb, they are termed 'complements' rather than 'postmodifiers'. (A detailed account can be found in *Collins COBUILD Grammar Patterns 2: Nouns and Adjectives* 1998.)

A small number of adjectives that are used only predicatively take an obligatory complement. For example, *liable* (in the sense of 'likely', as in No. 6 above) has a *to*-inf clause as complement; *prone* (with a similar meaning) also takes a *to*-inf clause, as does *loath*. As a predicative adjective, *fond* is always followed by an *of* prepositional phrase.

Summary

An adjective phrase has the structure: (modifying adverb) adjective (complement). The brackets signify optional elements. In the case of the complement especially, it is also of restricted occurrence, found only after specific adjectives.

C6   TYPES OF CLAUSE

C6.1   Noun clauses

In Unit B6, we identified a number of types of subordinate clause. You may find it useful to reread the second part of that unit before beginning this one. In this and the other C6 subunits, we shall be looking in more detail at how subordinate clauses are used in the structure of complex sentences. In this subunit, we are considering specifically subordinate clauses that are used in positions where we would expect to find noun phrases, e.g. as Subject, as Object, or after a preposition. Such elements are termed 'noun clauses', or 'nominal clauses'.

Activity 1

The noun clauses in the following text (taken from the *Guardian*, 27.12.00, p.17) have been italicised. Sentence numbers have also been added, in square brackets, to ease reference.

Examine each of the marked noun clauses. Say what type it is (*that*-clause, *wh*-clause, *to*-inf clause), and what function (Object, or prepositional complement (i.e. following a preposition)) it has in the sentence of which it is a part.

[1] Victor Borge, who has died aged 91, was not the first comedian to have con-trived his act *from sending up or mutilating serious music*. [2] But he did it with more style than anyone else, in a way which had more widespread and long-lived appeal. [3] He continued *to play his piano*, or hilariously failed *to play his piano*, on tours of the United States, where he mainly lived, and Europe, from where he originated, well into his 80s.

[4] Borge always claimed *that his deadpan humour succeeded because it was simple and drawn straight from life*. [5] If so, its simplicity was that of genius, *of being able to impose a thread of distorted but impregnable logic on to almost any set of circumstances.*

[6] 'What,' one TV interviewer asked, 'are you doing next?' [7] 'I guess *I'll be going straight to the bathroom.*' [8] Another interviewer asked *why he had bought a farm in Portugal.* [9] '*Someone,*' he replied, '*had to buy a farm in Portugal.*' [10] Even the ageing process was turned into a dismissive aside: 'It is much better than the alternative.'

[11] Borge the comic, whose command of the piano was (on stage) liable to grotesque accident, so that a simple piano stool could narrowly escape being a disaster area, turned even his imperilled past as a Danish Jew into the humour of mock conceit: [12] 'Only Churchill and me knew *how dangerous Hitler was.* Churchill was trying *to save Europe*, and I was trying *to save myself.*'

[13] Born in Copenhagen, Borge was the son of a violinist with the Royal Danish Philharmonic. [14] His mother introduced him to the piano from the age of three, and he made his stage debut at the age of eight. [15] There was one great prob-lem which he had to face in his early career – the quality of the on-site pianos he had to play. [16] Some were dreadful, so he developed tricks *for playing them* not taught by conventional teachers. [17] Out of that situation came his humor-ous movements and asides, always in a distinctive, unctious, throwaway voice.

[18] By the outbreak of the Second World War, Borge was a reasonably successful pianist and musical satirist in Denmark, well known for his guying of Hitler and other Nazis. [19] When the Germans invaded Denmark, newspapers reported *that his name was at the head of those destined for extermination.* [20] Fortunately for Borge, two Russian diplomats who had been amused by his act smuggled him aboard an American ship bound for Finland, from where he caught the last boat out to the free part of Europe.

Commentary

This text illustrates the range of noun clauses, both finite and non-finite. Let us begin with the *that*-clauses in the text, which are as follows:

[4] *that his deadpan humour . . . from life* – Object of *claim*
[7] *I'll be going straight to the bathroom*, with omitted *that* – Object of *guess*
[9] *Someone had to buy a farm in Portugal* – direct speech, Object of *reply*
[19] *that his name was . . . for extermination* – Object of *report*

In all these examples the *that*-clause is Object of a verb of communication or mental process, expressing either direct or indirect speech or thought.

We shall follow with the other type of finite noun clause, the *wh*-clause, of which there are three examples in the text:

[6] *What are you doing next?* – direct speech, Object of *ask*
[8] *why he had bought a farm in Portugal* – Object of *ask*
[12] *how dangerous Hitler was* – Object of *know*

The first two examples illustrate direct and indirect *wh*-questions, respectively. In the third, the *wh*-word (*how*) is, in fact, a modifier of the adjective *dangerous*. This clause could be paraphrased by *the extent to which Hitler was dangerous*, which is now a noun phrase with a relative clause (*to which . . .*). For this reason, this type of *wh*-clause is sometimes termed a 'nominal relative' clause, to distinguish it from *wh*-clauses that are direct or indirect questions.

Turning now to the non-finite noun clauses, this text has four *to*-infinitive clauses:

[3] *to play his piano* – Object of *continue*
[3] *to play his piano* – Object of *fail*
[12] *to save Europe* – Object of *try*
[12] *to save myself* – Object of *try*

Here there are two pairs of parallel structures, one where the *to*-inf clause remains the same but the verb of the matrix sentence varies [3], and one where the *to*-inf clause varies with the same verb in the matrix sentence [12].

Finally there is the other type of non-finite noun clause, the *-ing*-clause:

[1] *from sending up or mutilating serious music* – prepositional complement
[5] *of being able to impose a thread . . .* – prepositional complement
[16] *for playing them* – prepositional complement

All the *-ing*-clauses in this text follow prepositions. In the example in [1], the *-ing*-clause follows the *from* of the prepositional verb '*contrive* something *from* something'. In the other two examples, the *-ing*-clause follows the preposition in a postmodifer of a pronoun (*that*) or noun (*tricks*).

It is interesting that, in this text, all the *that*-clauses, *wh*-clauses and *to*-inf clauses function as Objects in the matrix sentence. This is the most common position for noun clauses, though their occurrence elsewhere is not precluded. We can illustrate this point with the *that*-clause.

Activity 2

What function does the *that*-clause have in the following sentences?

1   The problem is that he didn't know any English.
2   That he didn't know any English was of no consequence.
3   You haven't considered my proposal that everyone should be taught English.
4   It seems that he didn't know any English.
5   We suggest that everyone should be taught English.

Commentary

In No. 1 the *that*-clause (*that he didn't know any English*) functions as the Complement in the (SVC) sentence. No. 2 also has *be* as the main verb in an SVC structure, but here the *that*-clause functions as Subject. In No. 3, the *that*-clause (*that everyone should be taught English*) functions as part of the Object of *consider*, but it is 'in apposition' to *proposal* (compare the apposition of two noun phrases, e.g. *James Murray, the lexicographer*). It is termed an 'appositive' *that*-clause. Appositive *that*-clauses typically accompany nouns derived from verbs (deverbal nouns), as *proposal* from *propose* (for a fuller discussion, see *Collins COBUILD Grammar Patterns 2*, 1998). In No. 4, *that he didn't know any English* is the Subject of *seem*; it has been 'extra-posed' (see C4.3), which is obligatory for *that*-clause Subjects with *seem* and optional, though normal, in other cases – e.g. No. 3 might more naturally be expressed as *It was of no consequence that he didn't know any English*. Lastly, No. 5 illustrates the *that*-clause in its common Object position, here of the main verb *suggest*.

Similarly, *-ing*-clauses may function in a variety of positions, not just after prepositions as in our text examples. The following sentence, for example, occurs a little later in the same text:

Being asked to read lines for the warm-up of a radio show led to him being invited to do the same sort of job on air for the Bing Crosby Kraft Music Hall.

Here, two *-ing*-clauses fall either side of the main verb *led (to)*, as Subject and Object. The verb phrases in both *-ing*-clauses are in the passive voice (see B1), with the passive auxiliary as the present participle (*being*). Notice that the Object *-ing*-clause contains its own Subject (*him*).

Summary

Noun clauses are subordinate clauses that function in positions where noun phrases are typically found: Subject, Object, Complement. Additionally, *that*-clauses may function in apposition to a (deverbal) noun, and *-ing*-clauses may function as complements of prepositions.

Adjective clauses

In C5.1, in the discussion of the modification of nouns, we had a brief look at clause postmodifiers – relative clauses and non-finite clauses. You may like to reread the last section of that subunit, to remind yourself of the discussion. In this subunit, we take a further look at these clauses, under the heading of 'adjective clauses', because they fulfil the same kind of function as adjectives in the modification of nouns.

Activity 1

We begin with the same text as in C6.1, except that it is the adjective clauses that are now italicised.

List the adjective clauses. Say what type each is (relative clause, *-ing*-clause, *-ed*-clause), and comment on the internal structure of the clause (e.g. what function does the relative pronoun have – Subject, Object, etc.?).

[1] Victor Borge, *who has died aged 91*, was not the first comedian to have contrived his act from sending up or mutilating serious music. [2] But he did it with more style than anyone else, in a way *which had more widespread and long-lived appeal*. [3] He continued to play his piano, or hilariously failed to play his piano, on tours of the United States, *where he mainly lived*, and Europe, *from where he originated*, well into his 80s.

[4] Borge always claimed that his deadpan humour succeeded because it was simple and drawn straight from life. [5] If so, its simplicity was that of genius, of being able to impose a thread of distorted but impregnable logic on to almost any set of circumstances.

[6] 'What,' one TV interviewer asked, 'are you doing next?' [7] 'I guess I'll be going straight to the bathroom.' [8] Another interviewer asked why he had bought a farm in Portugal. [9] 'Someone,' he replied, 'had to buy a farm in Portugal.' [10] Even the ageing process was turned into a dismissive aside: 'It is much better than the alternative.'

[11] Borge the comic, *whose command of the piano was (on stage) liable to grotesque accident, so that a simple piano stool could narrowly escape being a disaster area*, turned even his imperilled past as a Danish Jew into the humour of mock conceit: 'Only Churchill and me knew how dangerous Hitler was. Churchill was trying to save Europe, and I was trying to save myself.'

[12] Born in Copenhagen, Borge was the son of a violinist with the Royal Danish Philharmonic. [13] His mother introduced him to the piano from the age of three, and he made his stage debut at the age of eight. [14] There was one great problem *which he had to face in his early career* – the quality of the on-site pianos *he had to play*. [15] Some were dreadful, so he developed tricks for playing them *not taught by conventional teachers*. [16] Out of that situation came his humorous movements and asides, always in a distinctive, unctious, throwaway voice.

[17] By the outbreak of the Second World War, Borge was a reasonably successful pianist and musical satirist in Denmark, well known for his guying of Hitler and other Nazis. [18] When the Germans invaded Denmark, newspapers reported that his name was at the head of those destined for extermination. [19] Fortunately for Borge, two Russian diplomats *who had been amused by his act* smuggled him aboard an American ship *bound for Finland, from where he caught the last boat out to the free part of Europe*.

Commentary

Let us begin with the relative clauses, which are in the majority in the text. Here, first of all, is a list, by sentence number:

[1] who has died aged 91
[2] which had more widespread and long-lived appeal

[3a] where he mainly lived
[3b] from where he originated
[11] whose command of the piano was . . . a disaster area
[14a] which he had to face in his early career
[14b] (that) he had to play
[19a] who had been amused by his act
[19b] from where he caught the last boat out to the free part of Europe.

In order to be a little more systematic, we will consider their internal structure not by the order in which they occur in the text, but by groups. We take, first, those with a relative pronoun in the *who* set (*who, whom , whose*), which refer back to a person: [1], [11] and [19a]. There is no example with *whom*, which occurs only rarely. Because this set makes a distinction between subject (*who*), object (*whom*) and possessive/genitive (*whose*) – see C2.1 – the relative pronoun itself should indicate its function in the clause. The problem with this assumption is that *who*, especially in speech and informal writing, is often used in both Subject and Object positions. In our two examples with *who*, however, the relative pronoun is the Subject of the clause; though note that in [19a] it is Subject of a passive Verb. The relative pronoun *whose*, as in [11], makes the antecedent noun (in this case *Borge*) a 'possessor' in a noun phrase within the relative clause, in this case of *command*, the head of the noun phrase functioning as Subject.

We take, second, the clauses with *which* as the relative pronoun: [2] and [14a]. This relative pronoun refers back to a non-personal noun, and it does not have different forms that might indicate its function in the clause. In fact, the two examples in this text show *which* used both as Subject [2] and as Object [14a], where *which* stands for *problem* and is Object of *face*. The 'possessive' form of this relative pronoun is *of which*, e.g. 'the piano, of which the keys often stuck' or 'the piano, the keys of which often stuck'. However, *of which* often sounds over-formal, even stilted; and so, with many non-personal nouns, *whose* is used instead ('the piano, whose keys often stuck') or some other construction that avoids the awkwardness of *of which*.

Before we look at the clauses with *where* as relative pronoun, let us take, third, the relative clause without a relative pronoun at [14b]. I have suggested *that* as the possible missing relative pronoun. This relative pronoun could also have substituted for *which* in [2] and [14a], and possibly for *who* in [19a]. You might also note that the relative pronoun could have been omitted from [14a]. There are two unrelated points here. First, a relative pronoun may be omitted if it functions as Object in the relative clause, as in [14a] and [14b]; but not if it functions as Subject, as in [2] or [19]. Second, *that* may be used as a relative pronoun only if the relative clause is 'defining' or 'restrictive' (see C5.1). The *who* set or *which* may be used for either 'defining' or 'non-defining' relative clauses, though it is a disputed point of usage whether they – especially *which* – should be restricted to non-defining contexts.

Fourth, we come to the clauses with *where* as the relative pronoun: [3a], [3b] and [19b]. You will have noticed that in each case the antecedent noun is the name of a place: *the United States, Europe* and *Finland*, respectively. This suggests, appropriately, that it is such nouns that require *where* as a relative pronoun in an associated relative clause. Similarly, nouns denoting points and periods of time may be represented by *when*, and *reason* may have *why* as its associated relative pronoun; e.g. 'the week when this happened', 'on Sunday, when Aunty Gladys came', 'the reason why we stopped visiting them'.

The other form of adjectival clause is the non-finite clause, either with present participle or with past participle. Non-finite clauses are, as this text indicates, not as common as relative clauses. There are two examples, both with past participle:

[15] not taught by conventional teachers
[19] bound for Finland

We suggested in C5.1 that non-finite clauses can be regarded as reduced forms of relative clauses; those with a present participle can be related to active clauses, and those with a past participle to passive clauses. [15], for example, could be expanded to: 'which were not taught by conventional teachers'; and [19] to: 'which was bound for Finland', though whether this is a true passive, or just a fossilised phrase (*be bound for*), is arguable. What is omitted from the relative clause, in the case of past participle clauses, is the relative pronoun and the passive auxiliary, and the relative pronoun would be the Subject of the clause.

It is also the case that present participle clauses are reductions of relative clauses in which the relative pronoun is the Subject. For example, the relative clause in [2] could be reduced to: 'having more widespread and long-lived appeal'; but that in [14], where *which* is Object, could not.

Summary
Adjective clauses may be finite (relative clauses) or non-finite (present or past participle clauses). They follow the noun that they modify. Relative clauses show a certain amount of internal variation, depending on the function of the relative pronoun, both in relation to its antecedent and to the structure of the relative clause.

C6.3

Adverbial clauses
In Subunit C4.2, we outlined the range of meanings and forms that elements may have when they express the circumstantial meanings associated with the adverbial slot in sentence structure (see A4). You will find it useful to reread C4.2, before you embark on this one. In this subunit, in the context of our discussion of clauses, we are focusing on one particular type of element: adverbial clauses.

Activity 1
We begin our look at adverbial clauses with a text (taken from the *Guardian*, 1.1.01, p.16). The sentences have been numbered, and the start of each adverbial clause has been marked by an italicised item, usually the subordinating conjunction. List the adverbial clauses, and say what meaning (time, place, reason, etc.) each of them has in the context of the sentence in which it is located.

[1] Aircraft maker Airbus has found itself in the middle of a row over the inaugu-
ration of the world's largest jumbo jet.

[2] Airline Emirates, the first customer to order the renamed A380, formerly
known as the A3XX, has protested to Airbus *after* it found it may not be the first
airline to fly the aircraft commercially.

[3] Industry sources said last night that Singapore Airlines will be the first,
even though it ordered the A380 after Emirates. [4] Singapore is a much larger
airline and has been given priority by Airbus over its Middle East rival.

[5] The row has not yet become public *because* Emirates hopes that the issue
will be resolved by negotiation. [6] But senior executives from the airline based
in Dubai feel let down by Airbus.

[7] Emirates' senior managers have told Airbus that they deserve better treatment *because* the company was prepared to commit itself to the project *when*
Airbus was concerned that it would not get the support it wanted and that the
project might collapse.

[8] Jubilant Emirates executives said that the first A380 would land at
Heathrow but were shocked *when* they heard that the prestigious first flight would
be offered to Singapore.

[9] Airbus executives are working on a compromise acceptable to Emirates,
which has placed 10 firm orders for the aircraft, valued at £2bn. [10] The most
likely solution is a simultaneous launch of the plane by Emirates and Singapore,
both *landing* at Heathrow. [11] *Since* the distance between Dubai and London is
shorter than that between Singapore and London, the Emirates flight would land
first, *so that* the airline would be able to claim it as the inaugural commercial flight.

Commentary

Here, first of all, is a list of the adverbial clauses, together with a general indication of
their meanings:

[2] after it found it may not be . . . aircraft commercially – Time
[3] even though it ordered the A380 after Emirates – Concession
[5] because Emirates hopes that the issue will be resolved by negotiation – Reason
[7a] because the company was prepared . . . project might collapse – Reason
[7b] when Airbus was concerned . . . project might collapse – Time
[8] when they heard that . . . to Singapore – Time
[10] both landing at Heathrow – Time
[11a] Since the distance between . . . Singapore and London – Reason
[11b] so that the airline would be able . . . commercial flight – Result

Let us now review the examples by meaning category. The text contains no examples
of Place or Direction adverbial clauses; the only possibility would be a clause introduced by *where*, and these are relatively uncommon. By contrast, the category of

Time is frequently expressed by an adverbial clause, and there are four examples in this text. Two ([7] and [8]) are introduced by *when*, indicating a point in time at which something happened. In [2] the adverbial clause is introduced by *after*, to set one action/event in a time sequence relation to another: the event of the adverbial clause introduced by *after* precedes that of the matrix clause. This contrasts with adverbial clauses introduced by *before*, where the action/event of the adverbial clause follows that of the matrix clause.

The fourth Time Adverbial is the present participle clause in [10]. Often, as here, an *-ing*-clause indicates a successive action/event; it could be substituted by *and* with a finite clause, e.g. '. . . a simultaneous launch . . . and both of them land at Heathrow'. Present participle clauses may also have the force of a finite adverbial clause introduced by *while*, e.g. 'Waiting for the call to the departure lounge, they noticed some friends by the gift shop' – alternatively 'While waiting . . .' or 'While they were waiting . . .'. Here the action/event of the adverbial clause is interrupted by that of the matrix clause.

The text contains three examples of Reason Adverbials, which are commonly expressed by adverbial clauses. Two of the examples ([5] and [7a]) are introduced by *because*, and the third [11a] by *since*. What is significant and interesting here is that the *because*-clauses follow their matrix clauses, while the *since*-clause precedes its matrix. The *because*-clauses add supporting reasons to the assertions made in the matrix clause; but in [11a] it is important to express the reason first, as the underpinning fact to support the matrix clause. Although an initial *because*-clause is not impossible, a reason adverbial clause preceding the matrix clause is more likely to be introduced by *since*.

There is one example of a Concession Adverbial, in sentence [3]. It is introduced by *even though*, where the addition of *even* adds emphasis to the strength of the concession. A simple *though* or *although* was, presumably, considered not to be sufficient for making the contrast forcefully enough. Concession clauses may precede or follow their matrix clause: you may like to consider the effect in this case of reversing the order of the clauses.

Finally, there is one example of a Result Adverbial, in sentence [11b], introduced by the compound conjunction *so that*. This conjunction is also used to introduce adverbial clauses of Purpose. The meanings of 'purpose' and 'result' are, arguably, closely related. A slight change to the text example can produce a 'purpose' meaning: 'The Emirates flight will land first, so that the airline can claim it as the inaugural commercial flight.' When *so that* has a 'purpose' meaning, it can be paraphrased by *in order that*; when it has a 'result' meaning, the paraphrase is *with the result that*.

You will have noticed that there are no examples of Manner adverbial clauses in this text. They do not occur frequently and are usually introduced by *as if* or *as though*, e.g. 'He swaggered in as if he owned the place.' The other major omission from this text is an example of a Conditional adverbial clause, introduced by *if* or its negative *unless*, e.g. 'If the Emirates flight lands first, the airline can claim it as the inaugural commercial flight', 'Unless the Emirates flight lands first, the airline cannot claim it as the inaugural commercial flight.'

Activity 2

You will have noticed that, apart from [11a], all the adverbial clauses follow their matrix clause. As we have noted before (A4), Adverbials have more flexibility in their positioning in sentence structure than do other slots. Go back to the examples in the text and determine whether it would be possible in each case to reverse the order of the adverbial clause and its matrix and what effect this might have on the overall meaning or effect of the sentences concerned. It may be necessary to swap the positions of noun phrases and their related pronouns in order to make best sense, e.g. in [2] to put *Airline Emirates . . .* in the initial *after*-clause and pronoun *it* in the following matrix clause.

Commentary

As implied above, the reversal is possible in [2], with the effect that the two actions/events are now expressed in chronological order. The concession clause has come first in [3], without necessarily swapping noun phrase (*Singapore Airlines*) and pronoun (*it*); the effect is to lay yet more emphasis on the contrast. The *because*-clause in [5] could possibly come initially, though it would be better with *since* (see above); the effect would be to alter the relation of reason and assertion, as discussed earlier. In [7a] the reversal is hardly possible without some extensive rewriting, partly because the *because*-clause is so long, containing, as it does, the *when*-clause, and partly because the reason needs to follow the assertion here for it to make sense. Similarly, the reversal of *when*-clause and matrix in [7b] is not possible, since it would produce the confusing introduction *because when . . .* In [8] however, the reversal could take place, with the insertion of *they* in the final matrix clause: '. . . but when they heard that . . . Singapore, they were shocked'. The effect is to delay and focus on the verb *shocked*. In [10], the succession in time is indicated by the order of the clauses, so no reversal is possible here. Similarly, in [11], reversal is not possible, because the matrix clause is sandwiched between a Reason Adverbial and a Result Adverbial, creating a nicely balanced sentence. The Result has to come last, for it to be interpreted unambiguously as 'result' rather than 'purpose', and the Reason therefore appropriately opens the sentence.

Summary

Adverbial clauses are a common means of expressing circumstantial meanings associated with time, reason, purpose/result, condition and concession. They may precede or follow the matrix clause, though following is the more usual position.

GRAMMATICAL RULES IN CONTEXT

C7

Spoken grammar

C7.1

Speech comes first, and writing second. That has been an axiom in linguistics since the beginning of the twentieth century. We all acquire speech before we learn to write; indeed, speech comes naturally – we are not conscious of 'learning' it – whereas we have to be taught to write. Even if we are fluent in both modes, we speak far more than we write. All languages have a spoken form, but many do not have a system of writing.

Despite the axiom, linguists have based their descriptions of language largely on the written form of the language, if for no other reason, because the data is more readily available and easier to collect. In more recent years, however, with the increased ease in the collection of spoken data and the possibility of storing large amounts of data in electronic form, linguists have paid more attention to the grammar of spoken language and how it differs from that of the written (e.g. Biber *et al.* 1999).

Activity 1

Examine the following transcript of an extract from a casual conversation (taken from Cheepen and Monaghan 1990: 116f). Intonation and other prosodic features are not marked, so you need to work out how you think it was spoken. There are two participants, K and C. I have numbered the turns, to aid reference.

First of all, rework the extract to make it look like a piece of writing, with complete sentences. Put brackets round the items you want to leave out, and underline or italicise any words that you want to add or alter.

---

[1] K: so what did I do this morning then start painting the skirting board white and when I opened the tin it weren't white was it was yellow says brilliant white on the [pr]

[2] C: you're kidding what the wrong colour

[3] K: the wrong colour inside the tin I don't ever remember that happening

[4] C: never known that before

[5] K: no oh sorry darling yeh

[6] C: crazy

[7] K: I couldn't help but laugh I mean you know me decorate

[8] C: well you think it's your eyes don't you

[9] K: you know me decorate it's taken me twelve years to actually admit that I will do some and the first thing I go to do

[10] C: it's silly

[11] C: and it really said brilliant white on the outside

[12] K: yeh – Carole said to me look Mum it's the wrong colour in that tin cause there was a little drip on the outside and I said oh no what's happened they've put the other ones on top cause it didn't look as though it dripped from from the in it wasn't in the rim it was just on the outside you know

[13] C: that's ridiculous

[14] K: yeh so I just said to (inaudible)

[15] C: must have been a whole batch

[16] K: I said I bought this yesterday and (inaudible) it ain't (laugh) oh oh said I'm terri I said it's not your fault he said I'm afraid we go by what's on the tin I said well of course you go by what's on the tin

[17] C: nobody expects them to open each one

Commentary

Here is a possible rewriting of the conversation, with excluded words bracketed and added or altered items in italics.

[1] (so) What did I do this morning (then)? *I* start*ed* painting the skirting board white, and when I opened the tin, it *wasn't* white (was it). It was yellow. *It* says 'brilliant white' on the *tin.*

[2] You're kidding! (what) *Was it* the wrong colour?

[3] *It was* the wrong colour inside the tin. I don't ever remember that happening.

[4] *I've* never (ever) known that before.

[5] (no oh sorry darling yeh)

[6] *That's* crazy.

[7] I couldn't help but laugh. (I mean) (you know) *For* me *to* decorate *is something.*

[8] (well) You think it's your eyes (don't you)?

[9] (you know) (me decorate) It's taken me twelve years to actually admit that I will do some *decorating,* and the first thing I go to do *turns out like this.*

[10] It's silly.

[11] (and) It really said 'brilliant white' on the outside?

[12] *Yes, it did.* Carole said to me: 'Look, Mum, it's the wrong colour in that tin', *because* there was a little drip on the outside. (and) I said: 'Oh no, what's happened *is that* they've put other ones on top', *because* it didn't look as though it *had* dripped from (from) the in*side.* It wasn't *on* the rim, it was just on the outside (you know).

[13] That's ridiculous.

[14] (yeh so) I just said to . . .

[15] *It* must have been a whole batch.

[16] I said: 'I bought this yesterday and it *isn't the right colour.'* 'Oh, (oh)' *he* said, 'I'm terri*bly* sorry.' I said: 'It's not your fault.' He said: 'I'm afraid we go by what's on the tin.' I said: '(well) Of course you go by what's on the tin.'

[17] Nobody expects them to open each one.

Activity 2

Go back over the original transcript and the rewrite and determine what kinds of item we have added. What is their syntactic function?

Commentary

We have needed to add a number of Subjects in order to complete sentence structures, e.g. *I* [1], *it* [1], *it* [15], *he* [16]. In some cases, we have also needed to add an auxiliary verb, or the verb *be*, e.g. *was it* [2], *it was* [3], *I've* [4], *that's* [6]. You will also have noted that in [1], the addition of the Subject (*I*) also necessitates adding an appropriate suffix to the verb (*started*). Omission of the Subject is quite common in ordinary speech, as this extract demonstrates.

Sometimes the speaker leaves a 'sentence' uncompleted, either because what they would have said is obvious from the context and flow of the conversation, or because the next speaker has already butted in with their turn. This happens at the end of [1], where I have added *tin*; another possibility would be *label*, though the speaker seemed to be beginning a word with 'pr'. At the end of [9], the sentence contains only a Subject (*the first thing I go to do*), and we have to supply the rest. In [12] we have to supply *side* to complete *the inside*, and in [16] the shop assistant is quoted as giving what looks like an apology, but only *I'm terri* gets spoken; we need to supply, presumably, *bly sorry*.

Occasionally, the situation is more complex still, as in the *me decorate* example in [7] and [9], where we read into this abbreviated phrase, uttered no doubt with the appropriate intonation, an expression of self-deprecating exclamation. In my rewrite, I expanded the first one by making it into a Subject infinitive clause, with its own Subject (*for me*), and adding a Verb and Complement (*is something*). The second, in [9], seemed to me to be unnecessary repetition.

We have also used italics for corrections, either because the written mode does not usually display the level of informality possible in speech (*wasn't* for *weren't* in [1], *because* for *cause* in [12], *isn't* for *ain't* in [16]) or because a speaker is deemed to have chosen an inappropriate word (*on* for *in* in [12]).

✪ Activity 3

Now let us look at the items that we have bracketed for omission. Examine the transcript and the rewrite again and attempt to classify the items that would be omitted from the written mode.

Commentary

First, there are what are called 'discourse markers', which serve either to introduce a turn or to provide continuity. Introductory items include the *so* in [1] and [14], *well* in [8] and [16]. Continuity is provided by *then* in [1], *and* in [11] and [12]. Second, there are the pause fillers or hedges, such as *you know* [7], [9], [12] or *I mean* [7]. Third, there are the tags, where a speaker appears to ask for confirmation from the other speaker, e.g. *was it* [1], *don't you* [8]. Also bracketed in the rewrite are: *ever* [4], as a case of conversational emphasis; *from* [12], which is repetition; *oh* [16], again repetition. The whole of [5] has been bracketed, because it looks as if it is an aside, addressed to someone else (a child, perhaps) in the situation, and therefore is not part of the text as such.

Summary

A grammar of speech has to take account of the fact that there may be incomplete sentence structures, as well as additions of discourse markers, filled pauses, tags, and the like. The context of the ongoing interchange, and the participation of the speakers in the developing conversation mitigates any danger of miscommunication. For further discussion of the grammar of spoken English, see Carter and McCarthy (1997), Biber *et al.* (1999: Chapter 14).

C7.2 Creative grammar

In this subunit, we shall consider how the grammar of English is exploited, adapted and sometimes extended by poets and advertisers. They do not so much 'break the rules', in the sense of Unit B7, but rather 'stretch' them to fit their particular purposes.

Activity 1

We begin with a poem by John Betjeman, entitled *Good-bye*. Identify the sentences in this poem, and say what the Subject and Verb is of each of them.

Some days before death	1
When food's tasting sour on my tongue,	
Cigarettes long abandoned,	
Disgusting now even champagne;	
When I'm sweating a lot	5
From the strain on a last bit of lung	
And lust has gone out	
Leaving only the things of the brain;	
More worthless than ever	
Will seem all the songs I have sung,	10
More harmless the prods of the prigs,	
Remoter the pain,	
More futile the Lord Civil Servant	
As, rung upon rung,	
He ascends by committees to roofs	15
Far below on the plain.	
But better down there in the battle	
Than here on the hill	
With Judgement or nothingness waiting me,	
Lonely and chill.	20

Commentary

There are only two full stops in this poem, one at the end of line 16, and the other at the end of the poem, suggesting that the poem contains only two sentences (lines 1 to 16, and lines 17 to 20).

The Verb in the first sentence is *will seem* in line 10. Its Subject is *all the songs I have sung*, and it is in an SVC pattern (A5). The poet has reversed the usual order, and the Complement (*more worthless than ever* – line 9) precedes the Verb. The pattern is then replicated three more times, except that the V is omitted:

Complement	*Subject*
more harmless	the prods of the prigs
remoter	the pain
more futile	the Lord Civil Servant as . . .

Lines 1 to 8 are a series of 'time' Adverbials (C4.2), beginning with a noun phrase (*some days before death*), and continuing with a number of adverbial clauses, introduced by *when*, though some of them have been contracted:

> *when food's tasting sour on my tongue*
> *cigarettes (have) long (been) abandoned*
> *even champagne (is) now disgusting*
> *when I'm sweating a lot from the strain on the last bit of lung*
> *and lust has gone out leaving only the things of the brain*

Notice how the structure changes between lines 2 to 4, where each line is a different *when*-clause, and 5 to 8, where each *when*-clause takes up two lines. This first sentence ends with a 'manner' adverbial attached to the last of the C(V)S structures, introduced by *as*.

The second, and much shorter, sentence of the poem (lines 17 to 20) in fact contains no Verb element. If we were to supply one, line 17 might read: 'But *it would be* better *to be* down there in the battle . . .' The poet has omitted elements that are not infrequently left out in speech (see C7.1). Finally, note that the poet has omitted the expected *for* after *waiting* in line 19 (normally either *awaiting me* or *waiting for me*), and how the adjectives of the final line (*lonely and chill*) are placed after the item they are modifying, i.e. *me*.

Activity 2

Consider now the text of the following advertisement, for *The Ramblers* organisation. What types of element occur in the written sentences (between a capital letter and a full stop) in this text?

Breathing Space.
(Don't take it for granted)
We don't. Help us keep Britain's breathing
spaces open. Footpaths and coastline, high places,
heaths and woodlands. For walkers.
For over 60 years, THE RAMBLERS' lobbying
and vigilance have been achieving wide-ranging
rights of access to some of our most beautiful
countryside. Go for a walk. Take a breather from
our crowded world. Think about the future; invest
in THE RAMBLERS.

Commentary

Breathing Space, with a larger typeface and, curiously, with a concluding full stop, is the headline; it is a simple noun phrase (C5.1), with pre-modifying participle as adjective (*breathing*) followed by the head noun. The bracketed instruction underneath is a negated imperative sentence (B1, C1.3), curiously without a concluding full-stop or exclamation mark, consisting of an idiomatic expression ('take something for granted') which has a number of manifestations, this being one of them.

The main body of text (in the actual advert, beneath a line drawing of two walkers on a hill) begins with a bold-face statement, involving ellipsis: *We don't*, i.e. 'take it for granted'. This is followed by a further imperative sentence: *Help us* ... The next two written units are not sentences in structure. The first is a series of nouns, one with a pre-modifying adjective (*high places*), and two pairs of them joined by *and*: they are examples of the 'breathing spaces' of the preceding sentence. The second is a prepositional phrase (*for walkers*), representing the beneficiaries of the imperative *help us*, and thus belonging to that sentence.

The second paragraph begins with a long (23-word) sentence, celebrating the successes of the organisation. It is a single clause, with the following elements: Adverbial of time, Subject, Verb (*have been achieving*), Object. The preceding and following sections of text each contain 19 words. The text is nicely balanced, with this self-congratulation taking centre-stage.

The text concludes with four imperative structures: *Go* ... *Take* ... *Think* ... *invest* ... The first three follow a full stop, but, curiously, the last one follows a semi-colon.

Advertisements often contain short and snappy units, and this is sometimes obtained by using phrase-type structures as if they were sentences. Imperatives are also typical of advertisements, and this one contains six in all.

Activity 3

We turn to another piece of poetry, the first three stanzas of a nine-stanza poem by E. E. Cummings. What is the poet doing to the grammar in order to achieve some of his effects in this poem?

anyone lived in a pretty how town	1
(with up so floating many bells down)	
spring summer autumn winter	
he sang his didn't he danced his did.	
Women and men (both little and small)	5
cared for anyone not at all	
they sowed their isn't they reaped their same	
sun moon stars rain	
children guessed (but only a few	9
and down they forgot as up they grew	
autumn winter spring summer)	
that noone loved him more by more	

Commentary

The poet is using indefinite pronouns (*anyone*, *noone*) as if they were proper names (B2). Interestingly, *noone* is a spelling that is usually regarded as incorrect; it is normally *no one* or *no-one*. Cummings' spelling reinforces its proper noun status. A number of the other effects arise from the reclassification of words: *how* in line one is used as an adjective, instead of an interrogative adverb; *didn't* and *did* in line 4 are used as nouns, instead of (auxiliary) verbs; the same is true of *isn't* in line 7, but its counterpart – (*their*) *same* – is an adjective, which works as a (pro)noun in the expression *the same*, but not here.

The passing of time is indicated either by listing the names for the seasons (lines 3 and 11) or by the list of celestial bodies plus *rain* in line 8. Line 5 has a strange collocation of synonyms (*both little and small*), where we would normally expect antonyms (*little and large, big and small*). Cummings creates a new phrasal verb in line 10 (*forget down*) in order to achieve the *down/up* symmetry. And in line 12, he replaces *and* with *by* in the expression *more by more*, presumably on the analogy of *little by little*.

We have overlooked line 2, which appears to be a rearrangement of the syntax (*with so many bells floating up and down*) in order to reproduce in the line the sound and movement of the bells.

Cummings stretches the grammar much further than Betjeman does in the poem with which we began, and as readers of it, we have to work much harder to make sense of it. In the end, though, the effects are more surprising.

C7.3   ## Humour and ambiguity

We delight in playing with language, exploiting the double meanings of words, punning, turning an expression into a joke. Much of the best comedy is of a verbal nature, from the games and jokes of the playground to the wit of playwrights.

Activity 1

Let us begin with Shakespeare! By what grammatical means does he create humour in the following exchange from *Twelfth Night*, Act 3, Scene 1? (Note: a 'tabor' is a small drum.)

Viola	Save thee, friend, and thy music! Dost thou live by thy tabor?
Clown	No, sir, I live by the church.
Viola	Art thou a churchman?
Clown	No such matter, sir: I do live by the church; for I do live at my house, and my house doth stand by the church.
Viola	So thou mayst say the king lies by a beggar, if a beggar dwell near him; or the church stands by thy tabor, if thy tabor stand by the church.
Clown	You have said, sir. To see this age! A sentence is but a chev'ril glove to a good wit. How quickly the wrong side may be turned outward!

Commentary

Later in the same scene, the Clown calls himself the Lady Olivia's 'corrupter of words'. In this extract, the expression *live by* is ambiguous, and the humour arises from the exploitation of this ambiguity. Grammatically, *live by* can be a phrasal verb, when it has the meaning 'earn one's living by means of'. Alternatively *live by* is simply a verb + preposition, with the preposition expecting some appropriate noun phrase to complete the expression ('live by the crossroads').

Viola then extends this ambiguity to the expression *stand by*: as a phrasal verb it means 'support' or 'be loyal to'; alternatively, it has the literal meaning, as verb + preposition, of 'be situated next to'. The Clown's final contribution is a telling analogy (of the glove turned inside out) of verbal wit.

Activity 2

Now go back to the titles of Units A7 and B7. Both those expressions – *grammar rules* and *breaking rules* – are ambiguous. What makes them ambiguous and how can you resolve the ambiguity?

Commentary

For both titles there is a choice of syntactic interpretations, between a phrase and a sentence. The primary interpretation of *grammar rules*, and the way in which you were supposed to take it when you studied that unit, is as a noun phrase, with *grammar* as a modifier of *rules*. Indeed, an adjective (*grammatical*) could have been used instead of the noun modifier (*grammar*), but there would then have been no ambiguity. The sentence interpretation makes *grammar* a Subject and *rules* a Verb; you might want to add *OK*, and make it into a grammarian's slogan.

In the case of *breaking rules*, you were expected to interpret this as a sentence fragment, so that *breaking* is a Verb and *rules* is an Object. But it could also have a noun phrase interpretation, with *breaking* as a participle modifier of the noun *rules*, by analogy with the expression 'breaking news', i.e. news that is just coming in. So, 'breaking rules' would be rules that are just being formulated or coming into acceptance.

Activity 3

Language play occurs in many contexts. On a daily basis newspapers often play with language in their headlines. Examine the following headlines taken from the *Guardian* and *The Times of India (Online)* newspapers. How are they playing with language?

---

1 Tellers count their blessings (The article was about the interruption to the counting of disputed votes in the American presidential election of 2000 caused by the Thanksgiving holiday.)

2 Tube derails capital's new year festivities

3 Greens fuel the debate

4 England lose Cork but not bottle (Dominic Cork was a member of the England cricket team.)

5   Tattooists' own goal leaves Beckham a marked man (David Beckham was a footballer.)
6   Bihar's village of women, weapons and woe
7   Officials send school's unisex toilets down the pan
8   Lastminute say patience will pay dividends (Lastminute was a 'dotcom' company.)
9   Net tightens around the hacktivists
10 Vajpayee minds his language at Sanskrit conference (Mr Vajpayee was Prime Minister of India.)
11 BJP tries to do a Tehelka on Cong in Karnataka.

Commentary

Many headlines exploit the fact that a large number of words have both a literal and a figurative meaning, or they make an allusion to an idiomatic expression or perhaps some cultural phenomenon, or they simply pun. Let us take these headlines one by one.

1   Tellers count votes at elections. *Count one's blessings* is an idiomatic expression, meaning 'be thankful for what you have', with religious overtones. Thanksgiving celebrates the first harvest reaped by the Pilgrim Fathers after they landed in America in 1621.
2   The 'Tube' is the underground rail network in London (the 'capital'). The verb *derail* has the literal meaning of '(cause to) leave the rails', but it has the figurative meaning of 'prevent or stop something from happening'. In this case, the early cessation of underground services on 31 December 2000 prevented new year celebrations taking place in London.
3   The 'greens' are environmental campaigners who lobby among other things for less pollution by motor vehicles. Motor vehicles run on (petrol or diesel) 'fuel'. *Fuel* has become a verb, with a figurative meaning of 'add to'.
4   Clearly, there is a 'bottle' and 'cork' metaphor at play here. But *lose bottle* is also an idiomatic expression meaning 'lose courage'.
5   There are tattooing and football allusions in this headline, but the expressions *own goal* and *marked man* have figurative meanings as well. An 'own goal' is when you do something to your disadvantage (in this case the tattoo on David Beckham wasn't quite accurate). A 'marked man' (Beckham was literally that) is someone who is under suspicion.
6   The alliteration of 'w' makes this a grabbing headline, over an article about young men having to leave their village to find work 'while the Kosi wastelands back home are stalked by Kalashnikhov-toting "strangers", who lord it over their wives'.
7   Toilets have 'pans', but the expression 'send down the pan' means 'reject'.
8   A number of allusions operate here. 'Lastminute' and 'patience' are in a kind of antonymy relation. 'Patience' is a card game, which if used for gambling could give a profit. 'Pay dividends' has both a literal meaning (in share ownership) and a figurative meaning ('bring advantage').

9   There is a new word here: *hacktivists*, formed by a blending of *hacker* and *activist*. They operate on the Internet, for which *net* is an abbreviation. But the expression *the net tightens* means that they are getting close to being caught.

10 This headline introduces an article about Prime Minister Vajpayee's use of Hindi at a conference on the Sanskrit language, when other speakers, according to expectation, were speaking fluently in India's ancient language. *Mind one's language* has the figurative meaning of being careful not to use inappropriate (usually coarse or vulgar) language.

11 You need to know Indian politics to understand this one! 'BJP' is a political party, recently the subject of a scandal (the Tehelka exposé). 'Cong' is an abbreviation for 'Congress', another political party. 'Karnataka' is one of India's states, in the south of the country.

Activity 4

Here now is the first stanza of a well-known 'nonsense' poem by Lewis Carroll (Charles Dodgson) – *Jabberwocky*. Many of the words are 'nonsense' words. But the poem makes some sense because the syntax is regular, so you can identify which word class each word belongs to – which is what you are asked to do.

> 'Twas brillig, and the slithy toves
> Did gyre and gimble in the wabe:
> All mimsy were the borogoves,
> And the mome raths outgrabe.

Commentary

Here is the answer: '*T* (i.e. 'it' – pronoun), *was* (verb), *brillig* (adjective), *and* (conjunction), *the* (definite article), *slithy* (adjective), *toves* (noun, plural), *did* (auxiliary verb), *gyre* (verb), *and* (conjunction), *gimble* (verb), *in* (preposition), *the* (definite article), *wabe* (noun), *all* (adverb), *mimsy* (adjective), *were* (verb), *the* (definite article), *borogoves* (noun, plural), *and* (conjunction), *the* (definite article), *mome* (adjective), *raths* (noun, plural), *outgrabe* (verb, past tense).

Activity 5

Finally, verbal humour is often an ingredient of puzzles. As part of an advertising campaign for its educational website <learn.co.uk>, the *Guardian* (for 3 January 2001) included the following familiar grammatical puzzle. What is the answer?

had had had had had had had had had had had
Put these in one grammatically correct sentence in the same order. Clauses, punctuation and calculators may be used.

Commentary

The following answer was given:

Peter, where John had had 'had', had had 'had had'; 'had had' had had the teacher's approval.

Do you get it?

C

C8   WORD-CHOICE IN USE

C8.1   Dialect

We introduced the term 'dialect' in Unit A8 to label variation in vocabulary that is based on geographical or regional differences. 'Dialect' differences may extend beyond vocabulary to grammar and encompass pronunciation, though the term 'accent' refers specifically to regional differences in pronunciation. We can use the term 'dialect' to include national varieties, such as British English, American English, Australian English or South African English, as well as varieties like West African English, Indian English or Hong Kong English. The term is used more familiarly to refer to regional differences within a national variety, such as West Midlands dialect, Yorkshire dialect or East Anglia dialect.

In Activity 3 in Unit A8, we gave a few examples of dialect words from New Zealand English and from Northern English dialect. In this subunit, we shall extend the range of dialect vocabulary for consideration and discussion.

Activity 1

Speakers of all varieties of English probably have some acquaintance with the vocabulary that belongs specifically to the variety of American English. We have heard it in American films and read it in American novels. Mostly we make sense of it because we can usually figure it out from the context, and in due course some of it becomes incorporated in our own lexicon. However, making sense of American English words in isolation may be more difficult. The following are marked as American English in the *Cambridge International Dictionary of English* (2000). What are their British English equivalents?

anklet	applejack	attorney	bangs	baseboard	billfold
caboose	carryall	cleat	cookie	diaper	eyeglasses
flashlight	garbage	homely	layaway	mobster	neat
penitentiary	realtor	ruckus	sidewalk	sneaker	sundown
tuxedo	vacation	yard			

Commentary

Here are the British English equivalents, listed in the same order as the American English words:

ankle sock	apple brandy	lawyer	(hair) fringe	skirting board	wallet
guard's van	holdall	(boot) stud	biscuit	nappy	spectacles
torch	rubbish	ugly	hire purchase	gangster	good
prison	estate agent	rumpus	pavement	plimsoll	sunset
dinner jacket	holiday	garden			

Activity 2

Here now are some examples (taken from *The Times of India (Online)*) of Indian English. What particular words or expressions would you identify as belonging to this variety? You will find some of them in the *Collins English Dictionary*.

1   If beer is fine, why should neera or toddy be taboo? Farmers and politicians are intensely lobbying with the government to allow neera and toddy tapping from coconut trees, especially in the wake of the fall in coconut output as well as prices.

2   The Chattisgarh government has sworn before the Supreme Court that it was ready to pay up Rs 552 crore to buy 51 per cent equity share in the Bharat Aluminium Company.

3   He was reacting to demands for his resignation from the post in the wake of allegations that he had accepted a bribe of Rs 20,000 from an unemployed youth in return for a zilla panchayat contract.

4   The recent busting of an online betting racket at Nagpur has revealed that satta operations, in keeping with the times, have turned truly cyber.

5   CITU on Thursday charged the International Monetary Fund (IMF) with trying to demolish the industrial sector of the country by dismantling public sector undertakings (PSUs).

6   Colour television sales have taken a massive beating this year, with a whopping 25 per cent drop in the first quarter ended March at just 11 lakh units.

Commentary

1   According to *Collins English Dictionary* (fourth edition (CED4)), one of the meanings of *toddy* is '(in Malaysia) a milky-white sour alcoholic drink made from fermented coconut milk, drunk chiefly by Indians'. This is presumably the sense of *toddy* here, and *neera* is similarly a mild alcoholic drink..

2   The term *crore* means '(in Indian English) ten million' (CED4). The use of *pay up* is perhaps also a feature of this variety.

3   *Zilla* is 'an administrative district in India' and *panchayat* 'a village council in India' (CED4).

4   *Satta* is used of 'speculation' on the stock exchange, but its use has been extended to the context of cricket match fixing. *Turn (truly) cyber* may not be unique to Indian English, but it is an unusual expression.

5   *PSU (public sector undertaking)* is a technical term of Indian politics and economics.

6   The term *lakh* means '(in India) the number 100,000, especially when referring to this sum of rupees' (CED4). The use of (colloquial) *whopping* in this context is perhaps a feature of the variety.

Activity 3

⊛

Let us turn now to a regional dialect of British English, and specifically Scottish, which has a rich vocabulary, some of it shared with northern English dialects. Unless you are Scottish, you are unlikely to have met most of this vocabulary, though it is represented to an extent in the works of a group of contemporary Scottish novelists. You will, therefore, need a good dictionary (*Collins English Dictionary* or *New Oxford Dictionary of English*, or *Chambers Dictionary*, which has traditionally had a good coverage of Scottish words) in order to look up the following words and find their Standard English equivalents.

agley	bairn	bawbee	birl	bonny	brae
chitter	corbie	couthy	cuddy	dreich	fankle
fash oneself	fou	halesome	hirple	howk	jaggie
kyte	lum	mickle	neep	scoosh	timeous

Commentary

The Standard English equivalents of these Scottish words are as follows:

agley: 'askew' or 'awry'

bawbee: 'coin of low value'

bonny: 'attractive', 'beautiful'

chitter: 'shiver with cold'

couthy: 'warm', 'friendly' (person)

dreich: 'dreary', 'bleak' (weather)

fash oneself: 'be upset or worried'

halesome: 'wholesome'

howk: 'dig out'

kyte: 'stomach', 'belly'

mickle: 'a large amount'

scoosh: 'squirt', 'splash'

bairn: 'child'

birl: 'spin', 'whirl'

brae: 'steep bank or hillside'

corbie: 'raven', 'crow', 'rook'

cuddy: 'donkey', 'stupid person'

fankle: 'entangle'

fou: 'drunk'

hirple: 'hobble', 'walk lamely'

jaggie: 'prickly'

lum: 'chimney'

neep: 'turnip'

timeous: 'in good time', 'early enough'

You may have been surprised at the meaning of *mickle*, because you are familiar with the proverb *many a mickle makes a muckle*, i.e. 'a lot of small things add up to something big', often used to encourage thrift. However, this is a misquotation of the saying *many a little makes a mickle*, where *mickle* has its original Scottish meaning.

Activity 4

Let us explore regional English dialects a little further by testing your own knowledge and usage of a few terms:

1   Which word do you use to refer to the footwear that you would put on to go into a gym or to play tennis. *Tennis shoe* or *gymshoe* are two possible terms, but there are several regional words as well. Which is yours?

2   The language contains a number of words to refer to people who are left-handed, or to left-handedness. Some of these are derogatory or slang, but there are regional terms as well. What would you say?

3   English has a large number of words to refer to 'a stupid person' (*berk, dickhead, nerd*, etc.), many of which are derogatory, even offensive, which is often their purpose. Do you have any dialect terms for this?

4   British English has a number of words to refer to being hungry, some of which are colloquial, and some dialect. What words do you use?

5   When you were a child playing games in the playground and you wanted to take time out and avoid being caught, which word did you use?

Commentary

1   If you come from southern or eastern England you are likely to use the word *plimsolls* to refer to this piece of footwear. However, if you are from the midlands

or the north-west, it is likely to be *pumps*; if from the Bristol area, *daps*; if from Merseyside, *gollies*; if from north-east England and Scotland, *sandshoes*; and if from Northern Ireland, *gutties*.

2   Words for left-handedness include *cack-handed*, which is fairly widespread, and then more restricted: *gallack-handed*, *gawk-handed*, *port-sider*, *southpaw*, *wacky*. An Australian English word is: *molly-dooker*. You may have another one.

3   For 'stupid person', Scottish and northern English words are: *souter* and *sumph*. North American English has *palooka* and *poopy*, among others. Australian and New Zealand English have *mopoke*, *nong* and *sook*. Anglo-Irish has *scowder*. But this is only a small selection of a much larger collection, and you have, no doubt, come up with many others.

4   The most usual word in British English regions is *hungry*, but *thirl* occurs in Cornwall and west Devon, *leery* in east Devon, Wiltshire and parts of Hampshire, and the variant *leer* further east along the south coast and as far north as Oxford. An area of the north midlands and south Yorkshire has the word *clammed* (Trudgill 1990: 107). There are also colloquial words such as *peckish* and *famished*, which are more widespread.

5   The most common 'truce word' is *fainites*, used in the south-east of England and in the south-west. Other terms include: *scribs* in east Hampshire and west Sussex; *exes* in East Anglia; *cruces* in Oxfordshire; *cree* in north Wiltshire, Somerset, south-east Wales and up into Gloucestershire and Herefordshire; *barley* in the west midlands, the north-west and south-east Scotland; *kings* in the east midlands and Yorkshire; *crosses* in Lincolnshire; *skinch* in the north-east of England; and *keys* in south-west Scotland. You may have an alternative term that may be quite local to your area. This information is based on work by Peter and Iona Opie on the language of schoolchildren, quoted in Trudgill (1990: 119).

Activity 5

Here, finally, is an anecdote from Peter Wright's little book on the Lancashire dialect (Wright 1972). The spelling has been adjusted to represent the Lancashire accent. Which words in this text would you identify as dialect, as against merely respelt for accent purposes?

At the Barber's

Ah slipped eht for a pow. As soon as ah wur in th' cheer an' th' barber wur clippin' wi' th' sithers rehnd mi lug-oil, ah sed, 'Ah'm lookin' for a noo car, 'Appen ah'll find one afoor lung . . . Ah've brunt aw th' papper off th' parlour an' it looks a reight mess . . . Ah knaw ah've rived mi yure but it'll easy comm eht. Thee 'urry up, mon, wi' this pow or ah'll be clemt. Ah con yet a 'orse's yed off. Ah could yet mi cap neb, an' if ah dooant be gerrin' a' pint o' 'ooam-brewed ah'll be 'evin th' bally-warch.' 'E nodded 'is yed but just finished me, took 'is brass an' said nowt. Ah geet mi cap off th' anger an' ses, 'Good mornin'!' Ah awlus thowt as barbers was talkative.

Commentary

The following glossary might help you to make some sense of this text:

pow – 'haircut'; *cheer* – 'chair'; *sithers* – 'scissors'; *lug-oil* – 'ear'; *brunt* – 'burnt'; *rived* – 'tangled'; *yure* – 'hair'; *comm* – 'comb'; *clemt* – 'very hungry'; *neb* 'peak (of cap)'; *bally-warch* – 'stomach ache'; *brass* – 'money'; *nowt* – 'nothing'; *awlus* – 'always'.

Whatever part of the United Kingdom or any other English-speaking country you live in, you will find that people local to your town or region have a vocabulary all their own. Listen out for local words. There may, indeed, be some interest in collecting local dialect words. Here are some words sent in recently to a Birmingham website <www.bbc.co.uk/birmingham>: *bostin* (splendid), *donnies* (hands), *napper* (head), *spuggy* (sparrow), *wassin* (throat).

C8.2

Topic

In Unit A8, we noted that an occupation, leisure pursuit, or any field of interest and endeavour, produces its own vocabulary. We developed this observation under the heading of 'jargon' in B8. Here, we are exploring it further under the heading of 'topic'. The fundamental insight is that what you talk about – your topic – may be characterised by a distinctive vocabulary. In part this may consist of words that are exclusive to the topic, in part it may consist of words that may be part of the 'common core' (A8) but with a sense special to the topic. Let us examine some examples from a number of diverse topics.

Activity 1

The following text is part of a credit card agreement. Which vocabulary items identify the topic? Are any 'common core' words being used with a special sense?

> We accept no responsibility if any other person, retailer or bank (or cash dispenser) refuses to accept any Card. You must advise us within 60 days of receipt of your statement of details of any Transaction you think has been incorrectly entered. We will only credit the Account with a refund in respect of a Transaction if we receive a refund voucher or other proof of refund acceptable to us. Subject to any statutory rights you may have, you may not use any claim against any other person as a defence or counterclaim against us. You may not transfer any rights you may have against us to any other person. If you want to stop a Continuous Authority Payment or similar arrangement to pay someone from your Account, you will be responsible for telling the other person or organisation you are paying that you want to cancel the authority or similar arrangement. Except in the case of Condition 9.9, you cannot in any circumstances stop a Transaction.

Commentary

This text is part of the 'small print'; it has a legal authority, and so its topic is a combination of the legal and the financial. Legal terminology includes: *statutory rights, claim,* defence, counterclaim. Words like *claim* and *defence* have a common-core meaning, but are used here in a special legal sense. Some of the terms have been specially defined for the purposes of the agreement; they are the ones with an initial capital letter: *Card, Transaction, Account, Continuous Payment Authority, Condition*. All of these words belong to the common core, but they have a special sense for this topic, or they have been joined into a unique compound, as *Continuous Payment Authority*. Similarly, *cash dispenser* and *refund voucher* are specialised terms, though their components are not.

Further ordinary words that are being used with a topic-specific sense include: *advise*, in the sense of 'inform'; *statement*, as a list of credit card transactions; *enter*, in the sense of 'include on the statement'; *arrangement*, in the sense of a 'financial arrangement' of a specific kind; *stop*, in the sense of 'prevent from being processed and entered on the statement'.

Activity 2
Our second example comes from the area of theology, whose vocabulary again has been partly coined for the purpose and partly taken from the common core and given a specialised meaning. Which are the words unique to theological language in the following text (taken from the *New Dictionary of Theology*, ed. Sinclair B. Ferguson and David F. Wright, Inter-Varsity Press 1988, p. 239)?

Evangelical theology goes back to the creeds of the first centuries of the Christian era, in which the early church sought to correlate the teaching of Scripture, penetrate its meaning and defend it. In concert with the thought of this period, evangelical theology affirms that: the Bible is the truthful revelation of God and through it the life-giving voice of God speaks; God is the almighty creator and we are his dependent creation; God has entered history redemptively in the incarnation of Jesus Christ; God's nature exists in Trinitarian expression; Jesus Christ is fully divine and fully human, the power and judgment of sin is a reality for all humanity; God graciously takes the initiative in coming to us savingly in Jesus Christ and by the Holy Spirit; Jesus Christ is building his church; and the consummation of history will be expressed in the second advent of Jesus Christ, the general resurrection, the final judgment, heaven and hell.

Commentary
The words, as against the senses of words, that are special to the topic of theology are, in my judgement, the following: *evangelical* (its use in ordinary language derives from its theological use), *creed*, *church* (as the people rather than the building), *Scripture, Bible, God, almighty, creator* and *creation* (almost consigned to theological language, as a minority viewpoint), *redemptive(ly), incarnation, Jesus Christ, Trinitarian, divine* (its other uses are derived from theology), *sin, Holy Spirit, (second) advent, resurrection, heaven, hell*. Words such as *truth, revelation, judgment* and *save*, with its associated words, are in ordinary language, but even there they often resonate their special theological meanings.

Activity 3

In general, we do not find great difficulty in understanding texts such as those in the previous two activities. We have enough acquaintance with the topic for the specialised vocabulary to be interpretable in context. For many of us, though, the language(s) of the natural sciences present more of a problem. In the following text (taken from *The Mitchell Beazley Joy of Knowledge Encyclopaedia*, 'Science and The Universe', pp. 80–1), is it the ordinary words with special meaning that cause problems of understanding, or is it the specialist words?

> The loudness of a sound can be measured with a decibel meter and the result given as a number of decibels (dB). Strictly, the meter measures the intensity of the sound, which is related to the pressure differences in the sound wave. The scale is logarithmic – an increase of 10dB is produced by 10 times the intensity. Loudness varies with the cube root of intensity, so that a sound 10dB greater sounds about twice as loud. The human ear does not hear all the frequencies of sound in the same way and a low sound is perceived as being less loud than a high sound of the same intensity. The number of compressions that pass in every second is called the frequency of the sound wave and is measured in hertz (Hz), equal to cycles per second. This scale is not logarithmic and a note of 440Hz (the A above middle C in music) sounds twice as high as, or an octave above, one of 220Hz (the A below middle C). In other words, the higher the frequency, the higher the pitch.

Commentary

There are, as it happens, few specialist words in this text, though that is not always the case with scientific language. Here we may identify only: *decibel, logarithmic, hertz, octave*. It is the ordinary words with specialist senses, and especially the high number of them and in combination, that makes this text 'scientific'. Such words are: *intensity, scale, pressure, sound + wave, cube + root, frequency, compressions, cycles, note, pitch*. The other, unrelated, factor is the measurement and calculation of loudness in terms of decibels and of frequency in terms of hertz, which increases the density of the text.

Activity 4

Sometimes advertisers and marketing people exploit our shaky acquaintance with the vocabulary of science and technology to impress us with the desirability of the goods they are offering for sale. Nowhere is this more blatant than in how computers are advertised. Consider the following, quite typical, example. How much of this means anything to you? But why do you find it impressive?

Mobile Intel Pentium III Processor
600MHz featuring Intel Speedstep Technology
64MB 100MHz SDRAM (Upgradable to 512MB)
10GB Removable EIDE Hard Drive
15″ XGA + (1024 × 768) TFT Display
256KB Integrated L2 Cache
Integrated Floppy Drive
High Performance ATI Rage 3D Graphics with 8MB Video Memory
3D Positional Sound with Wavetable
Integrated Touchpad
56Kb/s V90 Modem
Lithium Ion Battery
MS Windows ME
MS Works Suite 2000

Commentary

Someone mildly interested in buying a computer but not that knowledgeable would find most of this to be gobbledegook. If you are familiar with computers, some of it will make sense: the 'latest' processor (*Pentium III*), the speed of operation (*600MHz*), the amount of operating memory (*64MB* – 'megabytes'), the capacity of the internal storage (*10GB* – 'gigabytes'), the size and quality of the screen (*15″ XGA*), the speed of the modem (for internet connection) (*56Kb/s* – 'kilobytes per second'), and the quality of the battery (*Lithium Ion*). What impresses you, then, is, first, the size of the figures quoted (*600MHz, 64MB, 10GB, 56Kb/s*), and second, how state-of-the-art you think the specification is. I imagine that there are few of us, outside the computing fraternity, who can make sense of everything in this advertisement.

Concluding

We have looked at just four examples of topic vocabulary. This could be multiplied many times. If we are familiar with a topic, we may not even be aware that we are using specialist vocabulary. You may find it useful to reflect on a day-to-day basis about the range of 'jargons' that you have access to and those that you have active command of.

Formality

C8.3

We briefly introduced in Unit A8 the idea that vocabulary may vary along the dimension of formality, by noting that words may be labelled in dictionaries on a scale from 'formal' to 'informal' or 'colloquial' to 'slang'. Dictionaries, however, vary in the labelling decisions that they make: the *Cambridge International Dictionary of English* (2000), a dictionary for advanced foreign learners, labels over 3000 items as 'formal', whereas the *New Oxford Dictionary of English* has less than 1000 with this label. However, NODE marks more than 6500 items with the 'informal' label, as against 4500 in CIDE; NODE also has more words marked as 'slang' than does CIDE, but this may merely be a reflection of the fact that it is a bigger dictionary. What this means, though, is that, for the expression of certain ideas, we may have a choice of words, and our choice will be governed by our perception of the formality of the context and our relationship to the audience with whom we are communicating.

Activity 1

The following article appeared in the *Guardian*'s 'Editor' magazine on 5.1.01 under the title *Busting the bus jargon*. Consider why formal language might have been used in the first place. And do you consider the rewriting to be more appropriate to the context?

Guy Gibson, a training officer at Trent Buses in Derbyshire, was so unimpressed by the gobbledegook that filled his company's driving manual that he decided to rewrite it. He came up with some rather simpler, jargon-busting guidelines . . .

❑ Before: Ensure location factors and conditions in which manoeuvres are to occur are considered with regard to safety, minimal disruption to other road users, residents, legal constraints and regulatory requirements.
❑ After: Look where you are going, check mirrors, etc.
❑ Before: Ensure the vehicle is effectively manoeuvred to change direction.
❑ After: Turn the steering wheel when you reach a bend.
❑ Before: Ensure awareness and anticipation of other road users in the vicinity of the manoeuvre is maintained.
❑ After: Look where you're going.
❑ Before: Ensure vehicle is started from and stopped at a designated point.
❑ After: Use the bus stops.

Commentary

The vocabulary of the original manual, as given in these extracts, does not really fall into the category of 'jargon' (see B8, C8.2). It is, rather, somewhat overformal and overblown for its purpose. Possibly, its author thought that a manual for publication and intended to be taken seriously should adopt a suitably formal tone. It ran the risk, however, of failing to be effective, even to be counter-productive, because the formality of the language masks the important instructions that it is intended to communicate.

The rewritten instructions do not really do the job either. They now err so much on the side of being 'colloquial' that the intended meaning is partly lost. For example, 'Turn the steering wheel when you reach a bend' says rather less than the original sentence, which might have been expressed as 'Take care when you turn corners or take bends.' Similarly, 'Look where you're going' is rather less than the requirement to be aware of and to anticipate other road users. Changing some of the nouns to verbs would, in fact, help simplify: 'Be aware of other road users and anticipate what they will do when you are manoeuvring your bus.'

Activity 2

You will often come across texts – regulations, contracts, official documents – that are, of necessity, written in formal language. Plain English does not necessarily equal colloquial English. You may be called upon to interpret such texts for other people, and the solution may be to express them in simpler, less formal language. Here is part of one such text (a 'precept' from the Quality Assurance Agency for Higher Education's *Code of Practice on Collaborative Provision*). If you are to explain this to someone, which words would you identify as 'formal' and need expressing in simpler ones? Which less formal words would you choose?

> The agreements should include termination and arbitration provisions and financial arrangements and should describe the respective responsibilities of the contracting parties for academic standards and quality. They should include provisions to enable the Awarding Institution to suspend or withdraw from the agreement if the Partner Organisation fails to fulfil its obligations. The residual obligations to students on termination of the agreement should also be covered in the agreement or contract. Unreasonable confidentiality provisions which would preclude the Awarding Institution from sharing with other Awarding Institutions any concerns which led to its withdrawal from the agreement should be avoided.

Commentary

Part of the 'formality' of this text arises from the factor noted in Activity 1 that nouns are used instead of the verbs from which they derive (e.g. *provision, arrangement, withdrawal*), though the words themselves are not 'formal'. Similarly, the use of the passive voice (*should be covered*) adds to the formal tone. You may have noted some or all of the following as 'formal' words: *termination, arbitration, respective, suspend, obligations, residual, confidentiality, preclude*. In fact, only *preclude* is labelled as 'formal' in the *Cambridge International Dictionary of English*.

What possible simpler terms might be substituted? Here are some suggestions: *termination*: 'ending'; *arbitration*: 'resolution of disagreements' or '(provisions for) how disagreements are resolved'; *respective*: 'of each of'; *suspend*: 'stop for the time being'; *obligations*: 'what it should do'; *residual*: 'that are left or remain'; *confidentiality*: '(provisions for) keeping matters secret'; *preclude*: 'stop' or 'prevent'.

A simplification would involve more than just a change in some of the formal vocabulary. It would also require some syntactic simplification, as well as rephrasing to avoid some of the compounds, such as *termination provisions* and *confidentiality provisions*.

Activity 3

Let us now go to the other end of the spectrum. Here are some words and expressions that are considered colloquial, or even slang, and which made their appearance, according to Ayto (1999), in the 1990s. Do you know them, and can you gloss them?

as if, bad hair day, crustie, dadrock, DWEM, Essex girl, feminazi, hotting, internot, jelly, kit, get a life, lovely jubbly, luvvie, monster (adjective), mwah, off-message, saddo, slaphead, sorted, stormin, twoc, unfeasibly

Commentary

In case you have not yet caught up with late twentieth-century colloquialisms, here are some glosses, based on the explanations given by Ayto (1999):

as if:	used to express disbelief, usually in an ironic manner
bad hair day:	a day on which everything seems to go wrong
crustie:	homeless or vagrant young people who usually live by begging in cities and have an unkempt and unwashed look
dadrock:	younger generation's term for music played by ageing rock stars
DWEM:	an acronym for 'dead white European male', whose work is said to dominate the study of literature, history and culture in schools and universities
Essex girl:	an extension of earlier *Essex man* (brash, self-made young businessman who benefited from the 'wealth-creation' of the Thatcher era); *Essex girl* is vulgar, unintelligent, materialistic and promiscuous
feminazi:	formed by blending *feminist* and *Nazi* to denote contemptuously a radical feminist
hotting:	joyriding in high-performance cars – *hot* denotes both 'high-performance' and 'stolen'
internot:	someone who does not use the Internet and may even be opposed to it
jelly:	one of many slang terms from the drug culture, this one denotes a reformulation of the tranquillizer Temazepam
kit:	clothing, especially in the expression 'take one's kit off'
life:	in the expression 'get a life', said, scornfully, to someone who is considered to be dull, uninteresting, 'sad'
lovely jubbly:	money, wealth
luvvie:	a mocking term for an actor or actress
monster:	one of many 'approving' words, so 'outstanding' or 'successful'
mwah:	imitative of the sound made by an 'air kiss'
off-message:	said of a politician who is not representing the agreed party line
saddo:	a person who is 'sad', i.e. socially inadequate or otherwise worthy of contempt
slaphead:	a bald-headed or shaven-headed person

sorted:	well organised, under control, fully prepared (usually pronounced with a glottal stop in the middle, for the 't')
stormin:	another approval adjective, equivalent to 'wonderful', 'fantastic'
twoc:	the offence of stealing a car, an acronym of 'taken without owner's consent'
unfeasibly:	an intensifying adverb, equivalent to 'unbelievably', 'remarkably'

Activity 4

Take any two dictionaries, preferably from different publishers, and look up a few of your favourite slang words. What kinds of labels do the dictionaries use, and do they label them in the same way?

Commentary

Here are one or two examples from the *Concise Oxford Dictionary* (ninth edition (COD)) and the *Collins English Dictionary* (fourth edition (CED)):

arse is 'coarse slang' in COD and 'taboo' in CED

bum is 'British slang' in both

dick, in the expression 'clever dick' is 'British colloquial' in COD, but 'slang' in CED; and as a word for 'penis' it is labelled 'coarse slang' in COD and 'taboo' in CED

frog to refer to a French person is labelled 'slang offensive' in COD, but 'British slang' in CED, though the definition notes that it is 'derogatory'

shit is 'coarse slang' in COD, but just 'slang' in CED

twerp is 'slang' in COD, but merely 'informal' in CED

The status of words may change in a culture in the course of time, and there may not be any consensus about how to classify them. This exercise can be replicated historically by looking at the successive editions of the same dictionary. In the first edition of the *Concise Oxford*, published in 1911, neither *arse* nor *bum* have any formality label, but *shit* is marked as 'not decent' and *frog* as 'contemptuous for'. The others have no entry.

The classic treatment of slang is by the late Eric Partridge, whose *Dictionary of Slang and Unconventional English* was first published in 1937; the latest, eighth edition is edited by Paul Beale (Partridge 1984). A more modern treatment is Jonathon Green's *Cassell Dictionary of Slang* (1998).

EXTENSION

READINGS IN GRAMMAR AND VOCABULARY

HOW TO USE THE READINGS

The readings contained in this section are taken from the works of some key linguists who have written about the grammar and vocabulary of English. A couple of the readings are self-contained articles, but most are chapters or parts of chapters from books. They have been chosen because they expand on or provide an alternative perspective on the material in the corresponding units in Sections A, B and C, and in that context they can be understood, even though they may be plucked from other works.

Read each extract carefully, bearing in mind the related A to C sections that it follows on from. Some of the readings you will more readily comprehend than others, which you may need to read twice, or perhaps even more times. An introduction sets the reading in the context of its related units, and a follow-up section suggests how the reading may be applied to new data or in further investigation of grammar and vocabulary. Full bibliographical details are given of each reading, so that you may even feel inspired to go to the work from which the reading was taken and to see the extract in its original context.

D1

LINGUISTIC UNITS AND THE SENTENCE

The reading in this unit is taken from *English Syntactic Structures – Functions and Categories in Sentence Analysis* by Flor Aarts and Jan Aarts (1982), which is notable for its lucid exposition and wealth of examples. The extract is from the Introduction to the book and discusses the notion of 'sentence' and how we might characterise a sentence.

It reinforces the contention in Unit A1 that sentences have structure, and that of Unit B1, developed in the C1 subunits, that structure varies according to function or meaning, but it takes a different line of argument. It extends the discussion of sentences to encompass 'structural ambiguity', when the same sequence of words can represent more than one structure and more than one meaning.

D1.1

Linguistic units and the sentence

F. Aarts and J. Aarts (reprinted from *English Syntactic Structures – Functions and Categories in Sentence Analysis* (1982))

The description of the various components of a grammar has always concentrated on different sorts of linguistic units. Semantic descriptions, for example, have tended to concentrate on the meaning of individual words, and have only recently begun to pay attention to larger units than the word. Syntactic descriptions, on the other hand, have traditionally taken the **sentence** as their starting-point, smaller units being primarily regarded as 'building-blocks' of sentences. Since in this book we are in the first place concerned with syntax, we shall mainly deal with sentences and with smaller units as component parts of sentences.

Sentences consist of words. However, nobody would look upon (5a) as a sentence, although it is a string of eight English words:

(5) a. Lion cage this less in dangerous is the

Now, if we compare (5a) with:

(5) b. The lion is less dangerous in this cage

we will unhesitatingly accept the latter example as a sentence. It is true that in (5a) we are able to assign some sort of meaning to each word individually, but we fail to make any sense of the sequence as a whole; (5a), in other words, is not meaningful, whereas (5b) is. We shall therefore say that, if a sequence of words is to constitute a sentence, it must be meaningful.

Wordorder and sentence structure

The reason why we cannot make sense of (5a) is that we cannot tell which words should be grouped together. In (5b), on the other hand, it is perfectly obvious that *less* combines with *dangerous* to form *less dangerous*, rather than with *is* to form *is less*. Similarly *the* combines with *lion*, *this* with *cage*, and *in* with *this cage*. Thus, in (5b) we have three coherent groups of words: *the lion*, *less dangerous* and *in this cage*. Apart from being internally coherent, these groups also stand in a certain relation to each other. Thus *less dangerous* combines primarily with *the lion* rather than with *in this cage*. The latter group relates to the combination *the lion is less dangerous* as a whole. This network of relations between the words of a sentence is called its structure.

As appears from a comparison of (5a) and (5b), one of the factors that determines the structure of a sentence is the order in which the words are arranged. It is obvious that this order is subject to strict rules. For example, if in (5b) we keep *the lion* in initial position and examine the possibilities of arranging the other groups, we find that only (5f) has an acceptable wordorder:

(5) b. The lion is less dangerous in this cage
    c. *The lion is in this cage less dangerous
    d. *The lion less dangerous in this cage is
    e. *The lion less dangerous is in this cage
    f. The lion in this cage is less dangerous
    g. *The lion in this cage less dangerous is

The importance of the role played by **wordorder** appears not only from the unacceptability of four out of the six examples above, but also from the fact that the different order of the words in the two acceptable sentences (5b) and (5f) entails a difference in their structure and in their meaning. In (5f) *in this cage* now primarily combines with *the lion*, whereas *less dangerous* relates to the combination *the lion in this cage* as a whole. The difference in meaning is that in (5b) a particular lion (that the speaker has been talking about) is said to be less dangerous in this cage (than in another), but that in (5f) the lion in this cage is said to be less dangerous (than other lions in other cages). Other examples of the crucial part played by wordorder are the following pairs of sentences. In each pair the difference in wordorder results in a difference in structure as well as in meaning:

(6) a. Did he say who he was?
   b. Who did he say he was?
(7) a. He wanted to marry Jane
   b. He wanted Jane to marry
(8) a. I'll have it copied within a minute
   b. I'll have copied it within a minute
(9) a. Who has John rung up?
   b. Who has rung up John?

To comment only on the last pair, it is clear that in (9a) the agent of the action denoted by the verb is *John* and that *who* inquires after the identity of the person that John rang up. In (9b) *who* inquires after the agent of the action and it is John who has been rung up.

Differences in wordorder need not always have the effect that they have in sentences (6–9). In spite of differences in wordorder, we assign identical structures and identical meanings to the (a) and (b) sentences below:

(10) a. John ran away
    b. Away ran John
(11) a. On the horizon appeared a lonely horseman
    b. A lonely horseman appeared on the horizon
(12) a. I fail to understand this problem
    b. This problem I fail to understand

It will be noticed that in sentences (6–9) wordorder differences entail differences in the logical relationships between words and groups of words. This is not the case, however, in sentences (10–12), where these relationships remain constant and the different wordorder merely brings about a shift in emphasis.

Word-meaning and sentence structure

So far we have discussed sentence structure in terms of wordorder, giving examples of pairs of sentences containing the same words, and we have seen that a difference in wordorder often results in a difference in structure and meaning. Wordorder, however, is not the only factor that determines sentence structure. The structure of a sentence also depends on the individual meanings of the words or word-groups making up the sentence. Consider:

(13) a. He looked up the number
    b. He looked up the chimney

(14) a. Mary was waiting for two friends
     b. Mary was waiting for two minutes
(15) a. You shouldn't have left him so ill
     b. You shouldn't have left him so early
(16) a. She made him a good wife
     b. She made him a good dinner
(17) a. Peter had dreamt the whole night
     b. Peter had dreamt the whole story

In each pair the (a) and (b) sentences have different structures. This cannot be due to wordorder, but must be attributed to the fact that the last words are different and, consequently, contribute different meanings to the total meaning of the whole sentence. That the structures of the (a) and (b) sentences are different appears, for example, from the fact that in (13a) there is a close relation between *look* and *up*, which is absent in (13b); here we recognize a relation between *up* and *the chimney*. Again, in (14a) *for* goes with *waiting*, whereas in (14b) it combines with *two minutes*. Other structural differences can be detected in (15–17).

Structural ambiguity
Our examples so far have been ones in which structure is overtly indicated by wordorder (6–9) or by different lexical items (13–17). Sentence structure is, however, not always unambiguously derivable from overt marks like these, as can be seen from so-called ambiguous sentences like the following:

(18) Visiting relatives can be boring
(19) Freddy likes Susan more than Joan

An ambiguous sentence is one to which we can assign more than one structure and therefore more than one meaning. Thus (19) allows of the following two interpretations:

(19) a. Freddy likes Susan more than Freddy likes Joan
     b. Freddy likes Susan more than Joan likes Susan

The absence of any overt clues in sentence (19) makes it impossible for us to say whether it should be interpreted as (19a) or as (19b). Such structural ambiguities cannot be solved, then, by looking at the sentence in isolation. When the sentence is embedded in a larger context, however, the context will usually provide clues indicating which of the two readings is the intended one.

   Summarizing the major points of what has been said so far, we can say that:

1. if a sequence of words is to constitute a sentence, it must be meaningful;
2. sentences are interpreted not as strings of individual words but as sequences of groups of words;
3. between the words and word-groups of a sentence there exist certain relations;
4. the network of relations between the words and word-groups of a sentence is called its structure;
5. clues to the structure of a sentence can be found in its wordorder and in the meanings of the words in the sentence;

6. although wordorder provides a significant clue to the structure of a sentence, sentence structure is not always observed in the linear sequence of the words in the sentence.

Follow-up activities

Examples of how sentence structure determines meaning and interpretation can be found in all kinds of text. You might look particularly at advertisements and newspaper headlines, which will sometimes exploit structural ambiguity for effect, often humorous or ironical, e.g.

M&S goes west. So do profits.

Here, the headline writer has exploited the literal and figurative meanings of *go west*. The first part refers to the (literal) move of the firm's headquarters to west London; the second relates to the downturn in the company's profits.

Find further examples of sentences that are ambiguous, and resolve the ambiguity by explaining the different underlying structures, as suggested by Aarts and Aarts.

D2   GRAMMATICAL CLASS: THE PROBLEM OF LABELLING

We have examined the word classes of English in this series of units. One of the issues that we discussed in A2 concerned the criteria for establishing a class of words. We noted that traditional 'notional' definitions ('a noun is the name of a person, place or thing') are not adequate to rigorously establish a word class, and we proposed more reliable criteria, especially of a structural (morphological and syntactic) nature.

Classification is a general issue in the description of language. The reading in this unit addresses exactly that problem. It is from David Allerton's *Essentials of Grammatical Theory: A Consensus View of Syntax and Morphology* (1979), Chapter 7, entitled 'Grammatical class – the problem of "labelling"'. Allerton proposes that a class is a 'substitution list' of items that may occur at a particular position in structure, but he extends the notion beyond word classes to other kinds of grammatical element.

D2.1   Grammatical class – the problem of 'labelling'

D. Allerton (reprinted from *Essentials of Grammatical Theory: A Consensus View of Syntax and Morphology* (1979), Chapter 7.

Class and subclass

We have seen how the grammatical structure of a sentence needs to be described in terms of both the domain of the constructions involved in it and the relations between the constituents of those constructions. We now come to the question of what kinds of element those constituents are, or, more accurately, what classes of element they are. In any kind of syntactic description we have to provide labels for the different kinds of element like PREDICATE, VERB, TRANSITIVE, etc. But how are these arrived at? What does the concept of 'grammatical class' or 'label' involve?

How are classes identified? These questions need to be answered, whatever model of grammatical description we are working with. This means exploring the paradigmatic axis of grammar.

We are already familiar with the traditional word-classes, or 'parts of speech' (nouns, verbs, adjectives, etc.). But the traditional definitions were a mixed bag of imprecise, though not valueless, notional ideas (e.g. VERB: 'word denoting an action') and of only partially adequate procedures (e.g. PRONOUN: 'a word that replaces a noun'). Something more comprehensive and systematic is needed.

We may define the notion of class by reference to the first (and most important) grammatical operation we discussed earlier: SUBSTITUTION. A grammatical class is: (a label assigned to) a set of substitution lists (of grammatical elements appearing in different contexts) that have identical or broadly similar members. The vagueness of the phrase 'identical or broadly similar' is deliberate: it enables us to set up a small narrowly defined class at the one extreme, or a broad comprehensive class at the other. The generality of the phrase 'grammatical element' means that we apply it to classes of morphemes, words, phrases, clauses (and even sentences), regardless of the size of the element: thus the class of deverbal noun-forming suffixes, the class of prepositions, the class of noun phrases, etc.

If we attempt to list the simple (i.e. single-morpheme) words that could complete the following sentential contexts in English:

I noticed $\left\{\begin{array}{l}\text{the}\\\text{his}\end{array}\right\}\left(\left\{\begin{array}{l}\text{empty}\\\text{new}\end{array}\right\}\right)$ —— (yesterday).

we find that broadly the same substitution list emerges whether we choose *the* or *his*, whether we include the adjective *empty*, the adjective *new*, or neither, and whether we include the adverb *yesterday* or not. It comprises COMMON NOUNS. The list would include words like:

book, boy, bread, child, cow, loaf, oil, plan, pride, space, vigour

But the choice of adjective would make some difference to the list: after *empty* the word *bread* does not seem to fit; after *new* the word *sun* seems unusual. However, these differences are determined not so much by the grammatical potential of the words in question as by their lexical-semantic range or the state of those aspects of the external world they refer to. We do not need to stretch our imaginations too far to imagine uses for the concept of 'empty bread' or of 'new sun(s)'. So, broadly speaking, we disregard problems of semantic improbability when comparing substitution lists.

Some restrictions on substitution, however, are clear-cut and must be regarded as grammatical restrictions on the cooccurrence of items. For example, suppose we modify our original sentence frame by replacing *the/his* with *little* or *(not) much* or unstressed *some*, 'a certain quantity' (=/səm/ not /sʌm/), to give:

I noticed $\left\{\begin{array}{l}\text{little}\\\text{some}\end{array}\right\}\left(\left\{\begin{array}{l}\text{empty}\\\text{new}\end{array}\right\}\right)$ —— (yesterday).

Class of simple COMMON NOUNS

MASS subclass   NON-MASS
                                    (=COUNT) subclass
bread, ice, oil, pride,   book, boy, child, cow,
space, vigour, etc., etc.   loaf, plan, etc., etc.

Figure D2.1

The contribution of these new DETERMINERS (as we call *the* and the various alternatives to it) is to strongly restrict our substitution list, affecting our sample list as follows:

*book, *boy, bread, *child, *cow, ice, *loaf, oil, *plan, pride, space, vigour

In other words, if we wish to describe the class fully, we need to specify the SUB-CLASS that appears in this limited context, viz. after the mass determiners *little*, *(not) much* and *some*. We would have the scheme as shown in Figure D2.1.

It happens that the same nouns that fail to occur with *little, (not) much, some* – the NON-MASS nouns – are all nouns that readily do occur with *a, one,* and in the plural, with or without the numerals *two, three,* etc., all with the meaning 'a discrete quantity/discrete item (of the class)', e.g. *a book, one cow, two loaves,* but **a bread, *one oil, *two vigours* (except in the meaning 'a/one/two kinds of'). But notice that two items in the MASS noun list do have a COUNT use, viz. *one ice,* 'one icecream', *one space,* 'one discrete portion of space'. These nouns may be said to have 'multiple class membership'.

Grammatical classes almost invariably subdivide into subclasses, and very often the subclasses further divide into sub-subclasses, and so on. If we take as an example the class of English verbs, a typical context like the following would produce a list of verbs including those given below (allowing for individual differences in the realization of *-ed*):

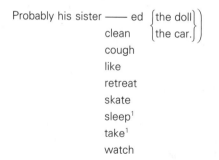

Now, out of this over-all representative list of verbs, some – the intransitive ones *cough, retreat, skate, sleep* – do not occur at all with a following noun-phrase object

---

[1] The combinations sleep + -ed and take + -ed are, of course, realized as slept and took respectively.

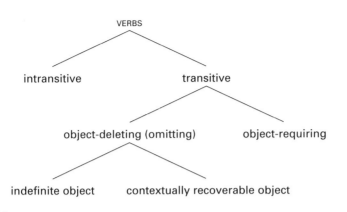

Figure D2.2

(like those given). Of the remainder that do, some – *like*, *take* – cannot occur without their object and the others – *clean*, *watch* – allow omission (or 'deletion') of their object, in the case of *clean* where the object is left indefinite, in the case of *watch* where it is contextually recoverable. This suggests a subclassification as in Figure D2.2.

If we adopted such a (sub)classification, it would be possible to describe 'transitive' as a subclass, 'object-deleting' as a sub-subclass and 'indefinite object' as a sub-sub-subclass; but such a cumbersome terminology tends to be avoided, and the word 'sub-class' is used throughout.

The more subtle a subclassification becomes, the more the classes seem to have a semantic coherence. In a simplified account, English non-sentence adverbials, for instance, could be divided up on the basis of syntactic criteria, as shown in Figure D2.3 overleaf.

Adverbials as a whole are characterized by certain properties, and, within the group, non-sentence adverbials, sometimes called ADJUNCTS, are identified by various syntactic criteria, such as their inability to occur initially in a negative sentence (Quirk *et al.*, 1972: 421f.), e.g.:

> *Carefully, he didn't open the door.
> (cf. Wisely, he didn't open the door.)

On the other hand, as we proceed (from left to right) through our subclassification, the subclasses become more and more semantically based, and the tests tend to be more semantic in nature, e.g. for TIME adverbials, the kind of question they answer – 'When?', 'How long (for)?', etc.

Follow-up activities

Allerton proposes a subclassification of verbs in this reading. Take a different structure and a selection of ten or so verbs of your own choice, and apply Allerton's method. Do you come up with the same classification, or do you need to make some adaptations to his framework on the basis of your evidence? Try the same experiment with other structure frames and other selections of verbs. You may like to compare your results with the discussion in Unit A5.

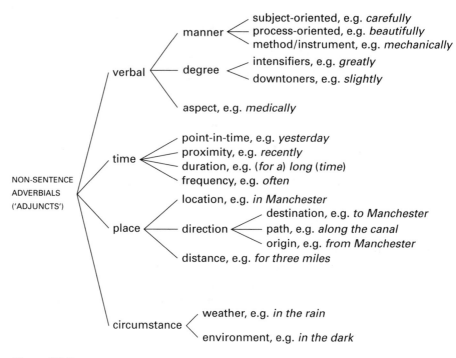

Figure D2.3

The reading concludes with a diagrammatic representation of a subclassification of Adverbials in English. For further discussion of Adverbials, see Units A4 and C4.2. Find at least one further example of each of Allerton's subclasses of Adverbial from an authentic text, e.g. newspaper, magazine or novel.

You can try Allerton's method on all kinds of places in structure, to see what kinds of substitution lists you can come up with. What kind of 'semantic coherence' do the resulting classes and subclasses have?

Allerton suggests that 'we disregard problems of semantic improbability when comparing substitution lists'. Look at the reading in Unit D5 for an alternative point of view on this question.

D3   LEXICALISATION

In Unit B3, having established in A3 that words have structure, we examined the various ways in which new words are created and added to the vocabulary of the language. In the C3 subunits we considered compounding and derivation, the major word formation processes, in more detail. Coining a new word is one thing, getting it accepted by your fellow language users, a process known as 'institutionalisation', is something else. The process may be a long and tortuous one, or a word may catch on instantly, as with much slang. But then, it may equally quickly go out of fashion.

What gives rise to new words, what we feel the need to 'name', and which coinages we choose for naming, are uncertain processes. The reading for this unit deals with such processes, which are called 'lexicalisation'. It comes from *A Comprehensive Grammar of the English Language* (Quirk *et al.* 1985) and is taken from Appendix I, which is devoted to the topic of word-formation in English. The section reproduced is I9-I12, which looks at lexicalisation processes, and it shows how unpredictable the process can often be.

Lexicalization

D3.1

Quirk *et al.* (reprinted from *A Comprehensive Grammar of the English Language* (1985) London: Longman, App I)

However new and unfamiliar it is, an entity, activity, or quality can be stated and described in sentences:

Let us convert our railways from having steam-engines to

using engines powered by $\begin{cases} \text{diesel oil.} \\ \text{electricity.} \end{cases}$ [1]

The nub of this suggestion might then be expressed by means of nominalization such as:

The use of $\begin{cases} \text{diesel-powered} \\ \text{electrically-powered} \end{cases}$ engines (is being investigated). [2]

This already presupposes some discussion of and familiarization with the notion. But as the proposal becomes more widely accepted as viable, such a nominalization will seem too clumsy on the one hand and too under-committed on the other. At this stage, we will not be surprised to find the notion institutionalized by means of (as it happened) the word:

$\begin{cases} \text{Dieselization} \\ \text{Electrification} \end{cases}$ (is feasible). [3]

We can now conveniently marshal arguments for and against *dieselization* or *electrification*, discuss how much it will cost to *dieselize* or *electrify* suburban trains, and whether the new locomotives might co-exist for a time with *undieselized* or *unelectrified* services. We have now LEXICALIZED a notion that could previously be discussed only in sentences and periphrases which varied from person to person. In lay terms, we now 'have a *word* for it'.

But the precise form of the lexicalizations [3] could not have been predicted. When it became possible to split atomic nuclei (and the consequent lexicalization, *nuclear fission*, came into use), there was some vacillation and even public debate as to the most appropriate adjective to lexicalize the property of a substance in being capable of undergoing such fission. Competing forms included *fissible*, *fissile*, and *fissionable*. It turned out that two lexicalizations were necessary; one for the general capability, the other for the capability in consequence of slow neutron impact; physicists are apt to use *fissionable* for the former and *fissile* for the latter. In more extreme cases, the unpredictability of a lexicalization is even more obvious: for example, Kerouac's attempt to sum up the demise of a soft and flabby entity (for which the word *crash* was thus inappropriate) as *sploopse*; or the lexicalization by the mathematician Kasner of a particular numerical value as *googol*.

The other noteworthy point about such lexicalizations as [3] is that their meaning is not recoverable from the form. In this way, as in the unpredictability just discussed, it is sharply distinguished from the expressions in [1] and [2]. We can surmise that *dieselization* and *electrification* refer to inceptive action concerning diesel oil and electricity respectively, but there is nothing in the words as such that takes us much beyond that. With *fissile* and *fissionable*, it is inevitable from the discussion above that not merely do they not proclaim that they are inherently concerned with *nuclear* fission; it is impossible to tell from their form what their precise meaning may be, even when we are told that nuclear fission is involved.

This is no more than we should expect if we reflect upon the concentration of presupposition that is packed into a lexicalization by the time it is successfully institutionalized. The coinage *racism* reflects in two syllables the conscience and the agonized sensibilities of a whole generation.

Of the two negative points just made about lexicalization, unrecoverability is far more endemic than unpredictability. Given the finite resources for lexicalization and the fact that some resources are more productive than others, there are various highly likely ways in which a lexicalization will be realized, and it is on these that we concentrate in this Appendix. Thus in the lexicalization of concepts that can be given nominal properties, it is very common to adopt a strategy based on noun-phrase structure. Compare:

> Some paper is shiny.
> *Paper that is shiny* is difficult to write on.
> Please don't buy me *shiny paper*.

We may postulate the way this strategy works in lexicalization:

[A] Oil comes from various sources, including vegetable matter. Such oil has functions and properties important for us and not shared with oil from other sources (*eg* mineral or animal matter). It is therefore worth distinguishing:

> This oil is from a vegetable source.
> *Oil from vegetable sources* is healthy for cooking.
> *Vegetable oil* . . .   [1]

[B] The engines of cars require oil; it has to be a special oil (*eg* from mineral sources, and of particular viscosity etc); since cars are relevant to our daily lives, such oil is worth distinguishing:

> This oil is for engines.
> *Oil for engines* is expensive.
> *Engine oil* . . .   [2]

But if such noun-phrase type premodification is so common in lexicalization as to challenge our earlier statement about predictability, it can readily be seen by comparing [1] and [2] that our statement stands concerning unrecoverability. Both [1] and [2] are of similar semantic and formal structure, but it is only by learning each as an idiosyncratic item that we can know that [1] 'means' oil *from* vegetables, [2] oil *for* engines. There is nothing inherently absurd about oil *for* vegetables, or oil *from* engines.

The latter point gains force in considering the lexicalizations that have in BrE clustered round *lighter* 'that which lights things' (itself a straightforward *-er* agential noun, based on the verb *to light*). On the one hand, we have *fire-lighter* 'something that helps one to light fires'; on the other hand, *petrol-lighter*, 'something that helps one to light (tobacco) by means of petrol'. But two independent lexicalizations give us *gas-lighter*: the one like *fire-lighter*, 'something that helps one to light the gas'; the other like *petrol-lighter*, 'something that helps one to light (tobacco) by means of gas'.

The idiosyncrasy of lexicalization needs to be borne in mind when one is considering, for example, conversion. When beside the noun *paper* there comes into use a verb *paper*, this is sometimes loosely referred to as the conversion of the noun into a verb. But this is not so. What normally happens (as in this instance) is the lexicalization of an action that is related to *one specific sense* of the noun, the sense concerned being selected on purely pragmatic grounds. Consider four of the senses of *paper* as a noun:

material in thin sheets made from wood or cloth	[1]
a newspaper	[2]
a piece of writing for specialists	[3]
wallpaper	[4]

The transitive verb 'formed' from this noun by conversion relates only to [4]:

John has papered the bedroom.

There would be nothing inherently absurd in derivatives from other senses, such as [2]:

(*)The Hearst organization has papered most of the mid-West.
['has supplied most of the mid-West with its papers']

or [3]:

(*)I'm papering part of my research in a specialist journal.
['publishing a paper on part of my research']

The position is simply that the social need for derivatives from the other senses seems not to have been felt and in consequence no lexicalization of the actions concerned has taken place.

By contrast, beside the noun *paint* ['liquid colouring matter'], two verb senses have been separately lexicalized:

Frank paints other people's windows but ignores his own.

['decorates with paint']   [5]

Frank paints other people's children but ignores his own.

['makes pictures with paint']   [6]

To each of these lexicalized actions the agential noun *painter* could equally relate:

Frank is a painter.

This example illustrates further the idiosyncratic nature of the lexicon. *A painter* could be predicated of Frank in [6] even if his normal occupation was as a car salesman and he painted only in his spare time, as a hobby. It could not be predicated of Frank in [5] unless house-painting was his regular paid work. We must contrast with these institutionalized uses of *painter* the affixation of agential *-er* in the environment 'The X-er of Y' which is simply a regular nominalization of '(NP) X-ed Y': in other words, a grammatical correspondence with no necessary lexicalization. Compare:

Augustus John was a painter of portraits. He was a well-known London *painter*.

Augustus John was a flouter of conventions. He was a well-known London ** flouter*.

As we have seen, conversion shows lexicalization having specific sense-orientation, in that only a particular sense of a word may be converted to another word class. But lexicalization also shows considerable item-orientation. Thus a conversion will apply to a specific formal item and not to any otherwise relevant synonym:

He offered her a $\left\{ \begin{array}{l} cup \\ mug \end{array} \right\}$ of coffee.

$\left. \begin{array}{l} \text{He } cupped \\ \text{(*)He } mugged \end{array} \right\}$ his hands and drank from the stream.

Compare also:

He has a $\left\{ \begin{array}{l} carpet \\ rug \end{array} \right\}$ in his bedroom.

He has $\left\{ \begin{array}{l} carpeted \\ \text{(*)}rugged \end{array} \right\}$ his bedroom.

It is noteworthy that, in both these examples, it is the lexical item of more general meaning that has lent itself to conversion.

Again, while the verb *burst* can be replaced by *bust* <nonstandard in BrE>, the converse is not true where *bust* is a (slang or very informal) lexicalization corresponding broadly to 'bankrupt':

Don't keep *bursting* in!

Don't keep *busting* in! <nonstandard>

The firm has gone *bust*. <slang>

*The firm has gone *burst*.

The point is further made by another slang lexicalization where *bust* refers to sudden intervention (especially by the police) and where the detachment from *burst* is additionally marked by regularization of the morphology:

The police $\left\{ \begin{array}{l} burst \\ *bursted \end{array} \right\}$ into the room.

The police *busted* him for possessing drugs. <slang>

Similarly, the verb *break* has two -*ed* participles, *broken*, and a largely nonstandard *broke*. But the latter is widely used adjectivally in the sense 'bankrupt', and though informal it is in educated use, even heard occasionally in broadcast news.

A comparable phenomenon of where two words are produced from one original is noticeable with 'back-formations'. Despite the well-established correspondence between the verb *destroy* and the noun *destruction*, the lexicalization of the concept *self-destruction* has led to the emergence of a new corresponding verb, as in:

The party is determined not to *self-destruct* on this issue.

Note that shortenings characteristically express in a specific form specific lexicalizations. Thus *lib* and *co-op* are not shortenings of *liberation* and *co-operative* respectively, as we see from

He advocated the **lib* of the prisoners.
She was very **co-op* and helpful.

but of (*women's/gay*) *liberation movement* and *co-operative* (*business organization*) respectively. Similarly, *exam* is a clipping of *examination* only in the sense of 'an (academic) test'.

Follow-up activities
New words are continually being coined or the use of old words extended, as new issues become central in current affairs, or as teenagers develop new terms of approval (*cool, boss*) or disparagement (*anorak, nerd*), or as marketing departments dream up new qualities for the products they are selling. Find some recent newcomers to the vocabulary of English and determine what has been the occasion of their creation and the possible process of lexicalisation that they have gone through. What process of thinking, for example, made a *refugee* into an *asylum seeker*?

Quirk *et al.* suggest that the word formation process of 'conversion' (see B3) is unpredictable in respect of which meaning of a word is converted to the new word class. Find some other examples like Quirk *et al.*'s paper, and determine which of the original meanings have undergone conversion, e.g. in the transfer of *book* or *partner* from the noun to the verb class.

Can you think of any other examples like Quirk *et al.*'s *carpet* to *carpeted*, but not *rug* to **rugged*, where a pair of semantically similar words lexicalise differently? For example, *rob* gives the noun *robbery*, but *steal* has no similar parallel; however, we have *stolen goods*, but not **robbed goods*.

VALENCY THEORY

In Unit A4, we identified a number of possible slots in the structure of sentences (Subject, Verb, Object, Complement, Adverbial), and we elaborated on the nature of those slots and the elements that may fill them in B4 and in the C4 subunits. We suggested in A4 that which slots may occur in any given sentence depended on the main verb in the Verb slot, and we noted that this insight derived from 'Valency Grammar'.

The reading in this unit is taken from an article by Thomas Herbst, entitled 'Designing an English Valency Dictionary: combining linguistic theory and user-friendliness', and published in *The Perfect Learner's Dictionary (?)*, edited by Thomas Herbst and Kerstin Popp (Max Niemeyer, 1999). The selected section of the article gives an outline of valency theory, which, as Herbst notes, has become the dominant approach to 'complementation' in German linguistics. By 'complementation', Herbst means the elements that accompany any given verb in the structure of a sentence; the term 'complement' encompasses any obligatory element, including what we have called Subjects, Objects, Complements, and some Adverbials.

Valency theory is an approach based on the operation of individual words, especially verbs, rather than classes or subclasses of words. It is therefore compatible with a 'lexical' approach to grammar, such as in the reading in D5, and as has been espoused in large part in this book.

Valency theory

T. Herbst (reprinted from "Designing an English Valency Dictionary: combining linguistic theory and user-friendliness", in *The Perfect Learner's Dictionary (?)*: T. Herbst and K. Popp (eds) (1999), Max Niemeyer Verlay, pp. 229–53)

The application of valency theory to English

The theoretical background to the dictionary is provided by valency theory – a theory that – as a result of a rather remarkable combination of work in foreign language lexicography and theoretical linguistics – has become the most established model of complementation in Germany over the last thirty years or so.[2] Nevertheless, it has to be said that the theory has so far been applied to English on a rather modest scale – for instance in the work of Emons (1974), Allerton (1982) and Matthews (1981).[3] This can in no way be compared with the attention that Anglo-American theories have received in Germany, of course, but this may say more about linguistic dominance than the value of the theory.

Valency theory and traditional approaches to sentence analysis

Types of complement

Valency theory, which would not claim to have the same theoretical scope as, for instance, transformational grammar, and which is relatively agnostic as to the wider theoretical framework in which it is to be used, presents in a number of important ways an attractive alternative to the more established ways of dealing with

[2]   Cf. Helbig (1992) or Herbst/Heath/Dederding (1980).
[3]   Cf. also Buysschaerts (1982), Herbst (1983).

complementation. Since it devotes a considerable amount of attention to the distinction between elements in a sentence that are specific to a particular word and those that are not, the theory is particularly attractive to lexicography.

On the other hand, it would be wrong to create the impression that the valency approach to complementation is radically different from, say, the approach taken in the *Comprehensive Grammar of the English Language* (1985) or what, from a valency point of view, can be seen as a superior version of that approach, the model employed by Aarts and Aarts in *English Syntactic Structures* (1982/1988). On the contrary, they share some very important basic assumptions:

The distinction that is crucial to valency theory is that between complements – or *actants* in Tesnière's (1959) terminology – and adjuncts or peripheral elements, as Matthews (1981) calls them, Tesnière's *circonstants*. It is the complements that are part of the valency of a verb. Thus in a sentence such as

[1A] *Following Ben Nicholson's first visit* to St. Ives, <u>he</u> painted <u>a number of</u> <u>landscapes and paintings of Porthmeor beach.</u>[4]

he and *a number of landscapes and paintings of Porthmeor beach* are classified as complements of the verb *paint*, which thus has a valency of 2, whereas *following Ben Nicholson's first visit to St. Ives* is a freely addible adjunct, which does not form part of the valency of the verb.

The distinction between complements and adjuncts is reflected in the classifications of CGEL or Aarts and Aarts in that the subordinate clause in [1A] would be classified as an optional adverbial in CGEL, which is not part of the complementation pattern. Terminologically, Aarts and Aarts come closer to the valency approach in that they do not, like CGEL, distinguish between obligatory adverbials and optional adverbials but between adverbials and complements – where the definition of adverbial corresponds to that of adjunct or peripheral element in valency theory and – with one exception – that of complement to that of complement in valency theory.

Table D4.1

	Following Ben Nicholson's first visit to St. Ives	<u>he</u>	**painted**	<u>a number of landscapes and paintings of Porthmeor beach.</u>
valency theory	adjunct	complement		complement
CGEL	optional adverbial	subject		direct object
Aarts/Aarts	adverbial	subject		complement: direct object

[4] The examples used in this section are mostly taken from the following works: Tom Cross (1994): The Shining Sands. Artists in Newlyn and St Ives, 1880–1930. – Tiverton/Cambridge: Westcountry Books/The Lutterworth Press; Tom Cross (1995): Painting the Warmth of the Sun. St Ives Artists, 1939–1975. – Tiverton/Cambridge: Westcountry Books/The Lutterworth Press; Mel Gooding (1994): Patrick Heron. – London: Phaidon Press.

Secondly, although valency theory over the years has developed a large number of criteria and syntactic tests to establish the distinction between complements and adjuncts, the overall success of such attempts seems doubtful. In practice there is perhaps little difference with respect to the actual patterns identified between a valency and, say, the CGEL approach to complementation.

Degrees of optionality

One important difference between a valency approach and the treatment of complementation in CGEL concerns the identification of the elements that carry valency or complementation. This is related to the distinction that is made in valency theory with respect to what I would like to call the degree of optionality of complements, which, in various modifications, plays a part in all valency accounts. Based on a classification made by Allerton (1982), it seems appropriate to distinguish between three types of complements:

Firstly, obligatory complements, i.e. complements which cannot be deleted if a word, or a particular sense of a word, are to be used in an acceptable sentence, such as *Newlyn* and *at the western end of Mount's Bay* in

[2] <u>Newlyn</u> lies <u>at the western end of Mount's bay</u>.

Secondly, optional complements, which need not be realised if the verb is to be used in an acceptable sentence:

[3A] In November 1958 he resigned as London correspondent to the magazine, privately determined never again to write <u>criticism</u>.
[3B] Heron had made it a condition [. . .] that he would write only when he felt his primary commitment, to painting, was satisfied.

Thus *criticism* is an optional complement as is *a number of landscapes and paintings of Porthmeor beach* in [1A], since its presence is not essential for the verb *paint* to be used in an acceptable sentence:

[1B] He was positively encouraging to Patrick, allowing him to paint in the afternoons.

Whereas [1B] and [3B] are perfectly self-sufficient sentences, in other instances the use of a word without one of its complements is subject to special conditions, as Allerton (1975) has pointed out. Comparing sentences such as

[4A] <u>Heron</u> was never to forget <u>the impressions of the light and landscapes of West Penwith</u>.
[4B] <u>We</u> must not forget <u>that the artist is also an ordinary man</u>.
[4C] How could I possibly forget?
or
[5A] Would <u>Heron</u> try <u>to discover within himself a gift for non-figurative painting</u>?
[5B] <u>He</u> ought to try.

[4C] and [5B] only seem acceptable in contexts where it is clear what the referent of the complement that is not realised syntactically is. Such complements thus form a third type, which can be termed contextually optional complements.[5]

---

[5]   For a discussion of these complement classes see Herbst/Roe (1996).

This way of looking at these syntactic phenomena is different from the CGEL account in two ways: Firstly, in valency theory the various occurrences of *paint*, *write*, *forget* and *try* are seen as two different uses of the same verb, whereas according to CGEL, where no distinction between obligatory and optional complements is made, they each represent two different verbs which are related by a word formation process, as is pointed out under the heading of 'change of secondary word class' in Appendix I (Herbst/Klotz 1998). Valency theory in general would take the lexical unit in the sense described by Cruse (1986) as the basis of a valency description.

Prepositional complements

The second area where valency and the CGEL or Aarts/Aarts approach differ with respect to the units they identify as carrying valency is of even more importance to lexicography. It is exemplified by sentences such as

[6] <u>She</u> drew <u>on these memories</u> in her sculpture.
[7] <u>No less than forty-four artists</u> were <u>showing their work to the public</u>.

Here, CGEL would analyse *draw on* and *show to* as complex lexical items termed prepositional verbs, whereas valency theory identifies a complement type prepositional complement, by which is meant a prepositional phrase that has complement status. As indicated in CGEL, there are indeed arguments for both analyses.[6] On balance, we tend to think it highly preferable to treat the occurrences of *write* with a noun phrase in [3C], with a prepositional phrase with *about* in [3D], *of* in [3E], *to* in [3F] and a *that*-clause in [3G] as instances of the same lexical unit *write*.

[3C] It was in *Arts* in March 1956 that <u>Heron</u> wrote <u>the celebrated article that recorded the first collective showing in London of the post-war New York School</u>.
[3D] Heron continued to write <u>about Braque</u>.
[3E] <u>He</u> could write <u>of Braque</u> now with a certain detachement.
[3F] <u>Zennor, he</u> wrote <u>to Middleton Murry and Katherine Mansfield</u> in the spring of 1916, '<u>is a most beautiful place: a tiny granite village</u>'.
[3G] <u>He</u> wrote <u>that he had found himself</u> 'compelled to refrain from jettisoning the figurative function entirely'.

This can, of course, only be done if a complement type prepositional complement is recognised and in fact it was the 'emancipation' of prepositional phrases to the same complement status as that of casemarked noun phrases that played a very important role in the early phases of German valency grammar.

Lexicographically, this has important repercussions. It is difficult to see why both COBUILD2 and LDOCE3 should deal with *decide on* in a sub-entry of *decide* thus splitting it off from *decide to do* and *decide that*. It is even more difficult to see the rationale behind depriving *decide against* and *decide in favour of* of that status.[7]

---

[6] Cf. Herbst/Klotz (1998).
[7] Busse (1998) reveals quite a number of inconsistencies of this kind in the new learners' dictionaries.

COBUILD2

decide /dɪsaɪd/ **decides, deciding, decided**   ♦♦♦♦♦   [S] 1
1 If you **decide** to do something, you choose to do   VERB   [W] 1
it, usually after you have thought carefully about the   =make up one's
other possibilities. *She decided to do a secretar-*   mind
ial course . . . He has decided that he doesn't want to   V to-inf
embarrass the movement and will therefore step   V that
down . . . The house needed totally rebuilding, so we   V against/in
decided against buying it . . . Its outcome will decide   V wh
whether Russia's economy can be reformed at all . . .   V
Think about it very carefully before you decide.
2 If a person or group of people **decides** some-   VERB
thing, they choose what something should be like
or how a particular problem should be solved. *She*   V n
was still young, he said, and that would be taken
into account when deciding her sentence . . . This is
an issue that should be decided by local and metro-
politan government.
3 If an event or fact **decides** something, it makes it   VERB
certain that a particular choice will be made or that there   =settle
will be a particular result. *The goal that decided the*   V n
match came just before the interval . . . The results will   V wh
decide if he will win a place at a good university . . .   V-ing
Luck is certainly not the only deciding factor, but it does
play an exceptionally large role.
4 If you **decide** that something is true, you form   VERB
that opinion about it after considering the facts. *He*   V that
decided Franklin must be suffering from a bad   V wh
cold . . . For a long time I couldn't decide whether the
original settlers were insane or just stupid.
5 If something **decides** you to do something, it is   VERB
the reason that causes you to choose to do it. *The*   V n to-inf
banning of his English play decided him to write   V n
something about censorship . . . What decided him   Also V n that,
was a cynical question: 'If I fail, I'll be no worse off   favour of n/-ing
than I am now, will I?'
decide on. If you **decide on** something or decide   PHRASAL VERB
upon something, you choose it from two or more   =settle for
possibilities. *After leaving university, Therese de-*   V P n
cided on a career in publishing.

LDOCE3

decide /dɪˈsaɪd/ v   **1** [I,T] to make a choice or judgment
about something, especially after a period of not knowing
what to do or in a way that ends disagreement: **decide to
do sth** *Tina's decided to go to Prague for her holidays.* |
decide that *It was eventually decided that four London
hospitals should be closed.* | **decide who/what/how
etc** *I can't decide what to do.* | **decide whether/if**
*Women now have greater freedom to decide whether or not
to get married.* | [**+ between**] *I'm trying to decide between
the green and the blue for the bathroom.* | **decide sth** *I'm
eighteen now – I have a right to decide my own future.* |
decide for yourself (=make your own choice or judgment, without asking anyone else to do it for you) *You must
decide for yourself whether to leave college.* – see also
DECISION (1)   **2** [T] to be the reason for someone making
a particular judgment or choice: **decide sb to do sth**
What was it that finally decided you to give up your job?
| **deciding factor** (=a very strong reason that forces you
to make a particular decision) *Money should not be the
deciding factor over who runs a TV station.*   **3** [T] If an
event, action etc decides something, it influences events
so that one particular result will happen: *A goal in the last
minute decided the match.* | **the deciding vote** (=the per-
son who has the deciding vote makes the final decision,
because all the other votes are equally divided)
4 decide in favour of/decide against a) to choose or
not choose someone or something: *After long discussion
they decided in favour of the younger candidate.*   **b)** if a
judge or JURY (1) decides in favour of someone or against
someone, they say in court that someone is guilty or not
guilty: *The jury decided in favour of the plaintiff.*

   decide on sth phr v [T] to choose one thing from many
possible choices: *Have you decided on a date for your
wedding?*

Summing up, it can be said that establishing prepositional complements in this sense
and treating patterns where optional complements are realised syntactically as instances
of the same lexical units as those where they are not results in a considerably
smaller number of lexical units identified.

The status of the subject

A third major difference between the valency approach and the complementation
approach is described in CGEL note 16.18 as 'valency [. . .] includes the subject of the clause, which is excluded (unless extraposed) from complementation'
and this is the one exception where the definition of the term complement by
Aarts and Aarts (1982/1988) does not coincide with ours.

   Subjects present a highly intricate theoretical issue. Valency grammarians usually classify the subject as an obligatory complement on the grounds that it cannot be deleted. This is quite obviously not true if one considers passive sentences
such as

[1C] They are painted in a variety of methods.

Of course, there still is a subject but it is not realised by the same complement
as the subject in [1A] or [1B].

This discrepancy can be resolved by distinguishing between structural neces-sity and valency necessity. The fact that active declarative main clauses need a sub-ject is part of structural necessity; whether a complement is obligatory or optional can only be resolved by considering active and passive uses of that verb. In other words, I would advocate a kind of intermediate position between canonical valency theory and the traditional subject-predicate-distinction in that I would consider the latter to be relevant at the level of structure but not of valency.

Table D4.2

	Following Ben Nicholson's first visit to St. Ives	he	**painted**	a number of landscapes and paintings of Porthmeor beach.
STRUCTURE	ADJUNCT	SUBJECT	PREDICATE	
VALENCY	ADJUNCT	OPTIONAL COMPLEMENT	PREDICATOR	OPTIONAL COMPLEMENT

Complements are to be seen as part of the lexical valency structure of a verb. Since their degree of optionality depends on whether they can function as subject, the formal specification of a complement class must in my view entail informa-tion on whether the complement can occur as the subject of an active clause, as the subject of a passive clause, or whether it cannot occur as a subject at all.

A very obvious justification for including subjects in an account of comple-mentation is, of course, that they can take different forms and that this is just as much dependent on the individual verb as the different forms elements such as objects can take. However, it has to be emphasized that this is a rather theoretical state-ment to make.

Follow-up activities

Take a number of verbs and, using example sentences (perhaps from dictionaries) con-struct a similar comparative table to Herbst's, to show the analysis under valency the-ory and that suggested in A4.

Valency information encompasses both which slots are possible, obligatory or optional, and what elements may fill them. Such information is of great importance to the learner of English as a second or foreign language, and it has been given con-siderable attention in learners' dictionaries. Compare the entries for a number of verbs in a native-speaker dictionary (e.g. *Collins English Dictionary, Concise Oxford Diction-ary*) and a learner's dictionary (e.g. *Collins COBUILD English Dictionary, Longman Dictionary of Contemporary English, Oxford Advanced Learner's Dictionary*). How do they deal with the 'valency' of verbs? Which one deals with it more adequately? The learner's dictionary should come out on top!

It is not only verbs that can be considered from the valency perspective. Some adjectives especially (e.g. *afraid, afraid of . . .*, *afraid that . . .*), but also a few nouns, particularly those derived from verbs (*assurance about . . .*, *assurance that . . .*), can also be said to take complements. You may like to investigate the valencies of members of these word classes further. A learner's dictionary would be a good source of reference.

D5   **PATTERN AND MEANING**

In A5, we identified the basic 'sentence patterns' of English, based on the obligatorily occurring syntactic slots (discussed in A4). The units at B5 and C5 explore the general patterning of phrases. The notion of 'pattern' is important to our conception of grammar, and especially when we consider the syntactic operation of individual words. This lexical approach to grammatical patterning is reflected in the reading in this unit, which is taken from *Pattern Grammar: A Corpus-Driven Approach to the Lexical Grammar of English*, by Susan Hunston and Gill Francis (John Benjamins, 2000). The extract comes from the final 'Summing up' chapter; it first of all defines what is meant by 'pattern', and then discusses the relationship between grammatical patterning and meaning.

For Hunston and Francis a pattern is not necessarily a sentence pattern, or even a phrase pattern, but a regularly occurring sequence of elements based on a verb, noun or adjective. It encompasses the 'complementation' of valency grammar (D4), but goes beyond it. The evidence for patterning comes from the searching of extensive computer corpora, in this case the *Bank of English*, with its 250 + million words of text. The patterns are given in detail in *Collins COBUILD Grammar Patterns* (1996, 1998).

D5.1   **Patterns and phraseologies**

S. Hunston and G. Francis (reprinted from *Pattern Grammar: A Corpus-Driven Approach to the Lexical Grammar of English* (2000), John Benjamins)

Put very generally, a pattern is a description of the behaviour of a lexical item, or one of the behaviours of that item, as evidenced in a record of large amounts of language use. This evidence is most readily obtained from a large, electronically-stored corpus. The term 'pattern' is sometimes used to describe everything about the phraseology of a word. For example, the pattern of *shred* in

(1)   *there was not a shred of evidence to support such remarks*

might be described as:

negative + a + *shred* + *of* + noun = abstract = assessment of certainty

This captures the fact that the phrase *a shred of* is typically followed by an abstract noun such as *evidence* or *truth*, which assesses certainty or truth, and that it typically occurs in a broadly negative clause (phrases such as *a shred of meat*, where the meaning is concrete rather than abstract, are found, but much less frequently). The pattern may be illustrated by a single example, but it can be observed as a pattern only when a large number of instances of *shred of* are seen together.

In this book, however, following the Collins COBUILD Grammar Patterns series (Francis *et al.* 1996; 1998), we use 'pattern' to describe a more generalised statement of behaviour. The pattern of *shred* as illustrated above is expressed as *a* **N** *of* **n**. That is, the noun *shred* follows the determiner *a* and is followed by a prepositional phrase beginning with *of*. The facts about the negative clause, and the nature of the noun in the prepositional phrase may be given separately, but they do not occur as part of the pattern statement.

Our use of 'pattern' has both advantages and disadvantages. As a description of the behaviour of an individual word (or sense of a word) it is clearly incomplete, and must be supplemented by other information (as is done, for example, in the definitions of the Collins COBUILD English Dictionary). On the other hand, it allows us to group together words which share pattern features, but which may differ in other respects in their phraseologies. For example, let us take the pattern **N** *as to* **wh**, where a noun is followed by *as to* and a clause beginning with a wh-word. A number of nouns have this pattern, including:

a.   *debate, discussion, guess, question, speculation*
b.   *confusion, doubt, uncertainty*
c.   *answer, clue, explanation, evidence, indication*
d.   *suggestion, advice*
e.   *idea, opinion*

There is, however, a considerable amount of further information that can be given about each of these nouns. For example:

a. *answer* in this pattern is often used with a broad negative, as in *no one has come up with a definitive answer . . . nor was there any easy answer . . . there's no right or wrong answer . . . there are no cut and dried answers . . . there seem to be more questions than answers.* The wh-word following *as to* is often *why*, though a range of other words is also found.

b. *debate* in this pattern is often modified by an adjective or determiner indicating a large quantity, as in *much debate . . . a lot of debate . . . growing debate . . . considerable debate . . . full and fierce debate.* The wh-word following *as to* is often *whether*; *why* is not often found here.

c. *advice* in this pattern often follows a verb indicating having or obtaining, as in *have some advice . . . seek professional advice . . . I wanted your advice . . . give him some advice . . . obtaining legal advice.* A range of wh-words are found after *as to*, though rarely *why*.

In other words, each of these nouns has its own specific phraseology, but a useful generalisation can be made about the pattern that they share: **N** *as to* **wh**.

The patterns that we discuss in this book and in Francis *et al.* (1996; 1998) are for the most part complementation patterns. That is, they describe what follows the verb, noun or adjective under discussion. There are some exceptions, notably the patterns with *it* and *there*, but complementation is the norm. For verbs, this is an adequate description. Little additional information needs to be given, except that in some cases the verb is reciprocal and has a plural Subject, and in some cases the verb group is typically negative or includes a modal. In the pattern **V that**, for example, one sense of *agree* has a plural Subject, indicating reciprocity:

(2)   *Scientists agree that these lumps of matter must originate in the asteroid belt*

mind is used in the negative:

(3)   *She tried not to mind that he was always late*

and *credit* is used with *cannot*

(4)   *I can't credit that he wouldn't tell me.*

In the case of nouns, however, the pattern may involve what comes before the noun rather than what follows it, and details of modification in the noun group itself may be part of the pattern. This is particularly true of patterns that begin with a preposition (*at* **N**, *by* **N**, *in* **N** and so on). For example, the pattern *at* **N** (Francis *et al.* 1998: 265–272) consists of the preposition *at* and noun group. That noun group sometimes has no determiner: *at church, at college, at home, at school, at sea, at university, at work* and so on. In some cases, the determiner can be specified: *at the airport, at the cinema, at the scene, at the station, at the super-market; at an angle, at a distance, at a junction; at my elbow, at my heels, at my side.* Other nouns are found in any kind of noun group, that is with any determiner, adjective and so on, following the preposition *at: ball, banquet, barbecue, ceremony, concert, conference, dinner party, festival, funeral, hearing, match, matinee, meeting, news conference, party, press conference, rally, reception, summit, talks, trial* and *wedding* are the nouns from one meaning group that behave in this way. Yet other nouns are always or often followed by particular prepositions: *at cross-purposes with, at log-gerheads with, at odds with, at variance with, at war with; at the bottom of, at the core of, at the heart of, at the root of.* Most complex of all are nouns which always occur in noun groups with pre- or post- modification. For example, *altitude, depth* and *distance* are used in noun groups following *at,* but not by themselves. Examples include: *at an altitude of twenty thousand feet, at a depth greater than that, at a greater distance.*

Where it is possible to reflect these details, we do so. Our coding, like any coding, is a compromise between the general and the specific, an attempt to describe the trees while keeping the forest in mind. The compromise for nouns appears to demand something that is closer to phraseology than that for verbs does.

Pattern and meaning

This book, and the research on which it is based (Francis *et al.* 1996; 1998), is in a sense an extended demonstration of Sinclair's assertion that '[t]here is ulti-mately no distinction between form and meaning' (1991: 7 and *passim*). We have argued that sense and syntax are associated, while raising the question of what exactly that association means. In this section, we will discuss two further issues: the lack of one-to-one correspondence between form and meaning, and the ques-tion of dictionary senses of words.

The argument that sense and syntax, or meaning and pattern, are associated, is based on two pieces of evidence. Firstly, when a word has more than one meaning, the meanings tend to be distinguished by having different patterns. For example, the verb *reflect* has three main meanings:

a. one has to do with light and surfaces, and is exemplified by

   (15) *The sun reflected off the snow-covered mountains* and
   (16) *The glass appears to reflect light naturally*;

b. another has to do with mirrors, and is exemplified by

   (17) *His image seemed to be reflected many times in the mirror*;

c. the third has to do with thinking, and is exemplified by

   (18) *We should all give ourselves time to reflect*
   (19) *I reflected on the child's future*
   (20) *Things were very much changed since before the war, he reflected.*

Examples are from the Collins COBUILD English Dictionary (1995: 1387).

   Each of these meanings typically occurs in a particular phraseology, that is, collocating with different types of noun or pronoun (*the sun, the glass*; *the mirrors*; *we, I, he*) and with a different complementation pattern: **V prep, V n;** *be* **V-ed**; **V, V** *on* **n, V** that. Although this alignment between meaning and pattern is particularly neat, we must point out that these patterns indicate only the most typical uses of the verb. It might well be possible to invent utterances which do not conform to the patterns given above and yet which are not unacceptable English, such as *The mirror was so scratched it would no longer reflect.* Such invented (or genuine) examples do not invalidate the generality, but they remind us that the given patterns indicate typical usage and tell us when a usage is unusual; they do not set unbreakable parameters.

   The second piece of evidence for the association of pattern and meaning is that words with the same pattern share aspects of meaning. This has been exemplified at length in Chapter 4. The argument will not be repeated here, but again we will draw attention to the limitations of this statement. A list of words that have the same pattern will be divisible in several ways, and different researchers would end up with different sets of groupings. The groupings will in most cases be of different sizes, including sometimes very small groups, and there may well be a 'ragbag' of words which do not fit into any other meaning group. We not believe that this indeterminacy in any way invalidates the assertion that words with the same pattern fall into groups based on meaning, but it does mean that the statement is not one that is provable in any objective way.

   From the above we can see that a description of the pattern/meaning association in English is not rule-governed in the sense that subject-verb agreement is rule-governed. It is a grammatical statement of a very different kind.

   We now turn to the first of the two issues we mentioned above: the lack of one-to-one correspondence between pattern and meaning. It is true that in many cases the meanings of polysemous words are distinguished by pattern, as in the example of *reflect* above. It is also true that a very few senses of words are identified by occurring in one pattern only. When the verb *eat*, for example, is used with an adverb such as *well* or *healthily* (in the pattern **V adv**), it has the meaning of 'habitually eat food that is good for you'. It is not possible to make this meaning of *eat* without using this pattern, or to use this pattern without making this meaning. (It is possible to use *eat* with an adverb but with a different sense, as in *She ate quickly*. In this case the occurrence of an adverb is not part of the pattern of the verb, because it is not typically associated with that sense of the verb. The pattern of *She ate quickly* is **V**, not **V adv**.) Such a one-to-one correspondence is rare, however. For example, the verb *dock* has two very different senses: it can refer to a ship coming into a dock, or to money or points being deducted. In the first sense, the verb has two complementation patterns: **V** and **V n** (the verb is ergative). Examples of these are:

> (21) *The vessel docked at Liverpool in April 1811* and
> (22) *Russian commanders docked a huge aircraft carrier in a Russian port.*

In the second sense, the verb also has two patterns: **V n** and **V n n**, as in

> (23) *He threatens to dock her fee* and
> (24) *She docked him two points for his mistake*

(Examples are from Collins COBUILD English Dictionary 1995: 488). The pattern **V** is exclusive to the first sense; thus,

> (25) *The vessel docked*

is correct, but

> (26) *Her boss docked*

is not. It appears that **V n n** is similarly exclusive to the second sense, so that

> (27) *She docked him two points*

is correct but

> (28) *He docked me my boat*

is not. However, because **V n n** has a productive use indicating that someone does something for someone (Francis *et al.* 1996: 274), *He docked me my boat*, while unlikely, is not absolutely impossible. The remaining pattern, **V n**, does not in itself distinguish between the senses (although the senses are, of course, distinguished by their collocations): both

> (29) *He docked the ship* and
> (30) *He docked the money*

are equally acceptable. In pattern terms, then, the overall behaviour of the two senses is different, but the behaviours do overlap.

Discussion of the relationship between meaning and pattern, such as that above, tends to rely on the divisions between senses that are made in dictionaries. The descriptions of *reflect* and *dock* above are based, more or less, on the divisions between senses that are made in the Collins COBUILD English Dictionary (1995).

A statement such as 'If a word has several senses, each sense has a different set of patterns' suggests that the identification of the sense is done separately from, and prior to, the identification of their patterns. And, indeed, this is the case when lexicographers compile dictionaries: the decision as to how many senses a word has, and where to draw the line between senses, is based on all the evidence of word usage, of which patterning is a part but not the whole. The lexicographer may, however, distinguish senses in a different way from someone coming to the evidence from a different perspective. Consider, for example, the verb *recover*. The Collins cobuild English Dictionary (1995: 1381) distinguishes six senses, shown here with their associated patterns:

1. When you recover from an illness or an injury, you become well again: **V from n/-ing, V**;
2. If you recover from an unhappy or unpleasant experience, you stop being upset by it: **V from n, V**;
3. If something recovers from a period of weakness or difficulty, it improves or gets stronger again: **V from n, V**;
4. If you recover something that has been lost or stolen, you find it or get it back: **V n**;
5. If you recover a mental or physical state, it comes back again. For example, if you recover consciousness, you become conscious again: **V n**;
6. If you recover money that you have spent, invested, or lent to someone, you get the same amount back: **V n**.

Clearly, two other divisions between senses are equally possible. One is made on the grounds of collocation and general meaning and might be expressed thus:

1. 'recover' means to become healthy or conscious after you have been ill, injured, or unconscious: the physical recovery sense (CCED senses 1 and 5);
2. 'recover' means to become happy or strong after a period of unhappiness or weakness: the metaphoric recovery sense (CCED senses 2 and 3);
3. 'recover' means to get back money or property that was lost, stolen, invested or lent: the re-obtaining sense (CCED senses 4 and 6).

The other is made on the grounds of pattern alone:

1. to recover (**V**) means to change from a poor state to a better state, either in terms of health, happiness, or weakness (CCED senses 1–3);
2. to recover from something (**V from n**) means to leave a poor state, either in terms of health, happiness, or weakness (CCED senses 1–3);
3. to recover something (**V n**) means to get it back, whether it is something physical such as money, or something abstract, such as health or consciousness (CCED senses 4–6).

Arguably, the CCED distinctions are the ones that are most useful to the learner, but if we ask the question 'Are the senses of *recover* distinguished by their patterns?', the answer must be 'It depends how you identify the senses'. As a hypothesis, then, it is not truly testable. A better question might be: 'If you distinguish between uses of the word *recover* based on its patterns alone, do the resulting categories make sense in terms of meaning?' In other words, is the third set of distinctions above at least as reasonable as the other two? This discussion is relevant to the practical problem of devising computer programmes that will distinguish between the senses of a word automatically. Such programmes tend to be written assuming the validity of dictionary sense-distinctions, and various parameters such as collocations or pattern are tested to see to what extent they fit the distinctions. It is worth pointing out, however, that a reverse procedure might be equally valid: that is, instances of the same word might be grouped according to pattern alone, with the sense distinctions following from that grouping. The idea of a dictionary in which, under each headword, there is a list of patterns and their associated meanings, rather than a list of senses with their associated patterns, remains an intriguing possibility.

Follow-up activities

Patterns can be investigated at a number of levels of detail. For example, the pattern 'a N short of a N' (*a sandwich short of a picnic*) has a number of realisations. More generally, 'cannot V to v' has a limited number of verbs in the V position – do they have the same kind of meaning? More generally still, 'our N that' will identify mostly nouns derived from verbs (*assumption, contention*) – again, with a similar range of meaning.

You can think of your own patterns to investigate. As Hunston and Francis do, you can mine a dictionary that has a lot of examples, in particular a learner's dictionary such as *Collins COBUILD Dictionary* or the *Longman Dictionary of Contemporary English*. Alternatively, if you have access to a computer corpus by means of a concordancing program or online, you can retrieve your own data. (The *Bank of English* allows online access for payment of a modest subscription; the *British National Corpus* can be accessed on line without cost, but the number of 'hits' given in the results is limited to 50.)

Hunston and Francis suggest, as did Allerton in the reading in D2, that there is a relationship, though not necessarily a straightforward one, between patterning and meaning. Again, this operates at a number of levels. In the pattern 'n spend N', the N position is normally a noun denoting either 'time' or 'money' – can you make the pattern more specific by extending it, e.g. with 'on n' or 'V-ing'? More generally, do all the adjectives in the pattern 'Adj-ed about n' all have a meaning of 'emotional state', e.g. *concerned, relieved, worried*?

D6 THE CLAUSE COMPLEX

In Unit A6, we distinguished between 'sentence' and 'clause', defining 'clause' as an element of 'sentence'. In B6, a distinction was made between 'main', or 'matrix', and 'subordinate', or 'embedded', clauses. The C6 units discussed and illustrated the major types of subordinate clause in English and noted their main functions. The reading in this unit continues the theme of clause relations and functions.

The major exponent in recent years of a functional approach to the description of grammar within the British linguistic community has been Michael Halliday. This reading is taken from his textbook, *An Introduction to Functional Grammar* (Edward Arnold 1985), from Chapter 7, 'Above the clause: the clause complex', in which he examines the 'functional-semantic' relations that clauses contract with each other when they combine into complex sentences.

Halliday's terminology is slightly different from that used in this book: his term 'clause complex', for example, is equivalent to our 'sentence'; Halliday reserves the term 'sentence' for the phenomenon in writing, using 'clause complex' for the structural sentence. He also uses the terms 'primary' and 'secondary' (clauses) as equivalent to our 'main' and 'subordinate', respectively.

The extract is from the beginning of Halliday's chapter, in which he focuses on the differences between 'parataxis' (co-ordination) and 'hypotaxis' (subordination). He outlines a scheme of basic types of clause complex (sentence) in terms of the relationships between the clauses that make them up.

Above the clause: the clause complex

D6.1

M.A.K. Halliday (reprinted from *An Introduction to Functional Grammar* (1985) Edward Arnold, Chap. 7)

'Clause complex' and 'sentence'

We said that a group – verbal group, adverbial group, nominal group – could be interpreted as a word COMPLEX: that is to say, a Head word together with other words that modify it. This is why the term GROUP came to be used. It meant 'group of words', or 'word group'; and it suggests how the group no doubt evolved, by expansion outwards from the word.*

However, because of the very diverse ways in which phenomena can be sub-categorized, groups developed their own multivariate constituent structures, with functional configurations such as the Deictic + Numerative + Epithet + Classifier + Thing of the nominal group in English. Treating the group simply as a 'word complex' does not account for all these various aspects of its meaning. It is for this reason that we recognize the group as a distinct rank in the grammar.

In the same way, a sentence can be interpreted as a CLAUSE COMPLEX: a Head clause together with other clauses that modify it. There is the same kind of relationship between sentence and clause as there is between group and word: the sentence has evolved by expansion outwards from the clause. So when we represent sentences in the grammar, the same question arises: does the notion of 'clause complex' allow us to account for all aspects of the meaning of the sentence? Or should a sentence also be interpreted as a multivariate constituent structure, with its own range of functional configurations?

---

* It is important to maintain the terminological distinction between GROUP and PHRASE, which is lost if a nominal group is referred to as a 'noun phrase'. Although group and phrase are both of intermediate rank as constituents, they have arrived there from different ends: a group is a bloated word, whereas a phrase is a shrunken clause.

The picture here is somewhat different. We certainly cannot account for all of sentence structure simply in terms of Head + Modifier; there are numerous kinds of modifying, and also other similar relationships. At the same time there is nothing like the structure of the nominal group referred to above, where the elements are (i) distinct in function, (ii) realized by distinct classes, and (iii) more or less fixed in sequence. A configuration of such a kind has to be represented as a multivariate structure. In a sentence, on the other hand, the tendency is much more for any clause to have the potential for functioning with any value in a multi-clausal complex. In other words, the relation among the clauses in a sentence is generally more like that of a string of nouns such as *railway ticket office staff*, which could be explained as a (univariate) word complex, than that of *these two old railway engines*, which could not.

We shall assume, therefore, that the notion of 'clause complex' enables us to account in full for the functional organization of sentences. A sentence will be defined, in fact, as a clause complex. The clause complex will be the only grammatical unit which we shall recognize above the clause. Hence there will be no need to bring in the term 'sentence' as a distinct grammatical category. We can use it simply to refer to the orthographic unit that is contained between full stops. This will avoid ambiguity: a sentence is a constituent of writing, while a clause complex is a constituent of grammar.

We shall interpret the relations between clauses in terms of the 'logical' component of the linguistic system: the functional–semantic relations that make up the logic of natural language. There are two dimensions in the interpretation. One is the system of interdependency, or 'tactic' system, parataxis and hypotaxis, which is general to all complexes – word, group, phrase and clause alike. The other is the logico-semantic system of expansion and projection, which is specifically an inter-clausal relation – or rather, a relation between processes, usually (but not always) expressed in the grammar as a complex of clauses. These two together will provide the functional framework for describing the clause complex. The unit that is arrived at in this way is that which lies behind the concept of 'sentence' as this has evolved, over the centuries, in the written language. Hence in the analysis of a written text each sentence can be treated as one clause complex, with the 'simple' (one clause) sentence as the limiting case. With a spoken text, we will be able to use the grammar to define and delimit clause complexes, in a way that keeps them as close as possible to the sentences of written English.

Types of relationship between clauses

Consider the following example:

> It won't be surprising if people complain if they don't punish him if he's guilty

This contains four clauses; each one other than the first modifies the one preceding it. We can represent this in Figure D6.1.

it won't be surprising	if people complain	if they don't punish him	if he's guilty
Head	Modifier		
α	β	γ	δ

Figure D6.1 Progressive modification

Usually the pattern is less regular than this; there are dependent clauses branching out at different places, and the clauses are not all of the same kind. A more typical example would be:

I don't mind if you leave as soon as you've finished as long as you're back when I need you.

Here there is a variation in the clause relationships: 'H if M', 'H as soon as M', 'H as long as M', 'H when M'. And the structure is no longer a simple dependency chain, with each clause dependent on the one preceding; the first three clauses form one block, and the last two form another which is dependent on it. This is shown in Figure D6.2.

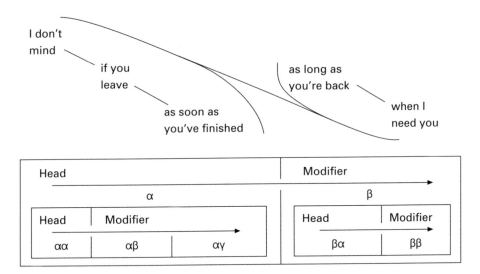

Head			Modifier		
α			β		
Head	Modifier		Head	Modifier	
αα	αβ	αγ	βα	ββ	

Figure D6.2 Modification with nesting (internal bracketing)

It follows from this that the order of the two blocks could be reversed; we could have

As long as you're back when I need you I don't mind if you leave as soon as you've finished.

Figure D6.3 shows the analysis of this second version.

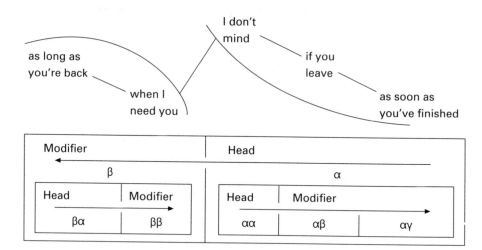

Figure D6.3 Modification with internal regressive bracketing

As a first step, therefore, we can interpret the relationship between these clauses as one of modification, the same concept that was used to explain one aspect of the relationship between the words in a verbal or nominal group. We have had to take account of the possibility of internal bracketing, or NESTING; but that too is a general property which we have already found in group structure. The question that arises at this point is: in what other ways does the concept of modification need to be refined and enriched in order to account for relationships within the clause complex?

The concept needs to be extended, we shall suggest, along two separate vectors, by introducing two distinct sets of alternatives: (i) the type of interdependency, or 'taxis'; (ii) the logico-semantic relation. We shall summarize these in the present section, and then go on to examine each in greater detail.

(i) Type of interdependency. The relation of modifying, whereby one element 'modifies' another, is not the only relationship that may obtain between the members of a complex.

Where one element modifies another, the status of the two is unequal; the modifying element is dependent on the modified. But two elements may be joined together on an equal footing, neither being dependent on the other.

The general term for the modifying relation is HYPOTAXIS. Hypotaxis is the relation between a dependent element and its dominant, the element on which it is dependent.* Contrasting with this is PARATAXIS, which is the relation between two like elements of equal status, one initiating and the other continuing.

---

* An earlier name for the higher term in the dependency relation, that on which something is dependent, was TERMINANT. The problem with this turns out to be that it is too readily misinterpreted as 'coming last in sequence'. The dependency relation, however, is neutral as regards the sequence in which the elements occur.

All 'logical' structures in language are either (a) paratactic or (b) hypotactic. The clause complex involves relationships of both kinds.

Hypotactic structures will be represented by the Greek letter notation already used for modification in the structure of the group. For paratactic structures we shall use a numerical notation 1 2 3 . . . , with nesting indicated in the usual way: 11 12 2 31 32 means the same as 1(1 2) 2 3(1 2).

A typical clause complex is a mixture of paratactic and hypotactic sequences, either of which may be nested inside the other; for example

I would	if I could,	but I can't
1 α	1 β	2

There is a paratactic relationship between *I would if I could* and *but I can't*, shown as 1 2; and a hypotactic relationship between *I would* and *if I could*, shown as α β.

We will refer to the members of a pair of related clauses, in paratactic or hypotactic relation, as PRIMARY and SECONDARY. The primary is the initiating clause in a paratactic structure, and the dominant clause in a hypotactic; the secondary is the continuing clause in a paratactic structure and the dependent clause in a hypotactic. This is set out in Table D6.1:

Table D6.1 Primary and secondary clauses

	primary	secondary
parataxis	1 (initiating)	2 (continuing)
hypotaxis	α (dominant)	β (dependent)

For most purposes we shall be able to refer to 'primary' and 'secondary' clauses and avoid using the more specific terms.

(ii) Logico-semantic relation. There is a wide range of different logico-semantic relations any of which may hold between a primary and a secondary member of a clause complex. But it is possible to group these into a small number of general types, based on the two fundamental relationships of (1) EXPANSION and (2) PROJECTION.

(1) Expansion: the secondary clause expands the primary clause, by (a) elaborating it, (b) extending it or (c) enhancing it.
(2) Projection: the secondary clause is projected through the primary clause, which instates it as (a) a locution or (b) an idea.

If we return to the examples given above, in Figures D6.1–3, these were all of the same type of interdependency (hypotaxis) and same logico-semantic relation (expansion: enhancement).

An example of a projecting complex (projection: locution) would be

John reported that Mary had told him that Fred had said the day would be fine.

The analysis of this is given in Figure D6.4:

| John reported ———— | that Mary had told him ———— | that Fred had said ———— | the day would be fine |

Head	Modifier		
α	β	γ	δ

Figure D6.4 Clause complex of the 'projection' type

Within the general categories of expansion and projection, we recognize first of all a small number of subtypes: three of expansion, and two of projection. The names of these, with suggested notation, are as follows:

(1) Expansion:
    (a) elaboration   = ('equals')
    (b) extension   + ('is added to')
    (c) enhancement × ('is multiplied by')
(2) Projection:
    (a) locution   " (double quotes)
    (b) idea   ' (single quotes)

This symbols combine with those for parataxis and hypotaxis:

$$= 2 \quad = β \quad + 2 \quad + β \quad × 2 \quad × β \quad ``2 \quad ``β \quad `2 \quad `β$$

Below is a brief definition of each of these categories, with examples:

(1a) Elaboration: one clause expands another by elaborating on it (or some por-
    'i.e.'   tion of it): restating in other words, specifying in greater detail,
                  commenting, or exemplifying.

(1b) Extension: one clause expands another by extending beyond it: adding
    'and'   some new element, giving an exception to it, or offering an
                  alternative.

(1c) Enhancement: one clause expands another by embellishing around it: qualify-
    'so, yet, then' ing it with some circumstantial feature of time, place, cause
                  or condition.

(2a) Locution: one clause is projected through another, which presents
    'says'   it as a locution, a construction of wording.

(2b) Idea: one clause is projected through another, which
    'thinks'   presents it as an idea, a construction of meaning.

Examples are given in Table D6.2:

Table D6.2 Basic types of clause complex

		(i) paratactic	(ii) hypotactic
(2) Projection	**(a)** elaboration	John didn't wait; 1 he ran away. = 2	John ran away, α which surprised everyone = β
	(b) extension	John ran away, 1 and Fred stayed behind. + 2	John ran away, α whereas Fred stayed behind. + β
	(c) enhancement	John was scared, 1 so he ran away. × 2	John ran away, α because he was scared × β
(1) Expansion	**(a)** locution	John said: 1 "I'm running away" "2	John said α he was running away. "β
	[b] idea	John thought to himself: 1 "I'll run away" '2	John thought α he would run away. 'β

In hypotaxis, the two clauses, primary and secondary, can occur in either order: either α ^ β or β ^ α. But it is always the secondary clause that is dependent, that does the expanding or gets projected. Examples of the β ^ α sequence are:

While Fred stayed behind,	John ran away	+ β ^ α
Because he was scared,	John ran away	× β ^ α
That John had run away	no-one believed	'β ^ α
β	α	

The logical symbol is always attached to the symbol for the dependent clause.

In parataxis, only the order 1 ^ 2 is possible – because the question of which is the primary clause in a paratactic relation is simply a matter of which comes first.

In a paratactic expansion, therefore, it is always the secondary clause that does the expanding; if we say

John ran away;	he didn't wait	1 ^ = 2
1	2	

the structure is still 1 ^ = 2.

With a paratactic projection, on the other hand, it is possible for the primary clause to be the projected one, as in

"I'm running away,"   said John "I $^\wedge$2
        1   2

This is because projection is inherently a directional (asymmetric) relation.

Parataxis and hypotaxis are discussed in more detail in the next section. Following that we take up the more specific categories of expansion and projection.

Follow-up activities

First of all, having read the Halliday extract, make sure that you understand the differences in terminology between his description and the one in this book.

Sentence complexity and the kinds of relations between clauses vary enormously for different types of text. There are several comparisons that you could make. For example take two or three news articles from different types of newspaper (e.g. a tabloid and a broadsheet) and: (1) calculate the proportions of simple and complex sentences; (2) examine how the clauses are related in the complex sentences (you may like to use Halliday's notation). Do the articles from one of the newspapers have more parataxis or hypotaxis than those of the other?

Alternatively, take a novel and an academic textbook, and do the same kind of investigation. Is there variation according to the type of text? For example, is there more parataxis in a narrative text such as the novel, and more hypotaxis in the academic textbook?

You can repeat the exercise with other pairs of texts, either of a similar type (e.g. classic novel vs. blockbuster), or of different types (e.g. advertisement vs. instruction manual) and you will find that sentence complexity is one of the indicators of text type, as well as of differences in style.

D7   STANDARD ENGLISH

In Unit A7, we attempted to define what is meant by a 'rule' of grammar, and in some of the examples we examined in B7 we suggested that they might be regarded by some people as 'non-standard' English. We did not discuss what we meant by 'standard' grammar or 'standard English', and the discussions of spoken grammar, creative uses of grammar and ambiguity in the C7 units did not address this question either. But it is a question that has been much discussed and debated, often with more heat than light, in recent years.

This reading, 'Standard English: What it isn't', by Peter Trudgill, is a contribution to a volume entitled *Standard English, The Widening Debate*, edited by Tony Bex and Richard J. Watts (Routledge, 1999). Trudgill argues that 'Standard English' is a social dialect, with some peculiarities of grammar, and with a vocabulary that contains no exclusive terms but which excludes words that are regionally restricted.

As you read Trudgill's article, think critically about it, and whether you agree with him at every point. Is he convincing? Does he use any 'knockdown arguments'?

Standard English: what it isn't

Peter Trudgill (reprinted from 'Standard English: What it isn't', in: *Standard English, The Widening Debate* (1999), T. Bex and R.J. Watts (eds) Routledge)

There is a reasonably clear consensus in the sociolinguistics literature about the term *standardised language*: a standardised language is a language one of whose varieties has undergone standardisation. *Standardisation*, too, appears to be a relatively uncontroversial term, although the terminology employed in the discussion of this topic is by no means uniform. I myself have defined standardisation (Trudgill 1992) as 'consisting of the processes of language determination, codification and stabilisation'. Language determination 'refers to decisions which have to be taken concerning the selection of particular languages or varieties of language for particular purposes in the society or nation in question' (ibid.: 71). Codification is the process whereby a language variety 'acquires a publicly recognised and fixed form'. The results of codification 'are usually enshrined in dictionaries and grammar books' (ibid.: 17). Stabilisation is a process whereby a formerly diffuse variety (in the sense of Le Page and Tabouret-Keller 1985: 70) 'undergoes focussing and takes on a more fixed and stable form'.

It is therefore somewhat surprising that there seems to be considerable confusion in the English-speaking world, even amongst linguists, about what *Standard English* is. One would think that it should be reasonably clear which of the varieties of English is the one which has been subject to the process of standardisation, and what its characteristics are. In fact, however, we do not even seem to be able to agree how to spell this term – with an upper case or lower case <s>? – a point which I will return to later. Also, the use of the term by non-linguists appears to be even more haphazard.

In this chapter, I therefore attempt a characterisation of Standard English. It should be noted that this is indeed a characterisation rather than a strict definition – language varieties do not readily lend themselves to definition as such. We can describe what Chinese is, for example, in such a way as to make ourselves very well understood on the issue, but actually to define Chinese would be another matter altogether. The characterisation will also be as much negative as positive – a clearer idea of what Standard English is can be obtained by saying what it is not as well as by saying what it is. My discussion of this topic will be both a sociolinguistic and a linguistic discussion. (But it will be specifically linguistic: the word 'ideology' will not appear again in this chapter.) And it will also, I hope, be informed by references from time to time to the nature of standard and nonstandard varieties in language situations beyond the English-speaking world.

Standard English is not a language

Standard English is often referred to as 'the standard language'. It is clear, however, that Standard English is not 'a language' in any meaningful sense of this term. Standard English, whatever it is, is less than a language, since it is only one variety of English among many. Standard English may be the most important variety of English, in all sorts of ways: it is the variety of English normally used in writing, especially printing; it is the variety associated with the education system in all the English-speaking countries of the world, and is therefore the variety spoken by those who are often referred to as 'educated people'; and it is the variety taught to non-native learners. But most native speakers of English in the world are native speakers of some non-standard variety of the language, and English, like other *Ausbau* languages (see Kloss 1967), can be described (Chambers and Trudgill 1997) as consisting of an autonomous standardised variety together with all the non-standard varieties which are heteronomous with respect to it. Standard English is thus not *the* English language but simply one variety of it.

Standard English is not an accent

There is one thing about Standard English on which most linguists, or at least British linguists, do appear to be agreed, and that is that Standard English has nothing to do with pronunciation. From a British perspective, we have to acknowledge that there is in Britain a high status and widely described accent known as Received Pronunciation (RP) which is sociolinguistically unusual when seen from a global perspective in that it is not associated with any geographical area, being instead a purely social accent associated with speakers in all parts of the country, or at least in England, from upper-class and upper-middle-class backgrounds. It is widely agreed, though, that while all RP speakers also speak Standard English, the reverse is not the case. Perhaps 9 per cent–12 per cent of the population of Britain (see Trudgill and Cheshire 1989) speak Standard English with some form of regional accent. It is true that in most cases Standard English speakers do not have 'broad' local accents, i.e. accents with large numbers of regional features which are phonologically and phonetically very distant from RP, but it is clear that in principle we can say that, while RP is, in a sense, standardised, it is a standardised accent of English and not Standard English itself. This point becomes even clearer from an international perspective. Standard English speakers can be found in all English-speaking countries, and it goes without saying that they speak this variety with different non-RP accents depending on whether they come from Scotland or the USA or New Zealand or wherever.

Standard English is not a style

There is, however and unfortunately, considerable confusion in the minds of many concerning the relationship between Standard English and the vocabulary associated with formal varieties of the English language. We characterise *styles* (see Trudgill 1992) as varieties of language viewed from the point of view of *formality*. Styles are varieties of language which can be arranged on a continuum ranging from very formal to very informal. Formal styles are employed in social situations which are formal, and informal styles are employed in social situations which are informal – which is not to say, however, that speakers are 'sociolinguistic automata' (Giles 1973) who respond blindly to the particular degree of formality of a particular social situation. On the contrary, speakers are able to influence and change the degree of formality of a social situation by manipulation of stylistic choice.

All the languages of the world would appear to demonstrate some degree of stylistic differentiation in this sense, reflecting the wide range of social relationships and social situations found, to a greater or lesser extent, in all human societies. I believe, with Labov (1972), that there is no such thing as a single-style speaker, although it is obviously also the case that the repertoire of styles available to individual speakers will be a reflection of their social experiences and, in many cases, also their education. It is of course important here to distinguish between individual speakers of languages and those languages themselves, but it is clear that languages too may differ similarly in the range of styles available to their speakers. In many areas of the world, switching from informal to formal situations also involves switching from one language to another. In such cases, it is probable that neither of the two languages involved will have the full range of styles available to speakers in monolingual situations.

English as it is employed in areas where it is the major native language of the community, such as in the British Isles, North America and Australasia, is a language which has the fullest possible range of styles running from the most to the least formal. This obviously does not mean to say, however, that all speakers have equal access to or ability in all styles, and it is generally accepted that one of the objectives of mother tongue education is to give pupils exposure to styles at the more formal end of the continuum that they might otherwise not gain any ability in using.

Stylistic differences in English are most obvious at the level of lexis. Consider the differences between the following:

Father was exceedingly fatigued subsequent to his extensive peregrination.
Dad was very tired after his lengthy journey.
The old man was bloody knackered after his long trip.

Although one could argue about some of the details, we can accept that these three sentences have more or less the same referential meaning, and thus differ only in style – and that the stylistic differences are indicated by lexical choice. It is also clear that native speakers are very sensitive to the fact that stylistic variation constitutes a cline: some of the words here, such as *was*, *his* are stylistically neutral; others range in formality from the ridiculously formal *peregrination* through very formal *fatigued* to intermediate *tired* to informal *trip* to very informal *knackered* and tabooed informal *bloody*. It will be observed that, as is often the case, the most informal or 'slang' words are regionally restricted, being in this case unknown or unusual in North American English. It will also be observed that there are no strict co-occurrence restrictions here as there are in some languages – one can say *long journey* and *lengthy trip* just as well as *lengthy journey* and *long trip*.

Formality in English is, however, by no means confined to lexis. Grammatical constructions vary as between informal and formal English – it is often claimed, for instance, that the passive voice is more frequent in formal than in informal styles – and, as has been shown by many works in the Labovian secular linguistics tradition, starting with Labov (1966), phonology is also highly sensitive to style.

As far as the relationship between style, on the one hand, and Standard English, on the other, is concerned, we can say the following. The phonological sensitivity to stylistic context just referred to obviously has no connection to Standard English since, as we have noted, Standard English has no connection with phonology.

Let us then examine lexis. I would like to assert that our sentence.

The old man was bloody knackered after his long trip.

is clearly and unambiguously Standard English. To assert otherwise – that swear words like *bloody* and very informal words like *knackered* are not Standard English – would get us into a very difficult situation. Does a Standard English speaker suddenly switch out of Standard English as soon as he or she starts swearing? Are Standard English speakers not allowed to use slang without switching into some non-standard variety? My contention is that Standard English is no different from any other (non-standard) variety of the language. Speakers of Standard English have a full range of styles open to them, just as speakers of other varieties do, and can swear and use slang just like anybody else. (It will be clear that I do not agree with the contention which is some-times heard that 'nobody speaks Standard English'.) Equally, there is no need for speakers of non-standard varieties to switch into Standard English in order to employ formal styles. The most logical position we can adopt on this is as follows:

The old man was bloody knackered after his long trip

is a Standard English sentence, couched in a very informal style, while

Father were very tired after his lengthy journey

is a sentence in a non-standard (north of England, for instance) variety of English, as attested by the non-standard verb form *were*, couched in a rather formal style. It is true that, in most English-speaking societies there is a tendency – a social convention perhaps – for Standard English to dominate in relatively formal social situations, but there is no necessary connection here, and we are therefore justified in asserting the theoretical independence of the parameter standard–non-standard from the parameter formal–informal. This theoretical independence becomes clearer if we observe sociolinguistic situations outside the English-speaking world. There are many parts of the world where speakers employ the local dialect for nearly all purposes, such as Luxembourg, Limburg in the Netherlands, and much of Norway. In such situations, a visit to the respective Town Hall to discuss import-ant local political problems with the mayor will not elicit a switch to Standard German or Dutch or Norwegian, but it will produce styles of greater formality than those to be found on Friday night in the local bar amongst a group of close friends. Stylistic switching occurs *within* dialects and not *between* them.

This theoretical independence of the notion of Standard English from style does not mean that there are not problems in individual cases of distinguishing the two, as Hudson and Holmes (1995) have pointed out. For example, I tend to regard the use of *this* as an indefinite in narratives as in

There was this man, and he'd got this gun, . . . *etc.*

as a feature of colloquial style, but other linguists might regard it as a non-standard grammatical feature.

Standard English is not a register

We use the term *register* in the sense of a variety of language determined by topic, subject matter or activity, such as the register of mathematics, the register of medicine, or the register of pigeon fancying. In English, this is almost exclusively a matter of lexis, although some registers, notably the register of law, are known to have special syntactic characteristics. It is also clear that the education system is widely regarded as having as one of its tasks the transmission of particular registers to pupils – those academic, technical or scientific registers which they are not likely to have had contact with outside the education system – and of course it is a necessary part of the study of, say, physical geography to acquire the register – the technical terms – associated with physical geography.

It is, however, an interesting question as to how far technical registers have a technical function – that of, for example, providing well-defined unambiguous terms for dealing with particular topics – and how far they have the more particularly sociolinguistic function of symbolising a speaker or writer's membership of a particular group, and of, as it were, keeping outsiders out. Linguists will defend the use of 'lexical item' rather than 'word' by saying that the former has a more rigorous definition than the latter, but it is also undoubtedly true that employing the term 'lexical item' does signal one's membership of the group of academic linguists. And it is not entirely clear to me, as a medical outsider, that using 'clavicle' rather than 'collar-bone' has any function at all other than symbolising one's status as a doctor rather than a patient.

Here again we find confusion over the term *Standard English*. The National Curriculum document for English in England and Wales (DfE/WO 1995) talks frequently about 'Standard English vocabulary'. It is not at all clear what this can mean. I have argued above that it cannot mean 'vocabulary associated with formal styles'. Is it perhaps supposed to mean 'vocabulary associated with academic or technical registers'? If so, this would not make sense either, since the question of register and the question of standard versus non-standard are also in principle entirely separate questions. It is of course true that it is most usual in English-speaking societies to employ Standard English when one is using scientific registers – this is the social convention, we might say. But one can certainly acquire and use technical registers without using Standard English, just as one can employ non-technical registers while speaking or writing Standard English. There is, once again, no necessary connection between the two. Thus

There was two eskers what we saw in them U-shaped valleys

is a non-standard English sentence couched in the technical register of physical geography.

This type of combination of technical register with a non-standard variety is much more common in some language communities than others. In German-speaking

Switzerland, for example, most speakers use their local non-standard dialect in nearly all social situations and for nearly all purposes. Thus it is that one may hear, in the corridors of the University of Berne, two philosophy professors discussing the works of Kant using all the appropriate philosophical vocabulary while using the phonology and grammar of their local dialect.

It would, of course, be possible to argue that their philosophical vocabulary is not an integral part of their native non-standard Swiss German dialects and that the professors are 'switching' or that these words are being 'borrowed' from Standard German and being subjected, as loan words often are, to phonological integration into the local dialect. This, however, would be very difficult to argue for with any degree of logic. All speakers acquire new vocabulary throughout their lifetimes. There seems no reason to suppose that technical vocabulary is the sole prerogative of standard varieties, or that while, if you are a non-standard dialect speaker, it is possible to acquire new non-technical words within your own non-standard dialect, it is sadly by definition impossible to acquire technical words without switching to the standard variety. After all, dialects of English resemble each other at all linguistic levels much more than they differ – otherwise interdialectal communication would be impossible. There is no reason why they should not have most of their vocabulary in common as well as most of their grammar and most of their phonology. If the Swiss example tells us anything, it tells us that there is no necessary connection between Standard English and technical registers.

So what is it then?

If Standard English is not therefore a language, an accent, a style or a register, then of course we are obliged to say what it actually is. The answer is, as at least most British sociolinguists are agreed, that Standard English is a dialect. As we saw above, Standard English is simply one variety of English among many. It is a sub-variety of English. Sub-varieties of languages are usually referred to as *dialects*, and languages are often described as *consisting of* dialects. As a named dialect, like Cockney, or Scouse, or Yorkshire, it is entirely normal that we should spell the name of the Standard English dialect with capital letters.

Standard English is, however, an unusual dialect in a number of ways. It is, for example, by far the most important dialect in the English-speaking world from a social, intellectual and cultural point of view; and it does not have an associated accent.

It is also of interest that dialects of English, as of other languages, are generally simultaneously both geographical and social dialects which combine to form both geographical and social dialect continua. How we divide these continua up is also most often linguistically arbitrary, although we do of course find it convenient normally to make such divisions and use names for dialects that we happen to want to talk about for a particular purpose *as if* they were discrete varieties. It is thus legitimate and usual to talk about Yorkshire dialect, or South Yorkshire dialect, or Sheffield dialect, or middle-class Sheffield dialect, depending on what our particular objectives are. Standard English is unusual, seen against this background, in a number of ways. First, the distinction between Standard English and other dialects is not arbitrary or a matter of slicing up a continuum at some point of our own choice, although as we have seen there are some difficulties. This is inherent in the nature of standardisation itself. There is really no continuum linking Standard English to other dialects because the codification that forms a crucial part of the standardisation process results in a situation where, in most cases, a feature is either standard or it is not.

Second, unlike other dialects, Standard English is a purely social dialect. Because of its unusual history and its extreme sociological importance, it is no longer a geographical dialect, even if we can tell that its origins were originally in the southeast of England. It is true that, in the English-speaking world as a whole, it comes in a number of different forms, so that we can talk, if we wish to for some particular purpose, of Scottish Standard English, or American Standard English, or English Standard English. (Bizarrely, the British National Curriculum document suggests that American and Australian English are not Standard English!) And even in England we can note that there is a small amount of geographical variation at least in spoken Standard English, such as the different tendencies in different parts of the country to employ contractions such as *He's not* as opposed to *he hasn't*. But the most salient sociolinguistic characteristic of Standard English is that it is a social dialect.

At least two linguists have professed to find this statement controversial. Stein and Quirk (1995) argue that Standard English is not a social-class dialect because the *Sun*, a British newspaper with a largely working-class readership, is written in Standard English. This argument would appear to be a total non-sequitur, since all newspapers that are written in English are written in Standard English, by middle-class journalists, regardless of their readership.

Stein and Quirk also fly in the face of all the sociolinguistic research on English grammar that has been carried out in the last quarter of the twentieth century (see for example Cheshire 1982). Standard English is a dialect which is spoken as their native variety, at least in Britain, by about 12 per cent–15 per cent of the population, and this small percentage does not just constitute a random cross-section of the population. They are very much concentrated at the top of the social scale (or, as some would prefer, 'the very top'). The further down the social scale one goes, the more non-standard forms one finds.

Historically, we can say that Standard English was selected (though of course, unlike many other languages, not by any overt or conscious decision) as the variety to become the standard variety precisely because it was the variety associated with the social group with the highest degree of power, wealth and prestige. Subsequent developments have reinforced its social character: the fact that it has been employed as the dialect of an education to which pupils, especially in earlier centuries, have had differential access depending on their social-class background.

So far we have not discussed grammar. When, however, it comes to discussing what are the linguistic differences between Standard English and the non-standard dialects, it is obvious from our discussion above that they cannot be phonological, and that they do not appear to be lexical either (though see below). It therefore follows that Standard English is a social dialect which is distinguished from other dialects of the language by its *grammatical* forms.

Standard English is not a set of prescriptive rules

We have to make it clear, however, that these grammatical forms are not necessarily identical with those which prescriptive grammarians have concerned themselves with over the last few centuries. Standard English, like many other Germanic languages, most certainly tolerates sentence-final prepositions, as in *I've bought a new car which I'm very pleased with*. And Standard English does not exclude constructions such as *It's me* or *He is taller than me*.

Grammatical idiosyncrasies of Standard English

Grammatical differences between Standard English and other dialects are in fact rather few in number, although of course they are very significant socially. This means that, as part of our characterisation of what Standard English is, we are actually able to cite quite a high proportion of them.

Standard English of course has most of its grammatical features in common with the other dialects. When compared to the non-standard dialects, however, it can be seen to have idiosyncrasies which include the following:

1   Standard English fails to distinguish between the forms of the auxiliary verb *do* and its main verb forms. This is true both of present tense forms, where many other dialects distinguish between auxiliary *I do*, *he do* and main verb *I does*, *he does* or similar, and the past tense, where most other dialects distinguish between auxiliary *did* and main verb *done*, as in *You done it, did you?*

2   Standard English has an unusual and irregular present tense verb morphology in that only the third-person singular receives morphological marking: *he goes* versus *I go*. Many other dialects use either zero for all persons or *-s* for all persons.

3   Standard English lacks multiple negation, so that no choice is available between *I don't want none*, which is not possible, and *I don't want any*. Most non-standard dialects of English around the world permit multiple negation.

4   Standard English has an irregular formation of reflexive pronouns with some forms based on the possessive pronouns, e.g. *myself*, and others on the objective pronouns, e.g. *himself*. Most non-standard dialects have a regular system employing possessive forms throughout, i.e. *hisself, theirselves*.

5   Standard English fails to distinguish between second-person singular and second-person plural pronouns, having *you* in both cases. Many non-standard dialects maintain the older English distinction between *thou* and *you*, or have developed newer distinctions such as *you* versus *youse*.

6   Standard English has irregular forms of the verb *to be* both in the present tense (*am, is, are*) and in the past (*was, were*). Many non-standard dialects have the same form for all persons, such as *I be, you be, he be, we be, they be*, and *I were, you were, he were, we were, they were*.

7   In the case of many irregular verbs, Standard English redundantly distinguishes
    between preterite and perfect verb forms both by the use of the auxiliary *have*
    and by the use of distinct preterite and past participle forms: *I have seen* ver-
    sus *I saw*. Many other dialects have *I have seen* versus *I seen*.

8   Standard English has only a two-way contrast in its demonstrative system, with
    this (near to the speaker) opposed to *that* (away from the speaker). Many other
    dialects have a three-way system involving a further distinction between, for ex-
    ample, *that* (near to the listener) and *yon* (away from both speaker and listener).

Linguistic change

There is also an interesting problem concerning which grammatical forms are and
are not Standard English which has to do with linguistic change, in general, and
the fact that, in particular, there is a tendency for forms to spread from non-
standard dialects to the standard. Just as there are some difficulties in practice in
distinguishing between features of non-standard dialect and features of colloquial
style, as was discussed above, so there are difficulties associated with standard
versus non-standard status and linguistic change. Given that it is possible for non-
standard features to become standard (and vice versa), it follows that there will
be a period of time when a form's status will be uncertain or ambiguous. For
example, most Standard English speakers are happy to accept the new status of
than as a preposition rather than a conjunction in constructions such as:

    He is bigger than me.

but less happy, for the time being, to do so in:

    He is bigger than what I am.

Similarly, American Standard English currently admits a new verb *to got* in

    You haven't got any money, do you?

but not (or not yet) in

    You don't got any money, do you?

Non-standard lexis

I have argued above that there is no necessary connection between formal vocabulary or technical vocabulary and Standard English. That is, there is no such thing
as Standard English vocabulary. There is an interesting sense, however, in which
this is not entirely true. We can illustrate this in the following way. It is clear
that there is such a thing as *non-standard* vocabulary. For instance, in the non-
standard dialect of Norwich, England, there is a verb *to blar* which means *to cry,
weep*. Not only is this verb regionally restricted, to the dialects of this part of the
country, it is also socially restricted – the small proportion of the population of
Norwich who are native speakers of Standard English do not normally use this word,
although they are perfectly well aware of what it means. This means that there

is a sense in which we can say that *to cry* is a Standard English word, whereas *to blur* is not. However, *cry* is by no means *only* a Standard English word, since there are very many other non-standard dialects elsewhere in which it is the only word available with this meaning, and even in the working-class non-standard dialect of Norwich, *to cry* is a perfectly common and frequently used word. Because Standard English is not geographically restricted to any particular region, its vocabulary is available to all. There are in any case also, of course, many cases in which Standard English speakers in different parts of England employ different but equivalent words, and hundreds of cases in which the vocabulary of English Standard English and American Standard English differ, as is very well known. The usage in the National Curriculum of the term 'Standard English vocabulary' in the sense of 'vocabulary that occurs in the Standard English dialect and no other' thus remains problematical.

Conclusion

From an educational point of view, the position of Standard English as the dialect of English used in writing is unassailable. (We should perhaps add, however, that it has nothing whatsoever to do with spelling or punctuation!) As far as spoken Standard English is concerned, we could conclude that the teaching of Standard English to speakers of other dialects may be commendable – as most would in theory agree, if for no other reason than the discrimination which is currently exercised against non-standard dialect speakers in most English-speaking societies – and may also be possible – which I am inclined, for sociolinguistic reasons (see Trudgill 1975) to doubt.

Either way, however, there is clearly no necessary connection at all between the teaching of formal styles and technical registers, on the one hand, and the teaching of the standard dialect, on the other.

Follow-up activities

Does your local dialect contain grammatical features (e.g. those mentioned by Trudgill) or words that are not shared by Standard English? Listen to local people talking to each other in the street, on the bus, in the shops; and note down any features you think might be local dialect.

Is there any writing in your local dialect, any local poets, for example? Ask in your local library if they know of anything. If you can find some, examine how the authors have represented local dialect features in writing.

Did you agree with everything that Trudgill says? Do you think that Standard English is purely a social class dialect? Write a rejoinder to Trudgill from an alternative viewpoint.

Do you use a regional dialect as well as Standard English? On what occasions, and with whom, do you use one rather than the other? If you do not know, keep a diary for a time and note down when you change from one to the other.

Do you find that your speech or writing is corrected by parents or teachers, or perhaps an older brother or sister? Are they objecting to a 'non-standard' feature in your speech, or are they merely displaying their prejudices against certain styles of speaking?

INTRODUCTION TO TWENTIETH-CENTURY WORDS

The units at A8, B8 and C8 have been concerned with various aspects of the vocabulary of English, examining the dimensions along which words vary and result in different 'vocabularies'. We have not as yet taken a historical view of the development of vocabulary. This lack is remedied by the reading presented here.

'Words are a mirror of their times,' says John Ayto, the lexicographer, in his Introduction to *20th Century Words* (Ayto 1999), which is reproduced here. Ayto shows how the new words that have come into English over the last 100 years illustrate that dictum. Ayto's monumental work looks at the vocabulary of the twentieth century decade by decade. We took some of the words from the list representing the final decade for Activity 3 of Subunit C8.3. Here Ayto explains the thinking behind his collection and reviews the growth in vocabulary during the twentieth century.

He notes the developments, in society, industry and culture, that have given rise to additions to English vocabulary in the twentieth century. He notes changes in sensibilities that have allowed some previously unrecorded words to find their place in the dictionary, and conversely some to be threatened with exclusion. And, relating to our discussion in Unit B3, he reviews the main word formation processes that have given rise to neologisms during the past century.

Introduction

J. Ayto (reprinted from *Twentieth Century Words* (1999), Oxford University Press)

On 1 January 1900 there were approximately 140 million native speakers of English in the world. A century later that figure has almost tripled to nearly 400 million. Add to them about 100 million who speak English as a second language. Consider how English has become the international language of communication, both conventional and digital, in the 20th century. Think, moreover, of the massive increase in literacy since 1900, the legacy of the spread of universal education in the late 19th century. The English language is in an unprecedented number of hands.

In that same period, the world itself has changed almost beyond recognition. In 1900, no powered heavier-than-air craft had left the Earth's surface; Dr Hertz's discovery of radio waves had yet to be put to practical commercial use; it was a mere three years since Joseph Thomson had detected the existence of the electron; and Claude Monet was painting his waterlilies. A hundred years later we look with complacency at pictures of the Earth taken from outer space; various forms of electronic communication have brought all corners of the globe into instantaneous touch with each other; the second half of the century has been lived in the shadow of the nuclear bomb; and avant-garde art proposes the dead sheep as an object of contemplation. The old European colonies have become independent nations. Two savage and prolonged world wars have claimed millions of lives and radically rearranged the planet's political geography. A clash of empires, East and West, has arisen and subsided. Sigmund Freud and his successors have delved into the recesses of the human psyche. The computer has grown, and shrunk, from a set of winking throbbing cabinets big enough to fill a room to a miniaturized component of everyday life, a progenitor of cyberspace, holding the threat and the promise of the future in its microcircuits.

Given that huge increase in the number of English-speakers since 1900, and the myriad new ideas, inventions, discoveries, and schemes that have proliferated in that period, it would be astonishing if the vocabulary of English had not grown substantially. And so it has. We shall never know how many new words were coined during the 20th century. Many were the inspiration of a moment, lost before they could be committed to paper (or recorded by any other means). Others were not common enough to catch the attention of dictionary compilers, or if they were, failed to convince the lexicographers that they deserved the stamp of approval. Those that slipped through the net are without number. But of the remainder we can speak with some confidence. The *Oxford English Dictionary* and its supplementary volumes record about 90,000 new words, and new meanings of old words, that have come into the English language in this century. In other words, every year on average 900 neologisms have come into existence which sooner or later make a sufficient mark to be considered as established in the language, and worthy of record in English's largest dictionary. The figure represents approximately a 25 per cent increase in the total vocabulary of the language as it had evolved in the thousand and more years up to 1900.

It is this newly minted lexicon of the 20th century that forms the basis of this book. It would have been unwieldy and ultimately unenlightening to list all the new words and usages. This is a selection, which attempts to present the most salient new English vocabulary of the past hundred years. The key new terminology of science and technology; the names of important new movements in politics and the arts; the vocabulary of fashion, in clothing, music, dances, hair-styles, food; the latest slang, most of it ephemeral but on everyone's lips at the time.

The words of each decade are given a chapter to themselves. They are listed alphabetically, with a brief introduction bringing together the main strands of lexical development within that period or setting them against their historical background. Each entry word has a date after it. I cannot emphasize too strongly that this represents the earliest date from which a printed or other written record of the word exists in the OED or its files – nothing more and nothing less. It is *not* meant to suggest that the word necessarily 'entered' the language in that year. It is not uncommon for words to escape immediate notice if they slip unobtrusively into the language rather than being announced with a fanfare; and slang and other colloquial items routinely take some time to find their way into the written record. Sometimes English is slow to adopt a term for a phenomenon, movement, etc. which to modern eyes seems the obvious one, and sometimes, no doubt, the record of an earlier adoption has yet to come to light (for example, Max Planck originated his quantum theory in 1900, but the terms *quantum* and *quantum theory* are not recorded in English until the second decade of the century; art nouveau was an important style of art of the last decade of the 19th century, but the term is not recorded as an English word until 1901). So, unless specifically documented details of a word's coinage are given, the date should be regarded simply as an indication of when a particular usage first appeared. The explanation of the word is followed by one or more examples of it in use, which often put further flesh on the bones of the definition. One of them may be the earliest recorded instance of the word in print, but this is not necessarily always the case.

Words are a mirror of their times. By looking at the areas in which the vocabulary of a language is expanding fastest in a given period, we can form a fairly accurate impression of the chief preoccupations of society at that time and the points at which the boundaries of human endeavour are being advanced. Table 1 summarizes the semantic fields which grew most rapidly in the succeeding decades of the 20th century. The new technology of cars, aircraft, radio, and film dominated lexical innovation in the 1900s (*dashboard, aerodrome, wireless, cinema*), along with the vocabulary of psychology and psychoanalysis (*libido, psychoanalysis*). These last two were not so dominant after the 1910s, but the others continued to be major sources of neologisms well into the 1930s. However, in the decade of World War I they were not surprisingly overshadowed by the broad spectrum of military vocabulary (*gas mask, shell shock, tank*), and in the 1920s the lexicon of national post-war relief, the bright young things and the Jazz Age, dominated the scene (*Charleston, Oxford bags*). Then in the 1930s the build-up to and start of a new war (*dive-bomb, Blitzkrieg, black-out*) put such frivolities in their place. In the first half of the 1940s, World War II was again providing the majority of new usages (*doodlebug, gas chamber, kamikaze*), but the return of peace brought other concerns to the fore: reconstruction, national and international (*National Health, Marshall Plan, superpower*), and the nuclear threat (*the bomb*). A small trickle of computer terminology (*electronic brain, hardware*) was to become a flood in the second half of the century. Similar small beginnings for the vocabulary of space exploration (*booster, re-entry*) reached their apogee in the 1960s.

The 1950s saw the first significant burgeonings of youth culture (*beatnik, teen*), which in its various manifestations has continued to be a prolific contributor to the English language throughout the rest of the century. It was also the decade in which television combined with other forms of communication and entertainment in a new vocabulary of the media (*hi-fi, transistor radio, videotape*) that would dom-

Table D8.1 Lexical growth-areas by decade

1900s	Cars Aviation Radio Film Psychology
1910s	War Aviation Film Psychology
1920s	Clothes/dance/youth Transport Radio Film
1930s	War/build-up to war Transport Film/entertainment
1940s	War Post-war society/international affairs Nuclear power Computers Space
1950s	Media Nuclear power Space Computers Youth culture
1960s	Computers Space Youth culture/music Media Drugs
1970s	Computers Media Business Environment Political correctness
1980s	Media Computers Finance/money Environment Political correctness Youth culture/music
1990s	Politics Media Internet

inate the next fifty years. Both had particular offshoots in the psychedelic sixties in the language of music (*the twist*, *Merseybeat*) and the language of drugs (*acid*, *speed*). In the 1970s, concerns about the destruction of the environment became a long-term source of new vocabulary (*green*, *global warming*), and the language of political correctness and its proponents began to get into its stride (*chairperson*, *herstory*). The 1980s were the decade of money, typified both by financial jargon (*dawn raid*, *white knight*) and by the lifestyle terminology of those who made and enjoyed it (*yuppie*, *dinky*). The major new player on the 1990s lexical scene was the Internet (*cybernaut*, *web site*).

Movements and trends in human affairs do not necessarily fit neatly into a particular decade, of course, and the terms we associate with them sometimes anticipate their high-water mark. We tend to think of *appeasement*, for instance, as essentially a phenomenon of the 1930s, and that was indeed the decade in which the negative connotations the word has today began to gather around it; but in fact the concept originated in the second decade of the century. Similarly that quintessentially Cold War expression *iron curtain* can be traced back to the 1920s. It is not at all uncommon for a new term to potter along for decades in obscurity (often as a piece of jargon known only to specialists), and then to find itself suddenly thrust into the spotlight: *greenhouse effect*, for example, was coined in the 1920s, but few non-climatologists had heard of it until the 1980s. Bear in mind, too, that one of the chief characteristics of human language is that it enables us to talk about things which do not exist yet: it can still cause a frisson to read H. G. Wells discussing the *atomic bomb* in 1914.

So although it may at first sight seem odd that some terms that are central to 20th-century life, and particularly to its technological culture (such as *car* and *aircraft*), are not represented in this collection, the answer in most cases is that they are pre-20th-century coinages. Table 2 gives a selection of high-profile or striking examples of this phenomenon, in chronological order.

But it is not only the areas of activity characterized by high vocabulary growth that give us clues about the direction the human race is going in. Our changing modes of social interaction have a lexical fingerprint too. Take, for example, the 20th century's rehabilitation of the notorious 'four-letter words', formerly so beyond the pale that no dictionary would print them. As their common (and often euphemistic) epithet 'Anglo-Saxon' suggests, they have been around a long time, and no doubt have been used very widely in casual speech, but the taboo imposed on them means that printed examples from the 19th century and earlier are quite rare. In 1896, for instance, J. S. Farmer became involved in a lawsuit when his publishers refused to let him include certain obscene words in his and W. E. Henley's *Slang and its Analogues* (1890–1904), an extensive and distinguished dictionary of slang. It appears to have been the great melting pot of World War I, bringing together people of all classes and backgrounds, that encouraged the spread of such words (see *fuck off* (1929)). You still ran a great risk if you printed them, though: between the wars, the likes of James Joyce and Henry Miller had their work banned when they tried to, and as recently as 1960 in Britain the use of 'Anglo-Saxon words' was one of the main issues in the trial of the Penguin Books edi-

Table D8.2 Pre-20th-century coinages

flying machine (1736)	**electron** (1891)
parachute (1785)	**ouija** (1891)
aircraft (1850)	**homosexual** (adj) (1894)
Communist (1850)	**spaceship** (1894)
acid rain (1859)	**automobile** (1895)
commuter (1865)	**feminism** (1895)
aeroplane (1873)	**modern art** (1895)
biplane (1874)	**motor car** (1895)
Venusian (1874)	**car** (1896)
benefit 'financial assistance' (1875)	**motion picture** (1896)
relativity (1876)	**motor** (verb) (1896)
phonograph (1877)	**moving picture** (1896)
old-age pension (1879)	**bad** 'good' (slang) (1897)
Labour party (1886)	**photosynthesis** (1898)
department store (1887)	**radioactive** (1898)
contact lens (1888)	**aspirin** (1899)
milk shake (1889)	**auto** 'car' (1899)

tion of D. H. Lawrence's *Lady Chatterley's Lover* for obscenity. When the critic Kenneth Tynan used the word *fuck* on British television in 1965 ('I doubt if there are very many rational people in this world to whom the word *fuck* is particularly diabolical or revolting or totally forbidden') it caused a brief but noticeable national convulsion. But perhaps a more significant straw in the wind was the publication in the same year of the *Penguin English Dictionary*, the first mainstream general English dictionary to include *fuck* and *cunt*. Its imprimatur was confirmed by that of the *Supplement to the OED* in 1972, and by the end of the century these words are included as a matter of course in any unabridged English dictionary.

This is not simply a matter of lexicographers catching up with reality. It represents a genuine change in public usage over the course of the century. In the 1990s, *fuck*, *fucking*, etc. are common currency in feature films, familiar enough not to raise an eyebrow on post-watershed television, and waved through on many newspapers (although some – generally speaking those aimed at the 'lower' end of the market – do protect their more unworldly readers with a well-placed asterisk, or the coyly euphemistic *f-word*); in 1992 *fuck* even appeared in a government-sponsored warning against Aids: 'So if you are going to fuck, it makes sense to use one of the stronger variety [of condoms]'. This state of affairs would have been quite unthinkable in the 1950s. It seemed that *cunt* was still holding the line (its taboo maintained, some claimed, not on account of its obscenity but because it was sexist), but in 1998 it was used on national television in Britain for the first time (in a dramatization of the life of Oswald Mosley on Channel 4). The last bastion had fallen.

What does this revolution in usage tell us about changes in English-speaking society? Given that World War I made these words much more widely available, what has happened, especially in the second half of the century, to sanction their more general toleration? It certainly seems to be part of a more widespread tendency to upgrade the status and acceptability of spoken English. Up to at least the 1960s, the notion of 'Standard English' was based exclusively on written English, and the colloquial language was regarded as an irrelevant but occasionally annoying or embarrassing offshoot that needed to be kept in its place. At the end of the century that is no longer so, and colloquial usages (both lexical and syntactic) are widely accepted in situations (including quite formal writing) where they would once have been considered inappropriate. Behind this may be perceived a more general breaking down of social barriers, a valuing of mateyness above reserve, a profound shift away from role models who found *fuck* distasteful or morally undermining. 'Four-letter' status seems destined for the history books. But a passing thought: English would appear to be in danger of depriving itself of some valuable letting-off-steam words for use in extremis, without any obvious replacements in sight. The only 20th-century coinage in this area to have caught on widely is *motherfucker*.

On the other hand, there are a good many usages which once went unremarked, but which we now dare not allow to pass our lips. In the 19th century, for instance, it was socially acceptable, if not positively desirable, to be fat, and there was no stigma attached to the word *fat*. It could even be used approvingly (Princess Alice wrote gleefully in 1864 'My fat baby is a great darling!'). At the end of the 20th century, however, thinness is fashionable, and to call someone fat is a monstrous insult. We have evolved a range of euphemisms, from the colloquial *chunky* to the ponderous *circumferentially challenged*, to avoid the direct accusation.

It sometimes seems as if the 20th century were the century of euphemism. Much of the doublespeak is counterbalanced by areas in which frankness has latterly become the rule (the earlier part of the century boasted a bewildering array of circumlocutions for 'menstruation', for example, whereas 1990s television advertisements for *sanpro* products are studiedly in-your-face), but there is no doubt that there are many areas which English-speakers have become embarrassed to talk about in the last hundred years. The one with the highest profile is probably racial differences. Post-colonial guilt has ensured that the casual, unconsidered racial insult of the first half of the century has become unmentionable in the second (in the 1990s it seems bizarre that Agatha Christie could have entitled one of her mystery novels *Ten Little Niggers* in 1939; it has now become *And Then There Were None*). But the usual lesson of euphemism applies: if underlying tensions remain, a change of name will not stick. The fragmented history of English words for black people down the decades illustrates this. Terms such as *black* and *nigger* fell under a taboo in the middle part of the 20th century. They tended to be replaced by *negro*, but this (even more its feminine form *negress*) went out of favour in the 1960s, perhaps on account of its anthropological overtones. Back stepped *black*, revived by blacks themselves as a term of pride. In the US it was joined by

Afro-American and later *African-American*, in Britain by *Afro-Caribbean*. The politically correct lobby enthusiastically revived the 18th-century *person of color*, and added its own rather unwieldy *member of the African Diaspora*. Then in the 1980s US blacks subverted the whole process by reclaiming *nigger*, in the assertive new spelling *nigga*.

The term *racism* dates from the 1930s, but the broader concept of *-ism*, in the sense of a censured discrimination on unacceptable grounds, is a creature of the 1960s. *Sexism* led the way (it is first recorded in 1968), but it was followed in the subsequent decades by many disciples. The era of non-discriminatory vocabulary was arriving (often labelled 'politically correct', especially by its detractors). It proved easy to ridicule (*person of restricted growth* for 'someone short' can surely only have been coined by somebody with a sense-of-humour deficit), but it was remarkably tenacious. Numerous examples are recorded in the sections on the 1970s and 80s. Its rise and subsequent chequered career maps neatly on to the idealism of the 60s, the militancy of the 70s, and the cynicism of the 80s.

In 1999, following representations, the American dictionary publisher Merriam-Webster withdrew an on-line thesaurus containing a section of words for homosexuals that included such taboo items as *faggot* and *fruit*. It further indicated that future editions of 'printed material' would be reviewed to remove these offending words. So at the end of the century the high tide of tolerance that admitted *fuck* to English dictionaries is seen to be receding, and the fingers of censorship are beginning once again to pick at the fabric of the lexicon.

By what mechanisms did English expand its vocabulary in the 20th century? There are fundamentally five ways in which neologisms are created: by putting existing words to new uses; by combining existing words or word-parts; by shortening existing words; by borrowing words from other languages; and by coining words out of nothing.

By far the commonest in English is the second – combining existing elements. It accounts for close on three-quarters of the new vocabulary coming into the language. It can be divided into two main categories, both of which are as old as the English language itself: two or more words can be combined in such a way that together, they mean something different from what they would mean separately (*dirty dancing*, *dreadnought*); or an existing word can have a prefix or a suffix added to it (*unbundle*, *beatnik*). But there is one particular sort of compound that is highly characteristic of the 20th century: the blend. To create a blend, you do not just put two words side by side; you concertina them together, so that the end of the first merges into the start of the second: for example, *motor* + *hotel* becomes *motel*. It is a pattern that seems to have had its beginnings in Victorian word-play, and certainly its most celebrated early exponent was the English mathematician and children's author Lewis Carroll. He created several still-famous nonsense-blends (such as *mimsy*, from *miserable* and *flimsy*), and he inspired the blend's alternative name – 'portmanteau word' ('Well, "slithy" means "lithe" and "slimy". . . You see it's like a portmanteau – there are two meanings packed up into one word', *Through the Looking-glass* (1871)). The pattern was establishing itself at the end of the 19th century (*brunch* is first recorded in 1896), and the

20th century has taken to it with great enthusiasm. Blends often have the air of journalistic jokes (for instance the ever-popular names for hybrid animals, such as *liger* and *shoat*), but many prove to have remarkable stamina (*chunnel*, *stagflation*), and not a few have become highly respectable members of the lexical community (*pulsar*). The 1980s and 90s in particular have been addicted to the blend's cool snappiness (hence all the cross-genre terms such as *infotainment* and *docusoap*).

The most effort-free way of expanding the vocabulary of a language is to put an existing word to a new use. This generally implies modifying its meaning. It is a phenomenon that is not easy to measure statistically, as there is often an element of subjectivity involved in judging whether the meaning of a word has changed sufficiently to qualify it as a new usage, but estimates of the percentage of such modifications among the total of neologisms are between 10 and 15 – a significant proportion. Much rarer, but also much more controversial, is the process known as conversion. This is when the word-class of a word changes, so that, for instance, a noun is used as a verb (e.g. 'to garage a car'). It is a long-standing feature of the language (Shakespeare was fond of playing with word-classes), but in the 20th century it has become a *bête noire* of the linguistic purists, who seem to see in it a threat to the coherence of the language. There is no sign that English-speakers have given up on it, though (for example, the verb *doorstep* and the noun *dry* from the 1980s).

If you want to shorten an existing word, the most straightforward way is to knock off the end (e.g. *hood* for *hoodlum*, *porn* for *pornography*, *recce* for *reconnaissance*). But there is a particular subset of these shortened words (nearly all verbs) that are created by deleting a suffix, thereby usually altering the word-class (*destruct* from *destruction*, *escalate* from *escalator*). They are known as back-formations, and they have proliferated in 20th-century English, particularly in US military and scientific jargon – a fact that perhaps has contributed to making them yet another target of the language police.

An extreme form of shortening a word is to leave only its first letter. This process of abbreviation produces what are often known as initialisms (*GI*, *LP*, *BSE*). When the resulting string of letters is pronounced as if it were an ordinary word, it is termed an acronym (*Aids*, *Cobol*, *Dora*, *NATO*, *PEP*). Acronyms have been the 20th century's great new contribution to English word-formation. They were virtually non-existent at its start, but by the 1990s they seemed to have seeped into almost every aspect of modern life). The main reasons for this are non-linguistic: the proliferation of organizations and other entities with multi-word names (a process which received a considerable boost during World War II), and an increasingly rushed world which prefers not to waste time on saying or writing such long names.

Foreign borrowing, which has so enriched the English language in previous periods, has provided it with approximately 5 per cent of its new words in the 20th century. The majority owe their adoption to some novel cultural influence. The Anglo-Saxon nations' attitude to foreign food, for instance, has undergone a sea change in the past fifty years. Cuisines once superciliously ignored have been enthusiastically assimilated, and they have brought an abundance of new culinary vocabulary with them: *balti, chow mein, ciabatta, courgette, doner kebab, pizza, quiche, tandoori*. Scientific and technological developments in a particular country can lead to a sudden inrush of foreign terminology (the prominence of France in early aircraft technology, for example, lies behind the abundance of French aerospace vocabulary in English – *aerodrome, aileron, fuselage, hangar, nacelle*). And interaction at a political or diplomatic level often contributes (admittedly time-bound) neologisms to English (*anschluss* and *führer*, *glasnost* and *perestroika*).

Dreaming words up out of thin air accounts for less than one per cent of English neologisms. The great majority of them are proprietary names or commercial names (*nylon, spam* (possibly a blend), *Teflon*), but some technical terms are devised in this way, either directly (*googol*) or by a piece of judicious borrowing from a literary source (*quark*). That leaves a tiny residue of strange coinages which sometimes catch the public imagination through their very outlandishness (*supercalifragilisticexpialidocious*).

Surveyors of the past are often tempted to sign off with a predictive flourish, outlining possible future developments. But not even the foolhardiest student of words would dare to guess at the state of English vocabulary in the year 2100. Words are the servants of events. Who in 1900 could have foreseen the combination of economic and social conditions that led in the 1980s to the craze for inventing *yuppie*-clone lifestyle acronyms (*buppie, guppie, Juppie, dinky, glam, woopie*)? And if by chance anyone had then possessed a working crystal ball, would it also have successfully predicted that it would be *yuppie* and not its original rival *yumpie* that took the decade by storm? All that can with confidence be said is that in the next century people will think new thoughts, have new experiences, make new discoveries, and that they will need new words to communicate them. Somehow, the English language will provide.

Follow-up activities

Words continue to be coined, often in unpredictable ways. Have you noticed any newcomers in the first few years of the twenty-first century? For example, *dotcom* or *dot.com* did not make it into Ayto's book.

Ayto suggests that one of the major phenomena of twentieth-century word formation has been the increase in initialisms and acronyms. Are there any that you use regularly? Note them down. Which vocabularies do they belong to?

One of the ways of creating new words is 'to put an existing word to a new use', and Ayto cites the example of *garage* in its use as a verb. Peruse a newspaper or magazine for verbs that started off their lexical life as nouns.

Ayto also makes a point about 'political correctness'. Are there any words that you are careful how you use, or that you avoid using, because you do not want to offend others' sensibilities? Discuss with your friends whether they share these sensibilities, and whether you behave differently according to the people you are with at any time. Have you noticed any change over time in which words are considered 'politically incorrect'?

THE LEARNING CENTRE
TOWER HAMLETS COLLEGE
ARBOUR SQUARE
LONDON E1 0PS

FURTHER READING

Some reference has been made to other works in the course of the book, and the full details of these can be found in the References. This is a more systematic guide to a few of the books that you could look at if you want to pursue your study of the grammar and vocabulary of English.

A GRAMMAR

A number of more advanced coursebooks in grammar are available, as well as many textbooks on particular aspects of grammar. One that shows the kinds of argument that grammarians use to reach their descriptive decisions is:

Aarts, B. (1997) *English Syntax and Argumentation*, London: Macmillan.

A carefully constructed overview of English grammar is contained in:

Huddleston, R. (1988) *English Grammar: An Outline*, Cambridge: Cambridge University Press.

Another way of following up the study of grammar is to look at the models of description, or theories, that are used to investigate and describe it. A well-argued survey, from the point of view of topics in grammar, rather than theories, is:

Matthews, P. (1981) *Syntax*, Cambridge: Cambridge University Press.

Halliday's 'Systemic Grammar' is expounded in:

Bloor, T. and M. (2001) *The Functional Analysis of English*, 2nd edition, London: Arnold.
Halliday, M. and Matthiessen, C. (2001) *An Introduction to Functional Grammar*, 3rd edition, London: Arnold.

'Valency Grammar' for English is given a lucid exposition in:

Allerton, D. (1982) *Valency and the English Verb*, London: Academic Press.

The relationship between grammar and meaning, which underlies much modern work in syntax, is given an innovative treatment in:

Dixon, R. M. W. (1991) *A New Approach to English Grammar, on Semantic Principles*, Oxford: Clarendon Press.

The attempt to develop a model of grammar that does justice to the structures of spoken English finds its expression in:

Carter, R. and McCarthy, M. (1997) *Exploring Spoken English*, Cambridge: Cambridge University Press.

The works that contain the most systematic and comprehensive treatment of the subject are the reference grammars. Until the 1970s, the most famous of these were completed by overseas scholars of English. Since then, there has appeared a series of Longman descriptive grammars, all based on corpora of texts, initially on the manual 'Survey of English Usage', and latterly on computer corpora such as the 'British National Corpus':

Quirk, R., Greenbaum, S., Leech, G. and Svartvik, J. (1972) *A Grammar of Contemporary English*, London: Longman.
Quirk, R., Greenbaum, S., Leech, G. and Svartvik, J. (1985) *A Comprehensive Grammar of the English Language*, London: Longman.
Biber, D., Johansson, S., Leech, G., Conrad, S. and Finegan, E. (1999) *Longman Grammar of Spoken and Written English*, Harlow: Pearson Education.

As the title suggests, the third of these pays considerable attention to the grammar of spoken English. Each of these 'big' grammars has generated more condensed offshoots, such as:

Quirk, R. and Greenbaum, S. (1973) *A University Grammar of English*, London: Longman.
Leech, G. and Svartvik, J. (1975) *A Communicative Grammar of English*, London: Longman.
Greenbaum, S. and Quirk, R. (1990) *A Student's Grammar of the English Language*, London: Longman.

One of the major drives towards the production of grammatical descriptions and reference grammars is the teaching of English as a foreign or second language. One of the most notable grammars from this stable is:

Collins COBUILD English Grammar (1990), London: Collins.

From the same project also come the works that have been mentioned a number of times in this book, edited by Gill Francis, Susan Hunston and Elizabeth Manning:

Collins COBUILD Grammar Patterns 1: Verbs (1996), London: HarperCollins.
Collins COBUILD Grammar Patterns 2: Nouns and Adjectives (1998), London: HarperCollins.

A number of Internet sites have information on English grammar. Of particular note is the *Internet Grammar of English* at University College London:

<www.ucl.ac.uk/internet-grammar/home.htm>

Various aspects of English are discussed on a regular basis in journals such as *English Today* (Cambridge University Press), which is a lively quarterly aimed at a broad readership, or the more academic *Journal of English Language and Linguistics* (Cambridge University Press).

B VOCABULARY

There is far less of an academic nature written on vocabulary than there is on grammar. A good place to start is with the lavishly illustrated:

Crystal, D. (1995) *The Cambridge Encyclopedia of the English Language*, Cambridge: Cambridge University Press.

Part II is about 'English vocabulary', though the structure of words (morphology) is covered in Part III, on grammar.

In terms of textbooks, the following provide different perspectives on the study of vocabulary:

Carter, R. (1998) *Vocabulary: applied linguistic perspectives*, 2nd edition, London: Routledge.
Jackson, H. and Zé Amvela, E. (2000) *Words, Meaning and Vocabulary*, London: Cassell.
Katamba, F. (1994) *English Words*, Routledge.
Singleton, D. (2000) *Language and the Lexicon*, London: Arnold.

The use of computer corpora has revolutionised the study of words and vocabulary, as lexicologists are able to investigate in new ways the company that words keep and the lexical patterns they enter. Studies from this perspective include:

Hoey, M. (1991) *Lexis in Text*, Oxford: Oxford University Press.
Moon, R. (1998) *Fixed Expressions and Idioms in English: A Corpus-Based Approach*, Oxford: Oxford University Press.
Sinclair, J. (1991) *Corpus, Concordance, Collocation*, Oxford: Oxford University Press.

The reference works on vocabulary are, of course, dictionaries, and the bigger the better, for example:

Collins English Dictionary (1998), 4th edition, London: HarperCollins.
The New Oxford Dictionary of English (1998), Oxford: Oxford University Press.

For a detailed account of the operation of words, especially in grammar, the learners' dictionaries give a more comprehensive treatment:

Cambridge International Dictionary of English (1995), Cambridge: Cambridge University Press.
COBUILD English Dictionary (2001), 3rd edition, London: HarperCollins.
Longman Dictionary of Contemporary English (1995), 3rd edition, London: Longman.
Oxford Advanced Learner's Dictionary (2000), 6th edition, Oxford: Oxford University Press.

Most of these dictionaries are available on CD-ROM, as well as in the print medium, often with additional features, and searchable in ways that would be tedious, if not impossible, with a book. The most comprehensive dictionary of all is the 20-volume historical *Oxford English Dictionary* (2nd edition, 1989), which is also available on CD-ROM, as well as online <www.oed.com>.

Some lexicographers chart the addition of new words to the vocabulary of English. The following, mentioned already in this book, are included here for completeness:

Ayto, J. (1999) *Twentieth Century Words*, Oxford: Oxford University Press.

Knowles, E. and Elliott, J. (1997) (eds) *The Oxford Dictionary of New Words*, Oxford: Oxford University Press.

Vocabulary matters regularly feature in the journal *English Today* (Cambridge University Press). A weekly email newsletter on lexical issues is produced by Michael Quinion; see his website at <www.worldwidewords.org>.

REFERENCES

Allerton, D. J. (1982) *Valency and the English Verb*, London: Academic Press.

Ayto, J. (1999) *Twentieth Century Words*, Oxford: Oxford University Press.

Biber, D., Johansson, S., Leech, G., Conrad, S. and Finegan, E. (1999) *Longman Grammar of Spoken and Written English*, Harlow: Pearson Education Ltd.

Cambridge International Dictionary of English on CD-ROM (2000), Cambridge: Cambridge University Press (CIDE).

Carter, R. and McCarthy, M. (1997) *Exploring Spoken English*, Cambridge: Cambridge University Press.

Cheepen, C. and Monaghan, J. (1990) *Spoken English: A Practical Guide*, London: Pinter Publishers.

Coates, J. (1983) *The Semantics of the Modal Auxiliaries*, London: Croom Helm.

Collins COBUILD English Dictionary (1995), 2nd edition, (ed.) J. Sinclair, London: HarperCollins.

Collins COBUILD Grammar Patterns 1: Verbs (1996) (eds) G. Francis, S. Hunston and E. Manning, London: HarperCollins.

Collins COBUILD Grammar Patterns 2: Nouns and Adjectives (1998) (eds) G. Francis, S. Hunston and E. Manning, London: HarperCollins.

Collins English Dictionary (1998), 4th edition (ed.) D. Treffry, London: HarperCollins (CED4).

Concise Oxford Dictionary Ninth Edition on CD-ROM (1996), Oxford: Oxford University Press (COD9).

Concise Oxford Dictionary (1999), 10th edition (ed.) J. Pearsall, Oxford: Oxford University Press (COD10).

Crystal, D. (1995) *The Cambridge Encyclopedia of the English Language*, Cambridge: Cambridge University Press.

Gram-Andersen, K. (1992) *Purple-eared monster – and its relations: a study in word formation*, Sussex: Book Guild.

Green, J. (1998) *The Cassell Dictionary of Slang*, London: Cassell.

Halliday, M. A. K. (1985, 1994²) *An Introduction to Functional Grammar*, London: Edward Arnold.

Halliday, M. A. K. and Hasan, R. (1976) *Cohesion in English*, London: Longman.

Herbst, T. (1999) 'Designing an English valency dictionary: combining linguistic theory with user-friendliness', in: T. Herbst and K. Popp (eds) *The Perfect Learner's Dictionary (?)*, Tübingen: Max Niemeyer Verlag, pp. 229–53.

Hunston, S. and Francis, G. (2000) *Pattern Grammar: A Corpus-Driven Approach to the Lexical Grammar of English*, Amsterdam: John Benjamins Publishing Company.

Jackson, H. and Zé Amvela, E. (2000) *Words, Meaning and Vocabulary*, London: Cassell.

Oxford Dictionary of New Words (1997) (ed.) E. Knowles with J. Elliott, Oxford: Oxford University Press.

Oxford English Dictionary (Second Edition) (1989) (eds) J. A. Simpson and E. S. Weiner, Oxford: Clarendon Press (OED).

Partridge, E. (1984) *A Dictionary of Slang and Unconventional English*, 8th edition (ed.) Paul Beale, London: Routledge.

Pike, K. L. and Pike, E. G. (1977) *Grammatical Analysis*, Arlington, TX: Summer Institute of Linguistics and University of Texas at Arlington.

Quirk, R., Greenbaum, S., Leech, G. and Svartvik, J. (1985) *A Comprehensive Grammar of the English Language*, London: Longman.

Scott, F. S. *et al.* (1968) *English Grammar: A Linguistic Study of its Classes and Structures*, London: Heinemann.

Svartvik, J. and Quirk, R. (eds) (1980) *A Corpus of English Conversation*, Lund: CWK Gleerup.

Tesnière, L. (1953) *Esquisse d'une syntaxe structurale*, Paris: Klincksieck.

The New Oxford Dictionary of English (1998) (ed.) J. Pearsall, Oxford: Clarendon Press (NODE).

Trudgill, P. (1990) *The Dialects of England*, Oxford: Blackwell.

Trudgill, P. (1999) 'Standard English: what it isn't', in T. Bex and R. J. Watts, *Standard English, The Widening Debate*, London: Routledge, pp. 117–28.

Tulloch, S. (1991) *The Oxford Dictionary of New Words*, Oxford: Oxford University Press.

Wright, P. (1972) *The Lanky Twang*, Settle: Dalesman Books.

GLOSSARY OF TERMS AND INDEX

auxiliary verb 44
a subclass of verb used as modifiers of main verbs to express tense, aspect and
modality, and passive

backformation 39
a word formation process, by which a word is derived by removing an affix,
e.g. *babysit* from *babysitter*

blend 38
the result of a word formation process that combines two words involving
the loss of letters/sounds from, usually, both of them, e.g. *motel* from *motor*
and *hotel*

borrowing 39
the misnamed process of taking a word from one language and importing it into
another, possibly with some modification to align its spelling/pronunciation to
that of its host

category 12, 15
the class to which an element of grammar belongs; contrasts with 'function'
(see below)

clause 12, 16, 20, 21–4, 45–7
a grammatical element functioning in sentences, either as a 'main' or 'matrix'
structure or as a 'subordinate clause'

cleft sentence 55–6
a structure that involves splitting (cleaving) a sentence and bringing one
element into particular focus, e.g. *It was Bill that Geraldine accused*

combining form 12
a bound element, usually from Latin or Greek, used to form neo-classical
compounds, e.g. *xeno- -phobe*

command 33, 59–61
a type of sentence function associated with giving orders, typically by means
of the 'imperative' sentence type

Complement 14, 84–5
a slot in sentence structure that expresses attributes of the Subject or Object

compound 37–8, 73–7, 82
a word resulting from a word formation process that combines, usually, two
free (root) morphemes, e.g. *roadside, six-pack*

conjunction 4
a class of words used mostly for joining clauses; it includes co-ordinating
conjunctions such as *and, but*, and subordinating conjunctions such as *because,
if, when*

conversion   38
a word formation process that derives a new word without any affixation,
but merely by changing its word class, e.g. *showcase* as a verb from the noun

co-ordination   45–6
the joining, usually of sentences but also of phrases and words, by means of a
co-ordinating conjunction such as *and*

declarative   32, 53–6
a type of sentence structure used typically for making 'statements', in which
the Subject usually precedes the Verb

derivation   38, 77–80
a word formation process by which a new word is coined by the addition of
an affix, e.g. *re-invent, smug-ness*

determiner   4, 5, 95
a class of words that modify nouns, including 'identifiers' and 'quantifiers'

dialect   29, 124–8
a variant form of a language spoken in a different part of the world (e.g.
Australian English) or a different part of the country (e.g. North Midland)

ellipsis   46, 119
the omission of an element, or part of it, from a structure

embedding   see 'subordination'

event   37
a type of meaning expressed by the Verb in which something 'happens' to
the Subject

exclamation   33
a type of sentence function associated with uttering surprise, satisfaction or
shock

exclamative   33
a type of sentence structure used for making 'exclamations', usually with an
initial *What* + noun phrase or *How* + adjective

filler   15–16
the element or category that goes into (fills) a 'slot'

finite clause   23, 47, 86, 105–6
a clause containing a finite verb phrase (with the initial verb in either present
or past 'tense') and having all the expected elements of sentence structure,
including Subject

formality   30, 131–5
a dimension of social variation that may affect vocabulary choice; some words
are labelled in dictionaries as 'formal', 'informal' or 'colloquial', 'slang', etc.